MACINTOSH PROGRAMMING SECRETS

Scott Knaster

Addison-Wesley Publishing Company, Inc.

Reading, Massachusetts   Menlo Park, California   New York
Don Mills, Ontario   Wokingham, England   Amsterdam   Bonn
Sydney   Singapore   Tokyo   Madrid   Bogotá

Library of Congress Cataloging-in-Publication Data

Knaster, Scott.
    Macintosh programming secrets.

    Includes index.
    1. Macintosh (Computer)—Programming. I. Title.
QA76.8.M3K683 1987   005.265   87–19374
ISBN 0–201–06661–0

Cover design by Doliber Skeffington
Text design by BMR, David Crossman
Set in 10/12 Palatino by BMR

0–201–06661–0 ABCDEFGHIJ–HA–8987
First printing, November, 1987

Foreword

Macintosh has the finest collection of software for any personal computer. You can pick from over 2,500 powerful, easy to use, and elegant applications. This achievement is the result of the hard work of many people—programmers, evangelists, writers, and testers, to name a few.

A few individuals made outstanding personal contributions to this achievement. Scott Knaster is one of them. For over two years, Scott was responsible for the technical support of Macintosh and Apple II developers. He managed a group of zealots who cajoled, coached, and scolded developers into creating great products.

There are two kinds of computer books. One is the result of ad hoc research on what a publisher thinks will sell. The other is the fruit of being immersed in a subject for years. This is the latter kind of book.

In this, his second book, Scott explains more about the art—and it is an art—of Macintosh programming. This book is the result of Scott's living and breathing Macintosh programming. He captures not only the how but also the why of Macintosh programming.

Scott's insights into Macintosh software are unique because he worked closely with Apple's software and hardware engineers and with all the Macintosh third-party developers. This book reflects his inside knowledge of Apple and the synthesis of the techniques of hundreds of Macintosh programmers.

Scott has written a most insightful book on Macintosh programming techniques. Read this book and you'll see that it's not just "how to program" but a treatise on the Zen of the Macintosh Way. Enjoy.

Guy Kawasaki
August, 1987

Acknowledgments

I created everything in this book. I wrote it, I edited it, I drew all the figures, I personally made the ink to print it, I chopped down the trees for the paper, I bound every copy, I sold it, I shipped it. I thank no one.

Just kidding.

Bill Dawson worked from a crazy idea to produce the Amazing Journey section, using a method of storytelling I've always wanted to try. Steve Stansel provided counsel and humor and once threatened to kill my dog—but I'm even with him because I still have his Laurie Anderson records. Carole Alden stayed with me and helped me find my way forward. Linda O'Brien is just the greatest. Alain Rossmann of Radius, former Apple Chief Evangelist, is the source for the FPI rule in Chapter 1. Jean-Louis Gassée is the inspiration for the section on making computers "more analog." Guy Kawasaki, my boss at Acius, let me go home from the startup wars at 7 o'clock often enough to finish this book. Barbara Knaster created the figures and helped with just about everything else. Jess Knaster, age one, helped by moving disks around, opening and closing books, and even trying to type something now and then.

This one is for my family: my parents, Shirley and David; my grandmother, Pearl Fox; my brother, Ken; my wife, Barbara; and my son, Jess.

Contents

Introduction

This book has two parts with an intermission between them, three appendices, a glossary, and an index. This introduction will give you an idea of what to expect.

Part One, "Concepts and Ideas," is the more abstract part of the book. It focuses on the standards, customs, and software that have defined Macintosh computers and their user interface since the Macintosh 128K appeared in 1984. Chapter 1, "Macintosh and Software," is about the evolution of the Macintosh and other personal computers. It includes a discussion of the user interface, and takes a practical look at which features are important in making software easy to use. Chapter 2, "Compatibility," tells about how you can write your software today so that it works on the Macintoshes that Apple will introduce tomorrow, saving you the trouble of bribing someone for inside information or digging through Apple's dumpster. After Chapter 2 you'll find the Intermission, an attempt to impart some important technical information without being desert dry about it. If you forget that it's educational, it will no doubt be more fun.

Part Two, "Technical Adventures," contains information on how things work in the Macintosh world and how you can do special tricks in your programs. It's organized by topic: most chapters are named after an appropriate part of the Toolbox and the chapters are arranged in alphabetical order by their names. Chapter 3 is the "Color" section (not like the color section in your Sunday funnies), which talks about the new stuff Apple has done in the Macintosh II to make color video possible. Chapter 4, "Event Manager," tells how you can set up your applications to work with both mouse clicks and keystrokes. Chapter 5, "Finder," discusses the technique of quitting from your application and launching another one directly, without running the Finder in between.

Chapter 6, "Printing Manager," discusses the trick of finding the icon for the currently selected printer, branches into a more general technique for finding any file's icon, and then gets into some of the special features of the LaserWriter and how to get at them from your programs. Chapter 7, "QuickDraw," describes the technique of drawing things quickly by using off-screen bit images and pixel images; it also covers a little about using color. Chapter 8, "Resource Manager," tells about how you can make your programs super-friendly by putting everything back the way it was when the user was last working. Chapter 9, "Window Manager," explains how you can deal with the proliferation of windows on giant screens that's happening in the Macintosh world.

Appendix A, "New Machines and System Software," presents an overview of the Macintosh SE and Macintosh II, plus information about new features in system files with version numbers of 4.1 or greater. As the navigator said in the movie *Dune:* "Many machines. New machines." Appendix B, "68020 Microprocessor Overview," goes into the 68020 that's built into every Macintosh II and is available as a third-party option for other Macintosh computers. Appendix C, "Macintosh Technical Note #110," is the saga of an interesting piece of technical information, which has been circulating among Macintosh techies for some time. After the appendices is a glossary of some important terms as well as an index.

Conventions

This is a guide to the way things are represented in this book. All words that are in **boldface** type have entries in the glossary. Hexadecimal numbers are always preceded by a dollar sign, as in $48, $FFFF, and $AD6. Numbers without a dollar sign are decimal numbers, unless it says otherwise.

You can watch for several kinds of special paragraphs that break up the prose. They look like this:

These paragraphs contain information that's a little bit off the subject, but interesting. If you're in a hurry or you don't care, you can skip these paragraphs without losing track of what's going on in the book.

A paragraph marked this way is warning you about something dangerous. It usually relates information that's vital to keep your program from crashing or your files from getting messed up, or something equally important.

As you probably guessed, paragraphs marked like this are about the Macintosh II.

This crystal ball icon marks information that will suffer from the time warp of writing a book. Between the writing and the book's appearance, months go by; more months intervene before you read it. The topics of paragraphs marked this way weren't perfectly defined when the writing was done.

Sincere Plea

Programs have bugs, and so do books about programming. If you find any, please let me know about them. If you have access to AppleLink, you can get me at address KNASTER2. Otherwise, you can use the U.S. mail, via Addison-Wesley, Reading, Massachusetts. Thanks, and have fun reading the book.

About This Book . . .

Welcome

This book is about writing software for Macintosh computers. If you've written Macintosh programs, or you're interested in learning how it's done, you'll be interested in the stuff inside. To get the most out of this book, you should be familiar with Pascal or C and you should have spent some time reading through *Inside Macintosh* (Addison-Wesley, 1985, 1986),the definitive Macintosh technical reference manual. If you know assembly language, have been writing Macintosh software for a while, enjoy listening to music, or have a sense of humor, you'll get even more out of this book.

This Book's Purpose

There are enough programmer's goodies in the Macintosh to fill a hundred books the size of *Inside Macintosh*. There's so much software, it does so much, and it's so tightly woven that you can approach it in many different ways. With *Inside Macintosh*, Apple supplies the absolutely necessary documentation: a reference manual describing how to use the tools and what they do.

With the release of new Macintosh technical documentation in 1987, Apple broadened its coverage: now, in addition to the information in *Inside Macintosh*, there are books to help you get started, to help you put all the pieces together, and to help you build hardware or write the software that will make add-on hardware work.

Even with all these thorough and well-written manuals, there's more to do (which is how I can get away with writing this book). The Macintosh software architecture is so rich that it can withstand many different approaches to documentation—even, I think, mine.

I've been working with Macintosh programmers for over three years providing technical support to software developers. I've been lucky enough to learn about how the Macintosh works by asking the people who've made it work. This book is about what I learned because I had to or because it was interesting.

Much of this book (especially Part Two) is written in a pretty nonlinear fashion. If you majored in literature, you might even call it anecdotal. It consists of lots of tips, ideas, techniques, pointers, fun facts, and obscure trivia designed to interest Macintosh programmers. Everything in the book meets at least one of these criteria:

- It's a vital fact that can really make a big difference in your software.
- It's a mysterious or misunderstood feature that deserves to be explained.
- It's a great capability that's little-known or underused.
- It's a commonly asked question or frequent complaint, problem, or pitfall.
- It's something interesting or fun.

If you've read my previous book, *How to Write Macintosh Software* (Hayden Book Company, 1986), you know I like to keep things interesting, even when they get heavy. A subject like programming the Macintosh—which has virtually no geopolitical implications and is not related to organized religion—deserves to be treated with a sense of humor. Since I believe you have a right to know as much about a subject as I can tell, I also try not to leave you hanging without telling the complete story.

The things in this book can make your programs better, more powerful, and easier to use. However, if you decide to give up programming, you can always use this book for gooshing spiders, and the laminated cover makes an excellent beverage tray.

P A R T O N E

Concepts and Ideas

In Part One, we'll discuss a little of the history and philosophy behind the Macintosh. We'll get technical at times, but we'll spend a lot of time just exploring the theories and ideas that have made the Macintosh what it is.

If you're into programming (and if you aren't, congratulations for deciding to read this book!), you may find a new perspective here. The idea is this: the Macintosh requires programmers to think about things they may not have thought much about before, including user interface design. Part One will help you figure out what things are important when creating Macintosh software.

C H A P T E R   1

Macintosh and Software

The history and early impressions of the Macintosh. The ill-fated but groundbreaking Lisa computer is recalled. The contents of the wondrous Macintosh ROM. The evolution of the Macintosh product line. A discussion of standards. Why ease of learning and ease of use are different and why that matters. What makes an open and a closed computer. The important parts of the famed Macintosh user interface. The invention, discussion, and application of the FPI rule. In which surprising reasons for software popularity are revealed. Software compatibility and what it means to you. Leaving the system file alone.

A Little History

Return with me now to those thrilling days of yesteryear . . . back, back to 1984, when Apple introduced the Macintosh to the world. It was a real milestone in personal computer history for several reasons. It was the first computer that had a radically different, easy-to-learn user interface, a price that lots of people could afford, and a company that could spend a lot of time and money getting people interested in it. Other computers fit one or two of these criteria, but the Macintosh was the first one that met them all.

Apple itself had introduced the Lisa just a year earlier, a system with a megabyte of memory (an amazing amount in 1983) and a user interface that would look pretty familiar to any current Macintosh user; but the Lisa retailed for $9,995, locking many people out because of price alone.

Many features that are a part of what we now call the Macintosh interface were originally invented by Xerox in its user interface research. Some computers available from Xerox before 1983 actually used elements of this interface, but they were even more expensive than the Lisa. When the Macintosh came out in 1984 with a list price of $2,495, it was the first time a system with this interface was priced in the mainstream of personal computers.

A lot of things made the Macintosh different from other computers when it was introduced. The first thing that people noticed was its unique industrial design. At the time, computers were put together two ways. The so-called portables usually had two disk drives to the right of the screen in a vertical orientation, and a keyboard that folded over. The other common construction was the three-box, used for almost all IBM PCs and clones; one box contained the computer's guts and disk drives, one box was the monitor, and the third box was the keyboard. The Macintosh, with its built-in monitor and disk drive and tall, vertical orientation, didn't look like anything else.

Its unique appearance prepared people for some of the other unusual things they'd discover about the Macintosh. The 3 1/2-inch disk drive was a pretty radical idea in 1984, but by far the most unusual thing about the Macintosh was the appearance of its software. The first strange thing users noticed about the software was the way the display showed black characters on a white background, the reverse of most computer displays. Back then, this was called inverse video even though it was designed to look like letters on a piece of paper.

Another funny thing was that all the applications looked very much the same: they all had a list of menu titles at the top of the screen and displayed their information in windows that could be moved around the screen. Most of these windows had little boxes and arrows allowing you to control their display.

The Macintosh was so different that it was hard to answer some of the conventional questions about computers. How many characters per line does it display? That's hard to say, since you can choose from different fonts and the characters are proportionally spaced. What printers does it work with? Just one, Apple's printer. How many function keys on the keyboard? None, but it does come with a mouse.

The Macintosh was unique mainly because of the decision to make the user interface a vital part of the computer. The original Macintosh had 64K of ROM and a good chunk of that was devoted to the **User Interface Toolbox,** a collection of routines that programmers can use to give their software all the familiar goodies like menus and windows.

The Soul of the New Machine

No other computer had ever paid so much attention to the user interface. Because the Toolbox was in ROM, programmers could use it without having to use up any valuable RAM space. In fact, since the original Macintosh had only 128K of RAM, programmers who wanted to reinvent some parts of the Toolbox were persuaded to abandon those plans due to the lack of available memory.

At first, it was tough to convince software developers that they should follow Apple guidelines for user interface design. One of the biggest strengths of the Macintosh user interface is its consistency—almost all applications use the same design. Of course, when there weren't any applications, selling this fact was pretty tough. Apple convinced many early Macintosh developers to follow the user interface through a unique form of evangelism, consisting of enthusiasm, hype, and gentle coercion.

As more and more Macintosh software became available, the user interface started to become a real standard and an important part of applications. Software reviewers began to knock off points if an application didn't follow Apple's user interface guidelines. The term *Macintoshlike* (or *Maclike)* was invented to describe software that seemed to use the interface in the proper way. The Macintosh user interface became an acceptable, even advanced, way of doing things.

The name game. In the early days of the Macintosh project at Apple, before it was released to the world, the nickname *Mac* became common usage for those in the know. Then, in late 1983, just before the computer was ready to ship, Apple employees were asked to stop using Mac and to stick to Macintosh, apparently because of trademark conflicts (rumored to be coming from McDonalds, as in the hamburgers). Finally, in 1986, Apple's gallant lawyers secured the rights to both names—just thought you'd want to know.

Another interesting phenomenon validated the Macintosh interface: lots of mutations and variations of it began to appear on other personal computers. Digital Research, inventor of the CP/M operating system that once dominated the industry, came up with GEM (graphics environment manager), one of the most prominent of these variations. After many delays, Microsoft came out with Windows, which seems destined to become the most popular of the MS-DOS-based systems that use a Macintoshlike user interface, especially now that Microsoft has announced that Windows will be built into a future version of OS/2. It's interesting to note that, according to published press reports, both Digital Research and Microsoft have licenses from Apple allowing them to use certain parts of the user interface.

The corporate world. If Microsoft licenses parts of the interface from Apple, and IBM licenses Windows from Microsoft, does that mean that Apple will hold the rights to a crucial part of IBM's operating system future? It doesn't seem likely but, as they say, only time will tell.

Apple itself has spread the user interface to the Apple II family of computers. The Apple IIgs, which was introduced late in 1986, includes many user interface tools that are similar to their Macintosh counterparts. An experienced Macintosh programmer moving to the Apple IIgs finds a lot of familiar concepts there.

Great moments in marketing. When Apple first used its advanced user interface, it was on the Lisa and it was called Lisa Technology. After the Macintosh was introduced and the Lisa was discontinued, it became known as the Macintosh interface. Now, with the same kind of technology available in the Apple II line with the Apple IIgs, Apple refers to it as the Apple Desktop Interface, or just the Apple Interface for short.

Hidden Factors

The user interface and the Toolbox that makes it available to programmers are the most obvious things that make the Macintosh unique. However, anyone who writes Macintosh software discovers that there's more than just user interface things in the Macintosh ROM. The Toolbox gives you tools for creating the user interface, but it also provides lots of ways to customize the behavior of things so that you can implement specialized features for your applications. You can redefine any of the Toolbox or operating system routines by putting in a **patch;** you can use **hooks** in the system to put in your own routines; and you can play with **low-memory globals** to modify the way the system works. Apple took a lot of heat because the original Macintosh had closed hardware, but it really didn't get a lot of credit for the open software architecture that allowed so much flexibility. There's a lot more on how these things work in Chapter 2.

The "carrot and stick" effect of having the Toolbox in ROM and not having very much RAM helped convince developers to do things Apple's way, but these weren't the only reasons. The most important factor was that most of the Toolbox software was really great. Also important was the flexibility provided by things like patches, hooks, and globals, allowing a programmer to make a choice to use certain parts of the software and not others. It's possible to use QuickDraw to do everything except, say, drawing rectangles. If you think you have a better way to draw rectangles, you can implement it and still use the rest of QuickDraw. This flexibility encouraged programmers not to reinvent too much.

Speaking of QuickDraw, it's another thing that makes the Macintosh a great machine for programmers. QuickDraw is used to draw all the text and pictures that you see on the screen and its power and flexibility have helped keep the Macintosh ahead of its competitors and imitators. Over the years, QuickDraw has been enhanced and extended to take advantage of bigger screens, color output, and the 68020 microprocessor.

The Macintosh II version of QuickDraw, called Color Quick-Draw, has been extensively revised. It now includes lots of support for color and the ability to work with video cards in slots and multiple screens. Because Color QuickDraw uses 68020 instructions extensively, it isn't available for other Macintosh models.

The Toolbox is the most visible part of the Macintosh for programmers, but other interesting features have helped make the Macintosh popular. Built into every Macintosh is the ability to live on an AppleTalk network; all you have to add is the cable. Because of this convenient connection to a reliable local area network and because of the popularity of the LaserWriter printer, which can be shared on AppleTalk, the Macintosh has become probably the world's most widely networked personal computer.

Another reason for the Macintosh's popularity is its easy connection via AppleTalk to the AppleShare file server, a device that allows all the users on a network to share files located on one central disk. AppleShare is a wonderful example of how the Macintosh interface can be applied to a fairly complicated operation like connecting to a file server. If you go through the process of connecting to an AppleShare file server, you can see that its designers really understood how to use the Macintosh user interface. The procedure could be made a bit easier, but if you don't appreciate the ease and simplicity of the operation as it is, ask someone to show you how to connect to a file server on a non-Macintosh system. You'll be fascinated.

If you dig deeper into the system, you'll find one of the most sophisticated implementations of a file system on any personal computer. The Macintosh's Hierarchical File System (HFS) is designed to work well with huge volumes and with file servers. It keeps track of files and directories with a system that's very much like a powerful database, using indexes called **b-trees** to locate the things it keeps on the disk. It also uses this system to keep track of each chunk of space on a disk. Because a big disk can hold thousands of files and directories, HFS becomes even more important as your disk fills up. In addition, HFS, along with the Disk First Aid utility program, works hard to make sure you don't lose information stored on the disk.

Success and Failure

The Macintosh product line has experienced more than its share of both success and failure during its brief existence. Because Apple has taken so many chances with its introduction, the Macintosh has given birth to an interesting history for a product that's just a few years old.

Introducing the original Macintosh computer was the biggest risk and most radical statement, of course. When it was introduced, Apple set out in a different direction from other personal computer manufacturers. The Macintosh contained a powerful, advanced microprocessor, the 68000, but rather than use the processor's power to do the same old things the same old way only faster, Apple decided to take a giant left turn and try to make the computer easier to learn. The result was the heavy emphasis on the user interface and the creation of the Toolbox.

The original Macintosh had plenty of drawbacks, too. One of the most serious was the small amount of RAM and disk space. Apple had only designed in 128K of RAM, which just wasn't enough for most programmers on the Macintosh, especially since the system took away about 40K for the video display and various other things like the stack and the system heap. To make the situation worse, Apple was desperately short of external disk drives when the Macintosh first shipped, and so most users had a single 400K disk drive. Early users cursed the Macintosh for making them swap disks in and out of the drive so frequently.

Always look on the bright side. Most early Macintosh users probably came close to heaving their computers down the stairs more than once because of frustration over disk swapping. The idea was that the operating system could have access to a disk that wasn't inserted just then merely by asking for it. It was a good idea but it turned out to be a big pain for users. If you think that was bad, though, imagine the results if Apple had had conventional disk drives, with doors that had to be opened and closed every time. Aaaaaargh!

There were some other holes in the original Macintosh. It wasn't designed to work with a hard disk drive; although several third party developers eventually created hard disks for the Macintosh, they had a lot of trouble fitting them in. The only way they could interface was through one of the serial ports or through the external disk port, which kept them from operating very fast. A bigger problem was the Macintosh's system software, in particular the Finder and the File Manager. Both of these guys were designed for small disks and both ran into serious trouble when trying to handle hard disks with many megabytes and hundreds of files. The Finder would slow to a crawl as it tried to see all the files on a big disk, and the File System's block allocation scheme was very wasteful for hard disks, allocating several thousand bytes even for the smallest file.

The original Macintosh also had an interesting marketing-type problem with printing. One of the things that made the Macintosh a very powerful system was its great graphics capability. In today's world of desktop publishing and fancy drawing programs, it can be hard to remember just how magical MacPaint was back when the Macintosh was new. To make it even more impressive, anything that you could create on the screen could be printed on the inexpensive Imagewriter printer that Apple sold.

Since printers use many different methods for printing graphics, software to do printing of graphics from the screen has to be rewritten for every kind of printer. Apple chose to support only the Imagewriter on the Macintosh, and took a lot of criticism for this decision, which locked users into buying an Apple printer to go with their Macintosh. The fact that the printer provided very good quality and performance at a reasonable price helped keep this from becoming too big a deal. However, for businesses that wanted to use daisywheel printers to create documents that looked typewritten, the lack of a higher quality printer was a big reason not to buy a Macintosh.

Daisywheel of fortune.   How could Apple have done something as foolish as neglecting daisywheel printers on a business computer? There were two reasons: first, during its formative days the Macintosh was never intended to be a business computer; second, Apple was cooking up the world's first inexpensive laser printer and felt that everyone would rather have one of them than some old daisywheel. Of course, the laser printer didn't follow the Macintosh until 14 months later. Eventually, Apple felt pressured to develop daisywheel support and created a daisywheel printer driver. Just as it was about to be released, the only copy of the source code was lost during one of Apple's many moves. Eventually, it was recovered and released through dealers; also, Apple's source code control got a lot better.

Many of the early Macintosh critics complained about the keyboard: it didn't have cursor keys or function keys, like the keyboards offered by you-know-who. Of course, these features didn't really fit with the new kind of interface the Macintosh presented, but their absence was criticized anyway. All these early objections were eventually answered by other Macintosh models, which you can read about later in this chapter.

Standards

A lot of press has focused on the Macintosh's failure to sell as well as expected, and eventually Steve Jobs was fired as head of Apple's Macintosh Division. But not nearly as much has been said about the Macintosh's real successes and the important ways it has changed personal computers. When the Macintosh was introduced, Apple's marketing called it the third standard in business computers, after the Apple II and the IBM PC. How accurate was this message?

There are several ways to look at what makes a standard in personal computers. Probably the most common way is by looking at how many different manufacturers make computers that can use a particular operating system. If you look at things this way, you have to say that the first standard was CP/M, and that it was replaced in the mid-1980s by MS-DOS. This seems to be a pretty narrow perspective, though, since it leaves out several million Apple II computers, not to mention more than a million Macintoshes. See Figure 1-1 for a look at some of the standards of their day.

Years	"Standard"	Primary reason
1976-1982	CP/M	Dozens of manufacturers
1977-1983	Apple DOS	Millions of computers
1981-present	MS-DOS	Hundreds of manufacturers
1983-present	Apple ProDOS	Millions of computers
1984-present	Macintosh O.S.	Over a million computers
1987-present	OS/2	Support from you-know-who

Figure 1-1. Personal computer "standards"

A more interesting criterion for a standard computer is the total number of computers in the world—not the number of different manufacturers—that support a particular operating system. This basis for judgment allows us to say that the Apple II was certainly a standard after CP/M in the early 1980s, since the total number of Apple IIs was probably greater than the total number of all CP/M machines from all manufacturers.

Another neat way to see whether a computer is a standard is by asking this question: does it run the current hot software? By applying this test, we can verify that the Apple II was really a standard, since it was the computer that ran VisiCalc, the first spreadsheet and the first application type uniquely invented for personal computers. When Lotus 1-2-3 surpassed VisiCalc in the mid-1980s, MS-DOS became a standard. Of course, this standard varies according to the area of computing involved. In desktop publishing, PageMaker is the standard, so both the Macintosh and the IBM PC qualify, but the Macintosh is the leader because it established its position first and provides a better solution.

The most important way that the Macintosh has established itself as a standard is in its greatest difference from the rest: the user interface. Because of the Macintosh, it's no longer acceptable for sophisticated software to have crummy, stupid interfaces. Making a program easy to learn and use is now an important part of software development. Specific elements of the Macintosh interface, especially windows, pull-down menus, and dialogs, are widely used in software that runs on other computers. The Macintosh has established a new standard in personal computers: a great interface is important for software.

Ease of Learning vs. Ease of Use

When someone who has never used a computer sits down with a Macintosh and learns the basics of using it within a few minutes, Macintosh shows that it's **easy to learn**. The interface is ideal for ease of learning. Commands are listed in pull-down menus, so you don't have to remember what they are. You make things happen by clicking on familiar objects on the screen like buttons and arrows. Once you learn the basic cut and paste operation, you know how to move information around, no matter what application you're using.

After you've had the computer for a while and you use it every day, an interesting thing starts to happen. You begin to remember some of those complicated commands. You know what buttons you want to click in a dialog even before the dialog is drawn on the screen. In short, you mutate into a (drum roll) . . . Power User! (sounds like a comic book superhero). When this happens, you find that you no longer have patience for those great little touches that made learning the program so easy. As the Macintosh made its way into the real world, it became obvious that most Macintosh software was easy to learn but started to cramp your style once you knew what you were doing; in other words, it was not **easy to use**. A few built-in features of the interface did make software easier for an experienced user: Command key equivalents on menu items, for example. But for the most part Macintosh software was heavy on ease of learning, light on ease of use.

Another problem was the message that Apple's marketing was pumping out at the time: the Macintosh was "the computer for the rest of us." This slogan helped establish the Macintosh's image as an easy-to-learn computer but it had a rotten side effect: it caused people to think that the Macintosh didn't have a lot of power, that it was a computer with training wheels you couldn't take off. This image caused people who wanted powerful computers to stay away from the Macintosh even though it was an incredibly powerful computer.

This had a real "chicken and egg" effect with software developers. They saw that the people buying Macintoshes weren't power users, so they assumed that they should come out with software that wasn't real powerful—that ease of learning was the only important feature for Macintosh software. This caused them to leave a lot of power out of their applications. Most of the applications that fit this description have not sold very well.

Eventually, the Macintosh got a reputation for wimpy software that lacked power features. Whether it was justified or not, the biggest boost to this reputation came when Lotus released its product, Jazz, in 1985. Although Jazz had six different integrated functions combined under a nice interface, it was better known for the fact that it didn't allow users to string a series of commands together in **macros** like the MS-DOS version of Lotus 1-2-3. Conventional wisdom usually blamed this on the non-fact that the Macintosh just wasn't capable of supporting powerful applications, ignoring the fact that some folks had figured out how to use the Macintosh for incredibly powerful applications.

Definition corner. Conventional wisdom is something that passes for the truth when (1) the truth isn't well known, (2) the truth isn't easy to understand, or (3) the truth isn't what a lot of people would like it to be. Conventional wisdom is almost never the same as the real truth. This has been a public service announcement.

The myth that powerful software couldn't be written for the Macintosh started to crumble in late 1985. Big blows were struck when Microsoft released Excel, generally known as the most powerful spreadsheet available for any personal computer, and when an unknown company called Aldus shipped PageMaker, creating a whole new industry.

Suddenly (or so it seemed), developers were figuring out how to use the Macintosh interface to create software that was easy to use *and* easy to learn. By 1986, there were a whole bunch of applications in almost every category that were at least as powerful as their counterparts in the MS-DOS world, outline processors (MORE), databases (4th Dimension), and even accounting software (Insight). The Macintosh also gained a wide variety of excellent development tools. These included several fast and powerful Pascal and C compilers, the TMON debugger, and Apple's own Macintosh Programmer's Workshop, which featured a powerful shell, Pascal and C compilers, an assembler, and MacApp, one of the industry's most advanced object-oriented development systems.

For the first time the Macintosh began to get the reputation for having the most powerful and most innovative software, rather than the most crippled. The image of the Macintosh as a toy was probably killed forever by the introduction of the Macintosh II in March 1987. This computer has features that can match anything else in its price range: a 68020 microprocessor, a minimum of one megabyte of RAM, with an option to expand to eight megabytes, an optional built-in hard disk, and expansion slots, just to name a few features. Even the truly narrow-minded have to think of the Macintosh II as a real computer—after all, it's made of three boxes and it can run MS-DOS if you really want it to!

The Closed Computer

One thing about the original Macintosh that surprised a lot of people was its so-called **closed architecture**—in other words, it lacked expansion slots, unlike the Apple II and the IBM PC. The expansion slots in other personal computers were used for adding disk drives, additional memory, printer interface cards, fancy video cards, clock/calendar cards, and lots of other neat stuff.

Though it didn't have slots, the Macintosh *did* have a lot of built-in features that had to be added as options to other computers: two serial interface ports, one of which could be used (eventually) for AppleTalk; a disk drive and connector for another drive; a mouse interface; advanced sound and graphics capabilities; and a clock and calendar. Even though the options most users would want were built-in, the Macintosh still took a lot of criticism.

The worst thing about not having slots is that it prevents a user from adding the great new peripheral that nobody had thought of when the computer was designed. For example, an expansion card with a hard disk on it became a hot item in the IBM PC world, but nobody could build one for the slotless Macintosh.

Another reason why a sealed computer without slots is criticized has nothing to do with engineering design, customer acceptance, marketing, or the phases of the moon. It has to do with how most personal computers are sold, especially Apples: by retailers. Retail computer dealers spend a lot of time in price wars with each other. One of the tools that smart dealers use is the ability to uniquely configure a system, either with a particular peripheral that adds value to the system or by installing a feature such as more memory or an internal hard disk that the dealer can get less expensively than the competition down the block.

With the original Macintosh, every dealer was selling exactly the same system. This forced the dealers to compete on price, which is initially a great situation for people buying computers but is ultimately not so great, because someone will not be able to keep up, and will go out of business. The original Macintosh's closed box prevented dealers from customizing it and making it more interesting to their customers. This knock against a closed machine may seem a little bizarre, but it certainly was a factor holding back the success of the Macintosh.

Why was the Macintosh a closed, nonexpandable box? The answer that seems to be most widely believed (conventional wisdom) is that the folks who designed the Macintosh were so arrogant that they figured they knew exactly what everyone would ever want, built just that much into the computer, then made sure that nobody could add anything to it that would mess up their masterpiece.

Actually, the original Macintosh was made the way it was for a fairly noble reason: to simplify things. At the time that the Macintosh was being designed, Apple's computer was the Apple II with its expansion slots. Into those expansion slots were plugged things never dreamed of when the computer was first designed: cards with other microprocessors on them, cards to provide a full 80 columns of text per line instead of the normal 40, cards with music synthesizers on them, cards to speed up the computer, and hundreds more.

An Apple II owner could add all these cards to enhance the system. Along the way to massive expandability, an interesting thing happened. Programmers had to start worrying about making sure that their software worked with all these different cards. There were at least six different 80-column cards, each behaving in a slightly different way. There were literally dozens of different printer interface cards, both serial and parallel. Expanding the memory of the original Apple II creates a memory map with more holes and switches than a mountain highway. Programmers were going nuts trying to keep up with all this.

Out of this mess came one of the fundamental ideas for the Macintosh, that it would have exactly one configuration for programmers to worry about. Every computer would have 128K RAM, a 9-inch black and white monitor with 512 by 342 resolution, an internal disk drive, two serial ports, and a mouse. Only the tiniest variations were possible: there might be an external disk drive, a modem, and a printer. This meant that the programmer didn't have to write a ton of special case code for lots of different kinds of devices.

Legend has it.   An old story says that the Macintosh design was so strongly committed to a single configuration that the expandability to 512K in the original machine was not supposed to be there. The 512K option, so the story goes, was snuck into the machine by its designer, Burrell Smith, fearlessly, in the face of certain death if discovered. As it turned out, the Macintosh 512K was absolutely vital for the Macintosh to be taken seriously.

Closing the computer to the outside world in order to make life easier for programmers turned out to be a mixed blessing, at best. It's true that developers didn't have to worry about different configurations, which simplified things; but designing powerful software with a good user interface was a whole new skill to learn, so the Macintosh made things hard for programmers in different ways.

An interesting phenomenon that occurred around the Macintosh was this: if you don't have slots, people will create them; it will just take longer and will be harder to do. By 1986, the original, slotless, so-called closed Macintosh could get a 68020 board, a color video modification, memory upgrades to a megabyte and beyond, and your choice of more than a dozen different internal hard disk drives. Clever developers figured out how to do this. Sure, it would have been easier and cleaner to do with slots (and it was, once the Macintosh SE came out) and more options would have been available, but it happened anyway.

For many Macintosh owners, maybe even the majority, expansion slots aren't necessary. The great number of things built into the box is enough power for most users and they never need to add anything that doesn't plug directly into the back. For these people, the original closed design of the Macintosh works just fine. This suggests that the closed hardware Macintosh was not necessarily a bad idea. In fact, Apple continues to sell the slotless Macintosh Plus and it's very popular. The difference is that now, potential customers have a choice: the compact, all-in-one Macintosh Plus, the compact but expandable Macintosh SE, or the modular, very expandable Macintosh II. Different people have different needs, and having several options to choose from simply lets more people use a Macintosh.

A Close Look at the User Interface

The computer industry really tries to destroy the English language. One of the most offensive terms that gets tossed around, though less and less these days, is **user-friendly**. This term always conjures up for me one of those happy faces you used to see all the time (see Figure 1-2). *User-friendly* can be bent to mean whatever you want it to mean, as can words like *relational database* or *freedom fighter;* so it really means very little. To define the Macintosh user interface, we'll try to use some more precise (or at least less obnoxious) terms.

Hi, I'm User-Friendly

Figure 1-2. Author's view of "user-friendly"

The standard Apple guidebook to the implementation of the user interface is the book *Human Interface Guidelines: The Apple Desktop Interface* (Addison-Wesley, 1987). In this section, we'll talk about some of the principles that are defined in that book.

The most famous principle of the user interface is ease of learning, which we've discussed a little already. In general, arbitrary terms, we can say that a program is easy to learn if a user can begin to

do useful work with it in less than an hour. The Macintosh user interface is obviously designed to help make things easy to learn. Pull-
down menus allow users to get an idea of what actions are possible.
Using the mouse to operate controls like buttons and scroll arrows is
pretty easy to figure out. Clicking on objects to select them is another
technique that can be understood quickly. In this section, we'll talk
about features of the user interface that make Macintosh software
easy to learn.

> **Terminology corner**.   There's some disagreement in the indus-
> try, and even within Apple, about which term is correct: *user
> interface* or *human interface*. Maybe the best way to compare
> the two is to ask which name is kinder to the person working on
> a computer, "human" or "user." I stick mainly with "user" in
> this book, but I really don't think it makes that much differ-
> ence. Which would you rather be, a user or a human? Several
> different terms are also used for the interface itself. It used to
> be the Macintosh user interface, but now that the Apple IIgs
> can do it too, Apple seems to prefer *Apple Desktop Interface*.
> People who aren't really familiar with the interface often
> talk about a windowing interface, or an iconic operating system,
> but these don't really describe what Apple is up to.

Consistency

One of the most important principles of the user interface is the
idea of different programs doing similar things in the same way:
consistency. There are two kinds of consistency: consistency within an
application and consistency across applications. An insane techie
terminology-inventor might call these **local consistency** and **global
consistency**, but I would never call them that.

Global consistency means that every program uses windows in a
familiar way—the windows look much the same and the same actions can be used to manipulate them, no matter what program you're
using. Any window that has a title bar can be moved around the
screen by letting the user drag the title bar. A window with a grow
box should allow the user to resize it. Scroll bars should work the
way that users (or humans) expect them to. The first three menus
should be the Apple, File, and Edit menus, and they should contain
familiar items, with familiar Command-key combinations that do
familiar things, and so on.

The benefit of this global consistency is obvious: once a user
knows how to use one Macintosh program, lots of others will look

pretty familiar. This doesn't mean that someone who learns Mac-Write will be able to churn out killer spreadsheets in Excel without learning anything new, but it does mean that people should get into new applications faster and more easily than they would on computers that lack a consistent interface.

Global consistency also means that you should sometimes give in to standards, even when you have a slightly better (or just a slightly different) idea. Momentum is very important when choosing a design, and standards have a lot of momentum. Maybe you think *bold* is a bad description for that particular text attribute and you'd rather call it *thick.* Maybe you even discovered an old textbook on typography that says that *thick* is the right term, not *bold.* Don't change it. Stick with *bold.* A little bit of correctness is not as important as a lot of consistency.

Local consistency means that applications do similar things in similar ways and that they don't make the same command mean different things at different times in the program. For example, any kind of window hanging around on the desktop, whether its a document, the clipboard, or a search window, should be able to be closed by clicking in its close box. Any button can be pressed just by clicking on it. Choosing Cut from the Edit menu should always remove whatever was selected and place it on the clipboard. If you're using Cut in part of your program to mean something slightly different, you should probably make it a new command instead.

Real World Metaphors

When you're designing a feature into your program, think about how it would be done in the real world—you know, the one outside the computer—and try to simulate that in your program. In the real world, documents are stuck in folders; the same thing happens in the Finder. Unwanted documents go to the trash; same in the Finder. If you accidentally throw something away, you can retrieve it from the trash if you don't wait too long; the Finder gives you the same chance, with the added advantage that there's no coffee grounds and orange peels all over it.

The real world is a good source for your design because people already know how to work with the real world—most of them live in it. Similarity to the real world makes your application better by making it easier for the user to learn and use. Sometimes, though, you have to put something in a program that isn't like anything the user would find in the real world. For example, there's really nothing like scroll bars in everyday life.

In these cases, you should be sure to follow the laws of physics in your design: don't create the metaphorical equivalent of a ball rolling uphill. For example, don't create a speed gauge that makes the computer slow down when you click on an up-arrow. Breaking the laws of physics in your application will cause your users to feel confused and out of control.

Half full or half empty?   You may find that the laws of physics vary from person to person. Switcher, the program-switching utility for the Macintosh, is a great example. Switcher draws a left-arrow and a right-arrow, and you click an arrow to switch to the next program. When you click the right-arrow, does that mean you want the program on the right to switch in, or does it mean you want the current program to slide to the right, bringing in the next one on the left? This question caused some debate while Switcher was being designed, so the program's author, Andy Hertzfeld, decided on the ultimate solution: the user can choose the correct reality in an Options dialog. It's a small matter, but it shows you how a program can be made really friendly.

Ease of Use

The next important feature of a program's interface, which is sometimes forgotten, is ease of use. Easy-to-use programs provide shortcuts for people who use them every day. The "cut and paste" metaphor for moving a paragraph from one place to another in a document is easy to explain and puts power in the hands of a novice, but a more advanced user may want a quicker way, such as somehow being able to drag the paragraph directly to its destination with the mouse.

When you implement more complicated, specialized features like this, it's important to hide them from the novice user. If you don't support the standard ways of doing things, you risk making your application hard to learn. The most common way to implement advanced functions is through special keys such as the Option and Command keys. For example, holding down the Command key while double-clicking on text might be used to select an entire sentence instead of a word; holding down the Option key might allow you to drag selected text in a word processor.

If you put in lots of power features and make use of the special keys, you may create some obnoxious-looking keyboard combinations. That's why you should make sure these features are only used for advanced operations, not simple ones. If your application uses an odd combination of keys to perform a complex operation that would otherwise take two or three menu selections, the user who has to perform that operation a lot will likely take the trouble to remember the keystrokes. If the user doesn't do that operation very often or forgets how to do it, selecting it from the menus should always be available.

When you add shortcuts, you should make sure to follow the standard way, if there is a standard defined for the feature that you're performing. Again, one of the most important features of the user interface is consistency. Because Macintosh programs are pretty consistent, a user can go from one to another with some idea of how things work in each. For example, in almost every Macintosh application, the user can open and close files with a file menu, make changes to text with the edit menu, or open desk accessories with the Apple menu. Most windows can be moved, resized, and scrolled in standard ways, too. This consistency is incredibly important in making Macintosh software both easy to learn and easy to use.

Direct Control and Feedback

Wherever you can, you should make actions happen as a direct result of something that the user does. Direct control makes the user feel on top of the program, leading to happier and more productive use of the software. Giving the user a choice about how to do things, rather than assuming a particular implementation and not offering any options, is one way of offering the user control, as in the case of Switcher's arrows.

If you have to make an arbitrary choice in your program, such as the size or arrangement of something on the screen, and it really doesn't matter to your program's logic what you do, see if you can let the user make the choice. This allows the user to customize the program's environment without costing you very much programming effort. Remember, you're not writing your application for yourself (usually); you're writing it for other people, so don't forget them.

To back up the notion that the user is in control, you must provide feedback to user actions. There are lots of standard examples of this kind of behavior in the user interface: menu items flash when they're selected, buttons light up when they're clicked, text lights up when it's selected, and so on.

When the user takes an action, draw something on the screen to show what's going on. For example, if the user asks to sort a database with 5000 records, a nice application will put up a dialog that shows the progress of the sort. It's pretty hard to estimate the actual time that an operation will take, since the computer may have any of several different microprocessors, RAM upgrades, disk drives, and who knows what else. A good alternative to showing the actual time of an operation is to show how much of the operation has been done and how much is left.

Figure 1-3 shows some techniques used by different programs to show an operation in progress. FileMaker uses words and numbers to show what's going on as records are added to a file. MORE provides a more visual indicator by filling up the picture of the document with black as the document is loaded. The AppleLink display shows both a graphic indicator and a time estimate.

A time estimate is a nice feature, but you have to be very careful when you indicate real time. Your application may be running on a Macintosh Plus with a 68000 or a Macintosh II with a 68020 running at twice the clock speed. In the case of AppleLink reading a message, the time estimate is accurate on any Macintosh, because the time it takes to read a message is limited not by the computer's clock speed but by the modem's speed, which is usually 1200 baud. If you want to show a real time estimate in your application, you can use a global called TimeDBRA to figure out how fast the computer's microprocessor is running. This is an arcane art—have fun trying it.

Avoiding Modes

A mode is an environment within an application that defines and restricts what the user can do. Traditional computer applications require the user to enter modes to take various actions. For example, a word processing program may have an editing mode for typing and revising text, a filing mode for working with files on disk, and a separate mode for printing documents. In each mode, certain actions are impossible: you can't edit a document while you're in printing mode, for example. This often confuses humans, since they don't work that way in real life.

Typically, each mode also defines its own set of commands, which can further confuse the poor user. The command that means "display directory" in filing mode may mean "delete paragraph" in editing mode. Oops. Another thing that makes modes harder for users is that you have to enter them and leave them. This adds extra commands that are only useful for navigating through the modes.

Modes *can* be used properly within the Macintosh user interface. Apple defines several cases in which modes are considered a reasonable way to implement something:

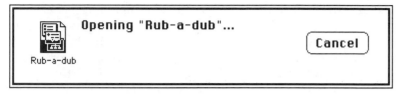

Opening "Rub-a-dub"...

Cancel

Rub-a-dub

MORE

20 records remaining to input from "Rub-a-dub".

To cancel, hold down the ⌘ key and type a
period (.).

FileMaker Plus

Receiving "Rub-a-dub".
To cancel, hold down the ⌘ key and type a period (.).

Percentage Complete:

◆

0   25   50   75   100

Time remaining: about 7 minutes.

AppleLink

Figure 1-3. Progress dialogs

- Long-term modes. When you want to write a letter, you go into "letter writing mode"—that is, you start a word processing program, a long-term mode. Each application, or each function within an integrated application, is a mode of this kind.
- Spring-loaded modes. This kind of mode must be actively maintained with some constant action, such as holding down a key or the mouse button. When you pull down a menu, you can only look at menus for as long as you hold down the button; you could say that you're in "menu selection mode." As soon as you let go of the button, poof: you're out of the mode. Spring-loaded modes are easy to get out of, so they're not painful to users.
- Alert modes. These modes come about when you have to tell the user something or ask the user to do something, for example to unlock a disk so that your application can write stuff onto it.
- Real life modes. Some things are modal in real life, like selecting which document you want to work on, picking a pencil or pen to draw with, or deciding to launch thermonuclear weapons. These kinds of modal real life actions should be duplicated by applications. Drawing applications like MacPaint and Full-Paint have palettes of tools to choose from that work something like real life.

The Macintosh user interface provides lots of tools and techniques for avoiding modes. For example, windows help choose long-term modes, since they allow the user to pick the right thing to work on. Pull-down menus also help avoid modes, since the user can choose virtually any action from a menu at any time. A more subtle technique that's used to help avoid modes is discussed next—don't stop reading now!

Select, Then Act

If you want to change the font of some text in a Macintosh program, you start by selecting the text you want with the mouse. Then, you choose a command from a menu to make the font change happen. The technique of selecting something and then acting on it is a fundamental feature of the Macintosh interface.

If you think about it, you'll find that this concept is behind almost all the work you do in a Macintosh application. Traditional computer programs work the other way: first, you figure out what you want to do, like deleting text; then you go and delete it. In fancy human interface terms, this technique (or **paradigm,** to use a ten-dollar word) is called **verb-noun.** The verb is what you want to do; the noun is what you want to do it to.

The Macintosh technique, of course, is **noun-verb.** What makes one more desirable than the other? In the previous section, we decided that modes should be avoided in general, since they confuse users and restrict their actions for no obvious reason. The verb-noun technique, in which the action is chosen first, leads directly to modes: to delete text, for example, you go into delete mode. The noun-verb technique—select, then act—is a way to avoid modes. In Macintosh text editing, you are never in delete mode. You select the text you want to work with, then choose the appropriate command from a menu. When you're done, there's no mode to get out of.

If you accept the argument that the arbitrary use of modes is bad for the user interface, it follows logically, as Mr. Spock would say, that you should use the "select, then act" technique in your user interface, because it helps you avoid modes. This principle of the user interface is subliminal to most users; they don't realize that they're using the noun-verb rather than the verb-noun technique, of course. Without this basic principle, though, the whole character of the user interface would change.

Using Graphics and Analog Indicators

The Macintosh has no text mode. Everything you see is drawn, not written. The dots on the screen are rectangular and there's no space between adjacent dots, so they bleed together. The Macintosh has QuickDraw, one of the world's most powerful graphics packages, in its ROM—you already know this, right? The point is that graphics are an integral part of the Macintosh interface, so use them.

Graphics can help convey an idea much more clearly than text can. For example, look at the way MORE shows the progress of a document being opened (Figure 1-3). Some people would have a hard time figuring out how far along they were with information like "12950 of 71440 bytes read," but a little document that fills up as the operation proceeds has obvious meaning to all users.

Pictures and icons can also convey information. The meaning of the Trash is obvious and every user soon figures out how to use it. However, you can go overboard with icons. Some complex concepts can be reduced to simplicity with insanely brilliant sets of pictures, but other ideas just get more complicated when you try to take away the words. The only way to find out if you've got it right is to try it out on real people.

> **Analog vs. digital.**   There are other advantages to using pictures instead of words and numbers. Pictures don't have to be translated into other languages, usually, and pictures are useful if your software's users can't read (like if they're very young kids).

The last decade or so has seen a massive increase in **digital** things: clocks, recording equipment, car speedometers, television channel indicators, stereo receiver volume controls, and oven temperature settings all often use numbers today. In the past, of course, all these things used knobs or dials and their values varied across a range rather than being set to discrete numerical values: they were **analog**.

Some interesting discoveries were made after the digital craze blossomed in the 1970s. Despite the absolute accuracy of reading a digital watch, lots of people preferred analog displays (or hands, as normal humans call them). Seeing a watch with hands indicating that it was almost 5 o'clock was more meaningful (though less accurate) than seeing that it was 4:58:37. The same thing happened with car speedometers: many people felt more comfortable with the old-fashioned needle than with a digital display.

Why are many people happier with analog displays, which are inherently less accurate than digital ones? One reason is the subconscious meaning attached to looking at a display. An analog display, such as a clock, can have many different appearances, so someone who looks at it all the time can attach subconscious, rapidly derived meaning to particular displays or times. A digital display must be interpreted more rationally: most people have to think about it more to grasp its meaning, despite its apparent pinpoint accuracy.

Another reason for the decline in popularity of some digital displays is that many people don't care for that much accuracy. Who needs to know that it's exactly 4:58:37? That's probably not the right time anyway! Most people don't care if they're going 56.8 miles per hour unless they get a ticket for speeding. In many cases, analog displays seem to be more human, and they provide all the information that we need.

Analog indicators in your programs, like the filling document in MORE or the time-remaining bar in AppleLink, are easily understood by users and have the added advantage of usually not needing to be translated to other languages. Computers are completely digital creatures. Making them more analog is a great way to help people figure out what they're doing.

WYSIWYG

One of the most common uses of computers is to generate pieces of paper. If a paperless office with everything stored in the computer and nowhere else is possible, it's a long, long way off. So for the time being you should keep in mind that people who use your application will probably want to print something eventually and they'll want it to look like what they see on the screen. This principle is somewhat awkwardly known as "what you see is what you get" or WYSIWYG, which is pronounced (yes, it's really pronounced) "wizzy-wig."

Traditionally, printers have been able to do much fancier things than personal computer screens. This is still true today: a Laser-Writer crams 300 dots into an inch, while the Macintosh screen shows 72. Still, 72 dots per inch, combined with enough inches, is enough real estate to allow a close approximation of what will be printed. The Macintosh lets you show different fonts, styles, and sizes, as well as all sorts of graphics. Your application can even get information about the printer—for example, its resolution and paper size—to make the screen display a more accurate picture of what will come out of the printer. Because of factors like the difference in resolution between the screen and the printer, exact WYSIWYG isn't really possible on a Macintosh, but it can be close enough so that most users won't really notice the difference. A good goal for your application is to show the user a preview of the output that's so accurate that it will rarely be necessary to do a test print.

Great moments in marketing. Just a couple of years ago, "what you see is what you get" was an expression (I think it came from a soul record of the early 1970s) that described programs that allowed you to see things on the screen just as they would look when you printed them. When the Lisa and Macintosh computers came out and mass-market computers were available that could approach WYSIWYG capability, some marketing person somewhere (probably at Apple) apparently decided that WYSIWYG was too programmerish, so a new term was coined: *visual fidelity*. Then in 1985 or so, WYSIWYG became an acceptable "word" to use outside the engineering department. In fact, to use real cool marketing lingo, WYSIWYG became a very **sexy** (ugh) feature. Also at that time it became popular to actually try to pronounce this thing, and it came out "wizzy-wig." I am not making this up.

Forgiveness

Most Macintosh applications have an Undo command that allows the user to reverse the action of the last command. For example, in a word processor, if you accidentally delete the selected text by pressing the backspace key, you can get it back by using the Undo command. This is a wonderful feature for anyone who's ever accidentally lost some work in a computer program—in other words, everyone.

Although it's not as commonly discussed as some other parts of the interface, the **forgiveness** feature is something that users love most, as you can imagine. It should be available for more than text editing, of course. You should try to make actions undoable whenever possible. Of course, some actions cannot be undone, like initializing a disk or drying your pet in a microwave oven. When the user wants to take some serious action that's not undoable, you should issue a warning (usually with an alert box) saying that the action can't be undone. This way, at least you give the user one last shot before performing the command.

Stability

Most people using computers don't understand how they work and they don't really care to know. The whole point of a user interface is to make work on a computer more familiar to users. To achieve this goal, you must provide an environment for your users that does not constantly change. You should try to keep the same menus and menu items throughout the program, for example. Your dialog boxes should be similar in style. Stick to your terminology: if you invent something in your program and call it a *potrzebie,* be sure to always call it that.

When an action is temporarily not available, like the Close item when no windows are open, the option is drawn in gray, not removed. Macintosh users are taught to understand this and it's useful any time you want to show that some option isn't available right now.

In general, you should avoid changing menus and menu items while your application is running. One exception is the Show/Hide menu item. This item says (for example) "Show Clipboard" to open the Clipboard window. When it's open, the item changes to say "Hide Clipboard."

User Interface Words To Live By

These are the general principles of the user interface. Always remember the principle at the heart of a good interface: the program is for other people, so keep them in mind while you're designing. Don't be afraid to innovate: try new things that are consistent with the standard user interface principles.

You should not consider the Apple definition of the interface the ultimate definition for every possible situation. That doesn't mean that you should contradict the guidelines just because you think that something is wrong or that you have a marginally better idea; but if you have an application that does something not thoroughly covered in the guidelines, try something clever and elegant that makes sense for the situation. You'll know you've done a great job if other programs start stealing your idea.

The FPI Rule

The Macintosh user interface is certainly one of the most important reasons why the Macintosh family of computers has been successful, but it's not the only reason. The advanced interface makes the Macintosh unique and the Macintosh is best known for its ease of learning, one of the fundamental principles of the user interface. But a great interface that makes software easy to learn will not make a computer successful when you try to sell it to businesses, as Apple learned in 1984 after introducing the Macintosh. It wasn't until software developers started coming out with beefier applications that many business computer users started considering using Macintoshes.

What things other than user interface are important in software? The most important consideration is amazingly obvious: the program's features. If a program doesn't have the features a prospective user is looking for, it doesn't matter how easy to learn the program is. As obvious as this little fact may seem, it was often overlooked by software developers creating their first Macintosh products. They got lost in the noise of ease of learning and forgot to put features in their software. Unfortunately, the customers they were trying to reach were not willing to trade features for ease of learning.

Once a prospective software buyer finds a program with the necessary features, the speed with which the program performs its tasks becomes very important. Many software developers don't pay close attention to the speed their of programs. A lot of programmers seem to think that the computer is pretty fast and it lets people work faster than they could otherwise, so they don't really need to work at making the program faster. Of course, some programmers work hard at speeding up their programs; this performance difference can separate a fair, functional program from a great one.

Programs that have been tuned for speed are often the most popular. In fact, many users of computers in business find speed so important that they're not willing to give up performance in order to have a better user interface; in other words, they think it's great if the interface makes the program easy to learn but it better not slow you down once you've become proficient.

For many Macintosh users, a program's features and performance are the most important factors in figuring out which program to use. They would rather have an application with a slightly cumbersome interface that does everything they want it to very quickly than a perfect implementation of the interface that leaves out crucial features or runs at glacial speed. It took software developers a while to realize this fact (some never did—may they rest in peace): the best and most popular applications have all three qualities—features, performance, and interface. This is the FPI rule, named after the three elements that make it up.

Of course, any Macintosh application with even the barest minimum of the standard user interface will have a better interface than a typical old-world program running on another computer. The FPI rule says you should make sure your programs have enough features to make them useful and run at a usable speed before you create exotic enhancements to the user interface.

This does *not* mean you should spend all your development time adding features and tuning performance and so little on the user interface that it makes a typewriter seem advanced. You must be sure not to break any of the fundamental rules of the user interface. In particular, if an interface for a feature exists that has been established as a standard by other applications, you should follow that standard unless you have a very, very good reason for doing it differently (thinking your technique is slightly better than the standard is not a good enough reason).

Remember that the best Macintosh applications are strong in all three areas addressed by the FPI rule. They have plenty of features, so they're useful to the widest possible range of users; they work fast, so the features are actually usable without having to wait forever; and they implement the Macintosh user interface, following the standards and extending them in reasonable, intuitive ways where there are no precedents. Applications that pay attention to all three FPI areas are the ones that become classics.

The final frontier. The original Macintosh computer, which had 128K of RAM and a maximum of 800K of disk space, was a great breakthrough because it had an advanced user interface and yet its price was in the same range as other personal computers. It became obvious that 128K of RAM and 800K of disk weren't nearly enough for this kind of computer, in part because of all the extra work that had to be done to keep track of the interface. In essence, the interface is an illusion created by the applications and system software. There's really no desktop, no windows, and no buttons inside the computer, of course: it's all an illusion that's there to make it easier for humans. This particular illusion is expensive and pretty difficult to maintain. Think of it this way: it's like one of the Star Trek episodes in which the Enterprise and crew visit a planet with an incredibly powerful being or force that holds them and won't let them go. In various episodes, this force was Landru, Vaal, or Apollo (the sun god, not the computer); in the end, Captain Kirk and friends would always find the power source for it and destroy the illusion. Unfortunately, this is what happened to a lot of software that ran on early versions of the Macintosh. They presented a great illusion (the user interface), but in the end, when the users challenged the computer by exercising the software, the power source (the Macintosh hardware) couldn't handle the illusion any more and eventually it was destroyed (the software slowed to a crawl or crashed). The fix for this was to make the power source more powerful; Apple has done this in more recent models of the Macintosh. If the aliens ever figure this out, the crew of the Enterprise may be in deep trouble.

Introduction to Compatibility

You'll find information in this book about maintaining compatibility with the various models in the Macintosh family of computers. This subject is very important, since new models of the Macintosh are coming out every year in addition to the seven different models already released by Apple (OK, since you asked: Macintosh 128K, 512K, XL, Plus, 512K enhanced, SE, and II). The best way to make sure that your application will work with future Macintosh computers is to think about compatibility while designing and writing the application. This section is a short introduction to the philosophy of compatibility among Apple's Macintosh computers.

Much of the Macintosh was designed with great **generality** in mind; in other words, the system software can be enhanced and expanded in many ways without breaking applications that work with the original system. This philosophy is very important to Apple when it designs a new computer. If a new Macintosh comes out and a significant amount of existing software doesn't work with it, people won't buy the computer—a situation Apple tries to avoid. So, in designing new Macintoshes, Apple first tries to design extensions and enhancements that won't kill existing applications and then spends a lot of time and effort testing non-Apple software to make sure the designed compatibility really works.

This commitment to generality and compatibility is obvious when you look closely at the system software. For example, when a program needs a chunk of memory, it calls the Macintosh Memory Manager, and the Memory Manager figures out whether enough memory is available to handle the program's request. This means that if the user adds more memory to the Macintosh, an application that asks for its memory chunks by calling the Memory Manager will now take advantage of the expanded memory with the same code that ran on the unexpanded machine. This is a great advantage over machines that don't allow programs to use expanded RAM automatically.

There are lots of tricks and techniques used in the Macintosh to give you a chance to make your software compatible with future members of the family. Even though no one, including Apple, knows exactly what kinds of features these new Macintoshes will have, if you take advantage of these tricks, your software may be compatible (or almost compatible) with future machines when they come out.

Hierarchical File System and Standard File

Another example of compatibility came with the introduction of the Hierarchical File System (HFS) in 1985. When this happened, Apple replaced a fundamental part of the operating system, the File Manager, converting it from a flat system to a hierarchical one. Despite this radical change, many applications continued to work well under the new system, because Apple had made sure that all the old File Manager calls were supported under the new system and because a clever trick allowed old applications to see files in directories (see Chapter 2 for more on how this works).

The user interface shields users from many of the raw facts of the system's hardware. This helps to make compatibility easier to maintain for many hardware and software changes. Adding a hard disk or changing from single-sided to double-sided disks is often a traumatic upgrade on many personal computers. On the Macintosh, most applications talk to files through the File System and the Standard File Package, which is the code that takes care of things when the user wants to open or save a file.

Standard File automatically lets the user look through the available disk drives and directories, eject disks and insert new ones, and even initialize new disks if necessary. Most applications don't have to bother knowing about the number, kind, or sizes of disk drives. If the programmer wants to know this stuff, there are clean ways to find it out.

The generality and high level of interface provided by Standard File and the File Manager make using file servers like Apple-Share almost invisible to application programmers. If the user is connected to a file server, Standard File will display the file server volume along with the other volumes when a file is opened or saved. Again, the programmer doesn't have to bother with the fact that a document is being saved on a file server instead of a local disk drive.

Using Global Variables

The Macintosh system software maintains an area of global variables. The size of this area depends on the version of the ROM, but the globals of each new ROM are a superset of the previous ones. In other words, once a global is defined in a certain location, it keeps its definition for future ROMs (at least, this has been true so far and it's likely to continue to happen). For example, location $9D6 is defined as a global variable called WindowList, and it contains a pointer to the frontmost window. This definition was made for the ROM in the original Macintosh and has remained valid for all the ROMs released since then. Although you can also find the frontmost window by calling FrontWindow, in many other cases, there's no other way to get the information that's in the global.

Is it likely that Apple will continue to maintain this variable, in the same location, in future versions of the ROM? That's an interesting question. There are probably hundreds of programs running around in the real world that depend on current definitions of various globals. These programs would fail if these globals no longer had the same meanings, and Apple is pretty fanatical about not making changes that will cause lots of applications to fail.

On the other hand, if Apple someday decides to make radical changes to the Macintosh operating system, some of today's globals may no longer be valid. If this happens, WindowList may be a good candidate for getting zapped, since there's a Toolbox call, FrontWindow, that does nearly the same thing but with a higher level interface. It's much easier for authors of future ROMs to make sure that Toolbox calls do the same thing than to guarantee that the globals will mean the same thing. This is especially true now that Apple is evolving the operating system to support multitasking.

What's the bottom line in this discussion? Right now, Apple is strongly committed to maintaining a high level of compatibility when each new ROM is released. No changes are made that would cause a lot of applications to fail on the new system. This means, among other things, that all globals have to maintain their locations and their meaning whenever possible. However, Apple someday may decide that it must change the operating system so radically that some globals will no longer be maintained. If this should happen, Apple will likely give plenty of notice and guidelines about the change.

It's not real likely that this radical change will happen all at once, though, so you shouldn't worry too much about it. It used to be that any feature documented without a warning in *Inside Macintosh* was all right, but with changes for multitasking that's not true anymore. To be on your best behavior, you should stick to the ROM calls and pay attention to new information from Apple. Also, watch out for those warnings. For example, *Inside Macintosh* tells you how to modify the Standard File dialogs, but it also warns you that "future compatibility is *not* guaranteed if you do not use the standard dialogs."

So there. As John Parker said, "Believe it!"

Don't Touch That File!

As you probably know, the ROM doesn't have everything in it that you need. When you start up a Macintosh, one of its first living acts is to open the file called System (or the system file) on the startup disk (if the disk doesn't have a file called System, it can't be a startup disk). The system file contains more important stuff that's needed to make the Macintosh work; how's that for a precise, scientific definition? Actually, System includes many common resources, including fonts, desk accessories, patches to the ROM, packages like Standard File and the List Manager, and much more. In short, System is a lot like Los Angeles: it's one big thing that's really composed of lots and lots of smaller things.

Whenever Apple issues an update to any of these pieces, System must be changed or replaced. Since the system file is so important to the computer and since it's open all the time, even while you're modifying it, and can't be closed, munging around with it can be a fairly delicate operation. For this reason, Apple has always advised developers not to make any changes to System. This advice is just fine, but what if you want to make some feature change that requires a modification to the system file?

Three tools are available to enforce the "don't touch the system file" rule that Apple preaches. The most common thing people do to System is to install fonts and desk accessories. Apple provides a standard tool for messing around with fonts and desk accessories, the well-known Font/Desk Accessory Mover. It doesn't matter if a font or desk accessory was created by Apple or by anybody else: Font/Desk Accessory Mover can install it.

Running numbers. The Font/Desk Accessory Mover has to be pretty clever as it shuffles those fonts and desk accessories around. Every FONT and DRVR resource, of course, has a resource ID. When the FDA Mover is told to move something from one file to another, it first must check in the destination file to see whether a resource with the same type and ID already exists. If so, it has to renumber the resource being moved in before adding it to its new file. That's not all. You may know that desk accessories are permitted to "own" other resources, such as pictures, controls, text strings, or anything else they use. This ownership is established by a special numbering scheme: every desk accessory owns all resources within a certain range of resource ID numbers. If the desk accessory is renumbered, the owned resources have to be renumbered, too. The FDA Mover takes care of this. And there's more. (This is getting to be like one of those TV commercials for the Ginsu knives.) Sometimes, resources contain the IDs of other resources embedded within them; for example, a DLOG resource contains the ID of the DITL that it uses. If these resources are also owned by the desk accessory, they have to be copied and, if the desk accessory is renumbered, they have to be renumbered too. Now you see why Font/Desk Accessory Mover is a fairly complex program.

The second tool Apple provides to allow you to leave the system file alone is the INIT 31 mechanism. The story is this: the original Macintosh system file contained resources of type INIT, which were little pieces of code. When the system was starting up, these INITs would be loaded and executed. By creating your own INITs, you could have any arbitrary code execute at system startup time, which is a very handy feature.

Unfortunately, in order to make your INIT work under this scheme, it has to be in System, and Apple tells developers not to put anything into System. What can you do? Well, in all versions of the system file released since January 1986 (version 3.0 and later), there's a neat trick added. Apple supplies a special INIT with ID 31 that comes as part of System. When it gets executed at startup time, it goes out and looks for any other files in the system folder that have the file type INIT. If it finds one, it opens the file and then searches in the file for resources with resource type INIT. If it finds any INIT resources, it loads them and executes them. This flow is illustrated in Figure 1-4.

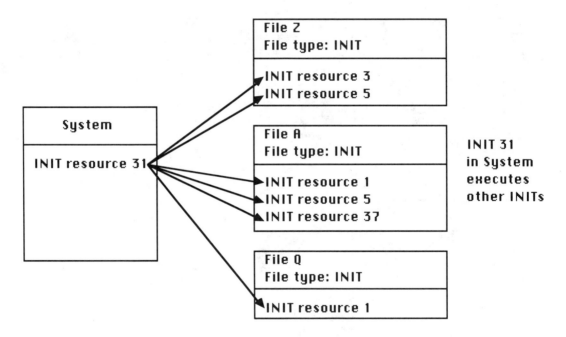

Figure 1-4 . INIT resource execution

The standard system file now contains INIT 31, so if you want to have an INIT resource executed when the system starts up, you don't have to modify the system file. All you have to do is create your INIT resource, put it in a new file of type INIT, then put it (or ask your users to put it) in the system folder. When the system starts up, your INIT will be run.

The Font/Desk Accessory Mover and the INIT 31 mechanism provide ways to avoid having to touch the system file, but only in highly specialized cases; they're only useful if the resources you're dealing with are fonts (type FONT), desk accessories (type DRVR), or INITs. What about more general situations, when you want to install or remove some other kind of resource? How can you avoid touching the system file then?

The answer is a slick utility called Installer. This program, released by Apple in 1986, allows you to add, replace, or remove any file or resource in a file. You can think of Installer as a sort of high-level interface for modifying system software. You tell Installer exactly what to do with Installer scripts, which are resource files that contain Installer instructions. Apple has used Installer for all its system software updates since early 1986. These include new releases of the system file, the Finder, printing software, and the AppleShare file server.

The neat thing about Installer is that it can be used to selectively copy or replace files and resources within files. If you're just copying or replacing resources, the rest of the file remains intact. Let's say you're releasing an update to your product consisting of some new CODE resources. It would be pretty simple just to put a copy of the complete new version on the update disk, but this presents at least one problem if you're a third-party developer: you'd like to be sure that people who buy the update already have the original software and aren't getting a complete package for the price of an update.

You can solve this problem by using Installer to do the update. By creating an Installer script to update the application, you can just provide a subset of the application instead of the whole thing. Even if you replace virtually all of the application's resources, you can still have Installer verify that the application is really there before performing the update. Sure, smart (and even semi-smart) people can get around this technique, but most won't bother. Macintosh Technical Note #75 describes how to create Installer scripts. You might find Installer useful if you have to create a software update.

Sometimes, creating an Installer script for a job can be overkill. If the installation process for your program is easy, you probably won't need to provide your users with an Installer script. For example, if all they need to do is put a file or two into the system folder, they don't need an Installer script. However, if you want to perform the delicate surgery of selectively replacing resources, or if there are several files to be replaced or modified, you should consider cooking up an Installer script to do the dirty work.

Other Apple Utilities

In addition to the Font/Desk Accessory Mover, the INIT 31 mechanism, and Installer, Apple provides a number of other neat tools and tricks you can use to your advantage when you're writing something for the Macintosh. This section describes some of the more interesting ones.

Control Panel

The Macintosh system software has always included a desk accessory called the Control Panel. It lets the user set such things as the desktop pattern, the correct time and date, and the speaker volume. With the release of the Macintosh II in 1987, Apple revised and extended the Control Panel's power. Now, the Control Panel groups its settings together by function or device. There's a group of settings for the mouse, the keyboard, the sound capabilities, and so on.

The best thing about the new Control Panel is that it's extensible. When the user opens the Control Panel, it checks for files of type cdev. If it finds any, it looks into them for resources that define the appearance of the Control Panel selections for that device. If you're creating any kind of device that requires the user to choose settings, you can create a cdev file that will present the choices in the Control Panel. This means you may be able to avoid writing a special control panel or preferences program of your own. Also, your user already knows how to use the Control Panel, which makes the process easier. For the official documentation on the Control Panel, see *Inside Macintosh*, Volume V (soon to be a major motion picture).

Chooser

When the LaserWriter was introduced in 1985, Apple released a desk accessory called Choose Printer, which let the user select between the directly connected ImageWriter and the AppleTalk–connected LaserWriter. This desk accessory was straightforward and specialized: it was used to select printers, period. Life was simple then.

As the utility of AppleTalk grew and more things became available for the network, Choose Printer was transformed into the more general Chooser. The Chooser is a desk accessory that allows the user to choose which specific devices will be used for various functions. The Chooser can be used to select a printer from among directly connected and AppleTalk–connected devices; it can select file server volumes to be mounted; and it can select a mail server. But it isn't really just for picking printers and file servers.

The Chooser is designed as a general-purpose friend to the user. It figures what to offer the user by communicating with files of type RDEV that it finds when the user selects Chooser from the Apple menu. The RDEV file contains code to tell the Chooser what to display for that device and what to do when the user chooses something.

By creating your own RDEV file, you can (you guessed it) have your own device show up in the Chooser, just like the standard Apple ones do. There's information on how to do this in *Inside Macintosh*, Volumes IV and V.

You might think that the functions of the Chooser and the Control Panel overlap somewhat. You're right. They both provide the user with a method for setting up devices and their characteristics. In fact, their functions are so similar that it's possible someday they'll be combined into a single jumbo-deluxe desk accessory that does it all. The Control Chooser? The Chooser Panel?

Until that happens, how do you decide whether to put your device-setup stuff into the Control Panel or the Chooser? In general, the Control Panel is used to set up how a device works, like the speed of a coprocessor card, the display characteristics of a video card, or the volume of the sound output. The Chooser is more appropriate for selecting one or more things from a whole list of things, like picking which printer to print on, which file server volumes to mount, or which AppleTalk–connected popcorn poppers to turn on.

If the functions of the Control Panel and the Chooser are ever combined into a single desk accessory, we can probably trust Apple's desire for compatibility with existing software to maintain the interface to the current Control Panel and Chooser. You should assume that things will continue to work as they're currently defined and that *Inside Macintosh* is the ultimate reference for how they work.

Things to Remember

To understand how to make your Macintosh software great, you have to know a little about the philosophy and history of this line of computers. You have to design things with your users in mind from the start. They're the ones that you're making your software for, so don't forget them.

C H A P T E R 2

Compatibility

What is compatibility and why should anyone care? A discussion on the great virtue of generality in computer design and what it has meant to the Macintosh product line. An introduction to good behavior as a way of life. The care and feeding of the medium-level interface. What you can get away with when customizing features like Standard File and the printing dialogs and what will come back to haunt you. What might change in the file system and what will likely stay the same.

Good Relations

In January 1984, Apple introduced the Macintosh. Its software was absolutely incompatible with every other computer ever built, even the ones built by Apple. Of course, there was a good reason for this: when you set off in a completely new direction, you allow yourself freedom from the constraints of the past.

If a new computer doesn't have to be compatible with anything else, its designers can be a lot freer and more revolutionary—and have a lot more fun—than they can when working on the evolution of an existing design. Apple has a lot of experience with both revolutionary and evolutionary computer design. The Apple II (often called the venerable Apple II, which is fine with me) was introduced in 1977. Since then it has undergone several face lifts, emerging at various times in the bodies of the Apple II Plus, Apple IIe, Apple IIc, and Apple IIgs. The most recent of these was introduced in 1986, nine years after the original Apple II. Yet Apple has managed to build a great deal of compatibility into every member of this product family. Every model has provided some improvements or different configuration but all of them can run a lot of late-1970s vintage software. Figure 2-1 tells you a little about the history of the Apple II.

Model	First year shipped	New Features
Apple II	1977	4K to 48K RAM, 40 column text
Apple II Plus	1980	Floating-point BASIC
Apple IIe	1983	up to 128K RAM, 80 column text
Apple IIc	1984	built-in disk drive & carrying handle
Apple IIgs	1986	256K RAM and up; 16-bit processor

Figure 2-1. Apple II models

Of course, all this compatibility doesn't come free or even cheap. Each Apple II is compatible with its predecessors because it was planned that way. Apple's commitment to making all its Apple II computers compatible has gone from strong to nearly fanatic in the last few years. A lot of time and money spent developing the Apple IIgs could have been saved if it hadn't had to be compatible with its predecessors.

Why spend this big investment in compatibility? Is it really so important? You bet it is. When a new computer ships, there's a group of people interested in it, whether or not it runs very much software.

When Apple introduced the Macintosh in 1984, a lot of interested folks bought one mainly on the promise of great software to come, a promise which took a while, but came through spectacularly. A really successful computer, though, must have lots of great applications software. Thousands of software packages are available for the Apple II. Inventing an Apple II that couldn't take advantage of most of these would be a big mistake and Apple knew it.

Apple faced a similar situation with the Macintosh Plus, which was introduced in January 1986, and the Macintosh SE and Macintosh II, which came out in March 1987. The whole point of an evolving product line is to take advantage of existing software and peripheral hardware. If Apple ships a new Macintosh that doesn't run the most popular existing Macintosh software, not many people would be interested in buying it.

Let a Thousand Flowers Bloom

There is another option available when you ship a new computer. Instead of ensuring that new machines work with existing software, a manufacturer can work with software developers in advance of a product's introduction, providing them with prototypes and technical help so they can have new software and peripherals ready by the time the computer is introduced.

This sounds like a great idea and in fact is exactly what happens. Months before a new computer is shipped, Apple's Evangelism group shows off plans and prototypes to developers. The lucky and talented ones become **seeded**; that is, they get prototype hardware and pre-release software and documentation. These brave souls then get to spend their days pounding away on a fascinating piece of exciting, not quite debugged new hardware, working feverishly to finish their products before the new computer is sent out into the world.

There are a couple of problems with this process. First of all, seeding periods are always too short. When a new computer is debugged, tested, and ready to be produced, it gets introduced to the world. This means that the prototypes that seeded developers work on are often ill-behaved beasts. Both the hardware and the software are changed and upgraded frequently, so the developer really has to know what's going on. Playing with a new Macintosh months before the rest of the world gets to see it may be fun, but it can also be trying.

Another problem with relying on seeded developers to produce all the software anyone would ever need is that only a select few developers get to be seeded. Seeding locks out the unknowns, the up and coming, and the Next Big Thing. Programs like PageMaker come from companies that Apple never heard of, once upon a time; and it's tough for unknown companies to get seeded with new hardware. Much of the real innovation in software comes only after a new computer has been out in the world for a while, when the machine's tricks and power have been discovered by the programming community (which, as you know, is somewhere near Berkeley). This is great for the new computer as it matures, but it doesn't help at all when it's struggling for acceptance.

So, if seeding isn't good enough, and the manufacturer wants to have lots of software available when a new computer ships, the only alternative is to make it compatible with something else. When the new computer just happens to be a Macintosh, like the Macintosh Plus was in January 1986, it seems like a reasonable idea to make it compatible with existing Macintosh software.

Designing Compatibility

How hard is it to make a new computer compatible with its parent? That depends on several things, including the original computer's design, the magnitude of changes in the new computer, the definition of *compatible*, and the designer's commitment to compatibility. Let's talk about each of these factors.

The best time to start thinking about a computer's future models is when the first model is being designed. In a sense, the designers of the original Macintosh were thinking about the Macintosh Plus, SE, and II when they were designing the original machine, although they really had no way of knowing what was going to happen that far in the future.

The first and most important way they accounted for future evolution was by recognizing that they couldn't possibly know about the changes and new features that would happen. That recognition allowed them to use one of the most powerful concepts in software: **generality**. When designers realize that *redesigners*, who will make modifications and enhancements, will follow them, they make the software for a particular task as modular and changeable as possible. Building in this generality allows future architects and developers to make changes and additions more painlessly.

Great moments in marketing: the XL story. After Apple gave up on the Lisa, it realized that a Lisa running MacWorks (the Macintosh emulator) was actually a pretty popular system. So, in 1985, Apple *renamed* the Lisa, calling it Macintosh XL. The hardware did not change—just the packaging and marketing. It was now obvious that this computer was intended to be used as a big screen, large-memory Macintosh. The funny thing is that it was a brilliant move; it worked. For the first time, Apple was selling a lot of Lisas. There was a problem though. Apple had already torn down the production facilities for the Lisa (or XL). Just at its height of popularity, the Macintosh XL (or Lisa) was killed.

There are zillions of examples of generality in the Macintosh's software architecture. The Window, Menu, Control, and List Managers are all written in wonderfully general ways that allow new features to be added just by writing **definition functions** to implement them. For example, the standard menu definition function draws the menus you see most of the time: lists of text items, some with command key equivalents, check marks, and other options. However, if you want to make your own kind of menu, such as a menu of patterns, you can do it by writing a menu definition function. The Menu Manager will still handle drawing the menu title, pulling down the menu, highlighting the items, and reporting back to the application which item has been selected. The Menu Manager is general enough to allow different kinds of menus to work properly. Because of the generality of its design, the Menu Manager (and the Control, Window, and List Managers) allow for future expansion. Building generality into software means admitting that the world will change in ways that the designer can't foresee, which is a humble and absolutely valid assumption.

The Macintosh system software shows its generality in lots of other ways. Most of the system's important features are accessed through **traps**, or calls to the ROM and RAM-based system software. Because of a clever scheme implemented by the ROM, the programmer does not have to know the address of a trap in order to use it— just its number. Making sure that a ROM routine keeps its address as the ROM is modified is very difficult; making sure that it has the same trap number is very easy (see Figure 2-2). If you want to know more about how this works, see the chapter "Assembly Language" in *Inside Macintosh*.

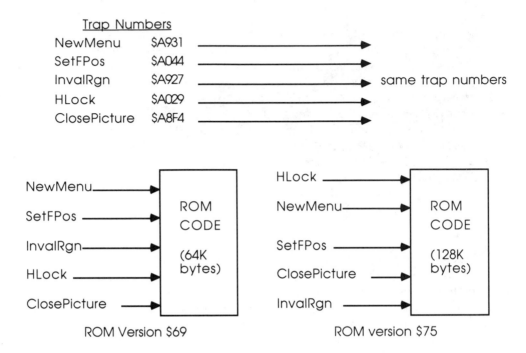

Figure 2-2. Addresses vs. trap numbers

The table that matches trap numbers to addresses is contained in RAM, not ROM. The system provides an easy mechanism for changing a trap's function or features by **patching** it. Actually, this particular feature wasn't implemented in the name of generality, just to be sure that there was a way to fix the bugs that inevitably crop up in a big ROM. Still, the fact that the basic features of the ROM can be changed in such a general way opens the door for lots of great software, such as the Japanese, Arabic, and Chinese Macintoshes, that would otherwise be very difficult or impossible to create.

Liquid ROM. One interesting benefit of having the operating system implemented as patchable traps is that the ROM can be "modified" with a disk. A bug in the ROM can almost always be fixed by implementing a new, patched trap that gets loaded from the System file on disk. In fact, this is exactly what Apple does with new releases of the Macintosh system disk. Numerous bugs in the 128K ROM (ROM version $75) were fixed by the accompanying System file version 3.2. This is how Apple can fix Macintosh ROM bugs without releasing a new ROM. Not every ROM bug can be fixed by a patch in the system file. In particular, any bug that does its damage before the system file is loaded during the startup process cannot be patched by the system file, which makes sense when you think about it. For example, the Macintosh Plus ROM (version $75) contains a bug that causes the system to hang when starting up from a non-SCSI device if a SCSI device is attached but powered off. This bug can't be patched from disk, since it occurs before anything is loaded from disk. The only way to fix it is to install a new ROM with the offending code repaired.

The generality of the Macintosh system software is extended even more by the use of **hooks** in almost every part of the system. Hooks are pointers to programmer-supplied routines (that is, addresses of routines) that allow a routine's function to be customized without hurting the general way things work. For example, a hook called EjectNotify contains the address of a routine that gets called whenever the user ejects a disk. This hook normally contains a zero, indicating that no special routine is called when a disk is ejected. By writing a routine, finding a place for it in memory, and putting its address into EjectNotify (which is at location $338), your routine will be called whenever a disk is ejected. Your application can use this as a sort of "disk-uninserted event" if you want to keep track of such things. The Finder uses this feature to clean up a disk before the user ejects it with Command-Shift-1 or Command-Shift-2.

As Apple moves toward a true multitasking operating system, some of the rules are changing. In particular, Apple now suggests that hooks like EjectNotify may change or go away in the future. Again, the best way to protect yourself is to watch the smoke coming out of Apple's chimney in the form of technical notes as time goes by.

Specializing

Generality in software is great because it allows for future variations and customization. *Generality* also describes code that implements a general, often elegant algorithm for handling a wide variety of cases. Just as for almost any design consideration in computer software, there's a tradeoff. The usual tradeoff for generality is speed. A very general piece of code is probably not taking advantage of special situations to the fullest possible extent.

As an example of this, consider a function like Line in Quick-Draw, which draws an arbitrary line. Line has to be able to handle drawing any requested line: horizontal, vertical, or diagonal with an arbitrary slope. By implementing a general algorithm, Quick-Draw can accomplish this task with a small amount of code, and it will work just fine. Are their other ways to do it? Sure there are.

The Macintosh, like many personal computers, uses **memory-mapped video.** This means that the dots (or **pixels**) you see on the screen correspond to bits in the computer's RAM. On monochrome (an ancient Aramaic word meaning "black and white") screens like those found on most Macintoshes, one dot on the screen is represented by one bit (or binary digit) in RAM. A bit can have two values: 0 and 1. A bit value of 0 produces a white dot and a 1 makes it black.

On computers with fancier video capabilities, like the Macintosh II, one pixel on the screen may be composed of several bits in memory. This allows for more complexity in the information displayed than mere black and white does, since gray scale and color are available. If you're using a Macintosh II with a video interface card that permits, say, two bits per pixel, each pixel can contain one of four different things: both bits can be 0, both can be 1, or they can be 0-1 or 1-0. These four combinations can correspond to four different colors or to four different shades of gray on a monochrome monitor.

On the Macintosh, as on most personal computers with memory-mapped video, the pixels are laid out horizontally in memory. That is, the upper left–most dots on the screen are represented by the first bits in video memory; as you move higher in video RAM, you move horizontally across the screen. When you reach the end of the line, you move to the start of the next line down. Figure 2-3 illustrates this mapping.

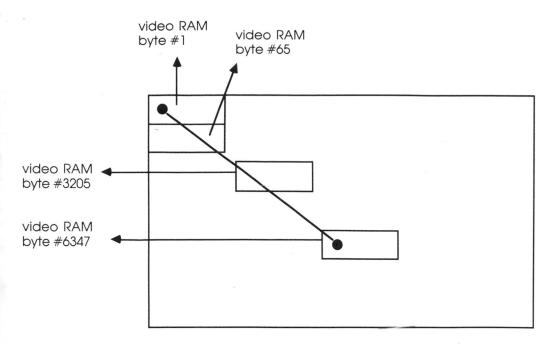

Figure 2-4. A line from 0,0 to 100,100

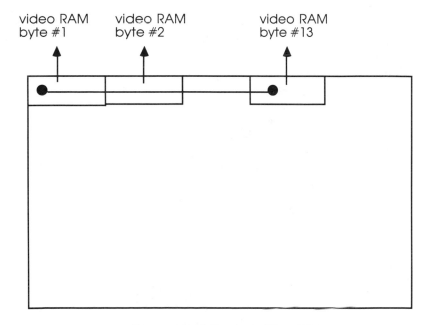

Figure 2-5. A line from 0,0 to 100,0

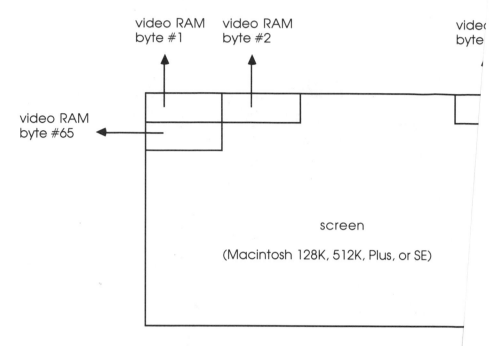

Figure 2-3. Screen mapping in RAM

Imagine some of the calculation necessary for drawing a line from point 0,0 to 100,100. As you can see in Figure 2-4, QuickDraw has to figure out where to place the dots on each horizontal line as it moves from line 0 to line 100; then it must determine which bits in memory correspond to each of these dots. This process involves storing data into 100 different bytes in memory. So, even without computation, 100 different machine language instructions must take place to make the right dots appear on the screen.

Now imagine that you're drawing a horizontal line from 0,0 to 100,0 (Figure 2-5). If a general drawing algorithm is used, placing the dots one by one, you would still need 100 different machine language instructions to make the dots light up to form the line. This is incredibly wasteful. The 68000 can address up to 32 bits of data, a long word, with one instruction. If the line drawing routine is smart enough to figure out when horizontally adjacent dots are being changed, the number of instructions required can be greatly reduced.

If the line drawing routine is really smart, it will determine in this case that the 100 bits it needs to set are all adjacent in memory. Since the 68000 can deal with 32 bits at once, all the dots in the line can be set with just four instructions: the first three can each set 32 bits, for a total of 96, leaving the remaining four bits to be set by a fourth instruction.

Let's ponder this discovery for a minute. This is important. This means something. We've discovered that by making the line drawing routine a little less general, by having it take special notice of horizontal lines, we can speed it up enormously. Drawing a horizontal line is said to be a **special case** of drawing lines. Adding special cases to a general routine has advantages and disadvantages. The advantage is obvious: performance for the special case is greatly enhanced. A horizontal line will be drawn much faster than it would have been without the special case code. This is the main argument in favor of adding special cases to general algorithms: speed.

There are a couple of problems with special cases in code. For one thing, special casing causes a loss of generality. In our example it was no big deal, because the structure of QuickDraw doesn't allow us to define different kinds of lines the way the Menu Manager allows for different kinds of menus.

There are other, potentially more significant drawbacks to adding special cases to our line drawing routine. The first is the fact that the code gets bigger. For each special case that's added, more code has to be written, using up more memory. Another drawback is that while special casing enhances the performance of the special case, it slows down all the others. How? Well, if every line has to be checked to see whether it's horizontal, that means that non-horizontal lines will take longer to be drawn while they're checked out by the special-case decider.

How can you tell whether adding special cases to a general routine is worthwhile? The important factors are the frequency of the special case, the amount of code necessary to implement it, and the performance benefits gained. If half of the lines drawn are horizontal lines, it's worth any reasonable amount of code to implement the special case, even if the performance improves only a little. On the other hand, if very few of the lines ever drawn are horizontal, this special case is worth doing only if the code required is small and the results are pretty impressive. When you're writing a general algorithm and have a chance to use special casing to improve performance, you should weigh the facts in your situation to see if adding the special case is a good idea. As Smokey says, "Only you can prevent forest fires." Of course, some situations seem to resist any attempt to find a generalized algorithm. If you get stuck with one of these, you can't do much but keep looking for those generalizations and keep improving the most important special cases.

Generality and Compatibility

Preserving compatibility across a product line means that new computers do a pretty good job of running software designed for the older members of the line. A computer manufacturer can try several good strategies when striving for compatibility. One is to define an architecture—a design specification—for an entire product line as soon as the first computer in the line is introduced.

With this approach, you define *compatibility* right from the start. When you ship the first computer, you tell the world exactly which features will and will not work in future versions. This doesn't mean you come up with and announce all the specifications of all the computers you ever intend to ship as soon as you introduce the first one. It just means that you lay out the ground rules and you warn that anyone who doesn't follow them will have software that doesn't work in the future.

When the original Macintosh was introduced in 1984, there was no official architecture announced by Apple. However, there was a very in-depth technical manual, *Inside Macintosh,* which served as a reasonable substitute. Apple had fought the compatibility wars many times with various models of the Apple II, and the Macintosh was designed with future compatibility in mind. *Inside Macintosh* contains suggestions and warnings about how to do things and what to avoid if you really want to be compatible with future machines.

Inside Macintosh became (and has remained) the main source of compatibility guidelines for the Macintosh. If a routine is documented there with no warnings or special guidelines, it's likely to be supported on future versions of the machine. On the other hand, a piece of software that thumbs its nose at a specific warning in *Inside Macintosh* is almost guaranteed to have problems working on future machines.

The problem with using *Inside Macintosh* as the guide for what's legal and what's not is that it really wasn't designed for that purpose. It provides a lot of information about how to stay compatible but since it wasn't meant to be the all-time compatibility directory, it can't tell you everything. At some point in the future, Apple may release a more complete specification on what is and is not legitimately available for use in the Macintosh. If you think it's too late for that because the Macintosh can't possibly undergo any more tortuous changes than it already has in its brief history, consider the Apple II, ten years old, still being enhanced, and still selling hundreds of thousands of computers every year.

If system software has lots of generality, it's easier to maintain compatibility for new computers. For example, on some computers, like the original Apple II, making a call to the system involves jumping directly to the address where the routine is located. This makes compatibility real hard when you're revising the system software because you have to make sure all the system routines have their starting points at the same place. This is a wonderful (and sometimes impossible) exercise in discipline for a programmer.

Later versions of Apple II system software, including ProDOS and the Apple IIgs Toolbox, have a better idea: system calls are made by jumping to a single dispatching location with a call number that tells what function to perform. Obviously, it's easy to make sure that this one location stays the same when the system is revised. Figure 2-6 shows how this works. The Macintosh trap system is similar to this, with a slight refinement: even the dispatching location can change when the system is changed, because of the neat way that the Macintosh implements trap calls. Macintosh programs don't even have to jump to a dispatching location to make ROM calls; they simply execute a special 68000 instruction that finds the trap dispatcher. This clever technique is shown in Figure 2-7.

```
LDA #13          Put call number in A-register
JSR  DISP        Jump to dispatcher
```

Dispatcher gets call number from A-register
Looks up routine address in dispatch table
Jumps to routine

Figure 2-6.   Apple II ProDOS call dispatching

```
MOVE.W #9,-(A7)  Push parameters on stack or load into registers
_TextSize        Trap word is an instruction
                 (Jumps to address pointed to by location $28)
```

Trap dispatcher gets call number from trap word
Looks up routine address in dispatch table
Jumps to routine

Figure 2-7.   Macintosh ROM call dispatching

Why would you want to be a bad guy and violate any of the compatibility guidelines? The most common reasons are to gain better performance in your software, because you don't know the "right way" to do it, or you do know the right way to do it, but you goofed. Obviously, the first reason is the only legitimate one. The way to avoid the second situation is just to learn as much as you possibly can about how the system works. The only way to avoid the third situation is through diligent testing. There's a great debugging tool called Discipline that helps expose these kinds of problems. Discipline is available as a standalone application or as a part of TMON, the super Macintosh debugger made by ICOM Simulations in Wheeling, Illinois.

Good Behavior

The legitimate reason for not playing by the rules, to make your software perform better, is another part of the generality vs. special casing argument. The authors of the system software have the difficult job of providing software that serves all applications, so it has to be general enough to handle all kinds of programs. Any particular application can probably write a special case version of a system function that will be faster than the standard one. For example, a MacPaintlike program could certainly rewrite parts of QuickDraw, or bypass QuickDraw and write directly to the screen's RAM, to make itself faster. Is it worth it to risk compatibility this way to improve your product?

This is an eternal computer science argument, especially when it is about personal computers. If the services provided by the operating system aren't fast enough or flexible enough, programmers won't use them, and their chance at staying compatible goes way down. In the IBM world, programs that obey the rules are called well-behaved, and it's interesting to note that many of the most popular and powerful programs are *not* well-behaved.

If *well-behaved* means "following the general guidelines Apple has provided for compatibility," a lot of Macintosh programs are pretty well-behaved. For example, if you ran the Macintosh Plus versions of some of the popular painting programs on the Macintosh II, you'd find they work pretty well when you use them in black and white, even on the larger screen (although some simply ignore the extra screen real estate). When you switch to gray scale or color, though, a few of them would freak out. This happens because they draw directly into the screen RAM and they always assume that one bit in memory corresponds to one dot on the screen, an assumption that's blown away when the Macintosh II draws in gray scale or color. I'd call that reasonably well-behaved.

Programs that work that well are doing several things right. They're probably doing their drawing through QuickDraw; if not, they're making use of global variables that give information about the screen. There's a global called screenBits, which tells how large the screen is and where in memory the screen RAM begins. If the program takes the trouble to check these variables when starting up, rather than blindly assuming that the screen has the same characteristics as the Macintosh Plus, it can be compatible with different screen configurations. You can see how this works in Figure 2-8.

Macintosh Plus   **Macintosh II with Apple monitor**

ScreenBits.bounds 0,0,512,342   ScreenBits.bounds 0,0,640,480

ScreenBits.baseAddr $FA700   ScreenBits.baseAddr depends on slot

ScreenBits.rowBytes 64   ScreenBits.rowBytes 128

Figure 2-8.   Using screenBits

Of course, if a program that bypasses QuickDraw doesn't bother to check screenBits to see where the video RAM begins, it will fail miserably when run on a Macintosh II. There's really no good reason to avoid checking the start of video RAM by looking at screenBits. There's no tradeoff involved: it costs virtually nothing in terms of speed and extra code and the benefits are great. This suggests that there are several levels of compatibility, depending on how a program works: it can do all its drawing through QuickDraw; bypass QuickDraw but still use globals like screenBits; or rely completely on the hardware never changing. We'll talk more about these three levels a little later.

Despite this fairly good behavior, programs that draw directly into screen RAM all croak when they try drawing in color or gray scale, where multiple bits in RAM are mapped to the same pixel on the screen. The main reason for this is that using multiple bits per pixel is a new technique for the Macintosh, and these programs had no way to anticipate how Apple was going to do it. If Apple had provided a specification of how all the bits would be mapped into each pixel when these programs were written (circa 1985), they would have had a chance to conform to the spec and might have worked without modification from the Macintosh Plus versions.

Of course, it was impossible for Apple or anyone else to know how the Macintosh II video would work in 1985 because it hadn't been invented yet. It's virtually impossible to guess all the possible twists that future models of a computer will take, making it very hard to specify a complete architecture for a product line when the first computer in the line is created. If the original Macintosh was taken as a thorough specification for all future models, it might not have been possible to implement major changes such as the hierarchical file system (the original Macintosh file system was flat) and color video.

Encore.   After Apple created the Macintosh 128K and Macintosh 512K, the people in the Macintosh division began to put together the next Macintosh. By most accounts, it was a powerful, expandable, 68020-based system. It never did come out, however, and after Steve Jobs left Apple the more modest Macintosh Plus was quickly designed and shipped. The two-year gap between the original Macintosh and the Macintosh Plus almost killed the product line. Apple seems to have learned this lesson well, since it took only 14 months to follow the Plus with the SE and the II.

It seems like it would have been nice for the original Macintosh specification to have had things like a hierarchical file system, color video, multitasking, and other neat innovations. There were several factors working against this, though. One was the Macintosh's **design center:** what it was originally designed to be and do. The original Macintosh was never designed to use a hard disk, so its file system was tuned to work very well with small disks. It was designed to be a self-contained box, so color video was not an issue.

Living color.   Actually, the original Macintosh implementation of QuickDraw includes some color functionality, which is documented in *Inside Macintosh*, Volume I. Programs that use these capabilities come out in color on a Macintosh II with a color monitor. However, no information was provided on just how the video RAM would look in a color Macintosh, so programs that bypass QuickDraw could not be ready for color.

Another important reason why it's tough to write a specification for an entire product line when the first one appears is that personal computer technology moves so fast. It's hard to know what will be available, interesting, or important in a year, let alone five or ten years.

A less obvious reason why it was difficult to have a complete Macintosh specification when the original Macintosh was introduced has to do with creativity. In working on the original Macintosh, the product's current "specification" consisted of whatever work had been done the night before. The discipline of writing things down can interfere with artistic creativity, and the creation of the Macintosh was definitely undertaken as an artistic effort. Writing specifications was not a big part of the original Macintosh design work. Making a computer was. This design technique has advantages and disadvantages, but that doesn't really matter here. That's just the way it was done.

If these programs work as well as they can even without going through QuickDraw, what's the penalty for going around the system and special casing? The penalty comes when the system is modified, either with new hardware or new software. In general, the higher a level of interface that software uses, the easier it is to retain compatibility with future versions.

In other words, software that relies on specific qualities of the hardware (the lowest-level interface), such as the location in RAM of the video, is the most likely to fail on future machines. Programs that skip QuickDraw but use global variables like screenBits work OK sometimes, but at other times they don't, like when using color or gray scale. Programs that stick to the highest-level interface available (QuickDraw calls only, such as LineTo, FrameRect, FillOval, and so on) will work fine in almost all cases, even when drawing in color.

Levels of Interface

QuickDraw and painting programs have been our example in this section, but the same rules and tradeoffs apply to all parts of the system. When Apple changed to its Hierarchical File System many programs had no compatibility problems, mainly those that stuck to the highest-level interface provided by the File Manager and the Standard File Package. Some other programs, which bypassed the File Manager but still made intelligent use of global variables, worked well most of the time but had subtle compatibility problems that had to be fixed. Finally, a few programs that relied on specific facts, like the structure of a disk directory, had to be rewritten.

If we sink lazily into broad generalities here, we can say that a programmer has three choices when thinking about a design strategy for a particular routine or feature.

1. Play completely by the rules, using only the highest level interface to the system software. The advantages to this choice are that the program stands the best chance of continuing to work when the computer's hardware or system software is changed and this interface is usually the best documented. The disadvantages are that the high level interface provided is usually pretty general and so does not provide the best possible performance.
2. Avoid all but the most minimal software interface and code directly for the hardware. This approach has the mixed blessing that you get to reinvent system software that will only be used by you. Since this is by definition a special case, you can make things work just as you want them to. Of course, you'll spend a lot of time redoing work that's already done and you virtually guarantee that your program won't work on any other flavor of this computer. This approach is rarely the best one to take.
3. Use a "medium-level" interface. This means you bypass the high-level calls so that you can special case and improve performance but you're intelligent about it, and you take advantage of things like patching traps and system globals to maximize your generality. Again, a good example of this is using screenBits to find the video RAM and its size, even if you don't use Quick-Draw for drawing.

Most Macintosh applications use a combination of the high-level and medium-level approaches. This gives them the ability to maximize their performance while still making smart decisions about compatibility. In general, you should avoid using the hardware-level interface in applications unless you can guarantee the exact configuration of the hardware, ROM, and system file that's going to be used, which is pretty difficult to do if your program is going to last more than a few months. In Figure 2-9 you can see examples of these three levels of interface.

Of course, just because a program bypasses the high level interface and violates the compatibility rules doesn't mean it's a bozo effort. A good programmer will try to stay within the guidelines as much as possible, as long as that doesn't have a terrible effect on the program's performance. Making a program faster by using the medium-level interface is a good way to enhance performance without completely sacrificing compatibility.

Level	Example	Comments
High	theWindow:=FrontWindow	should work forever
Medium	scrDmpEnb^:=$FF	Lomem global; may change someday
Low	BitClear (pointer($EFFFFE),2)	Works on 128K & 512K only

Figure 2-9. Three interface levels

Although the medium-level interface (relying on system global variables and not using the highest level) is usually immune to changes in a new system, it's definitely not guaranteed to keep you compatible. As a system evolves, it becomes more and more difficult to make sure the medium-level interface stays the same. Eventually, Apple may have to chuck the current arrangement of global variables kept in low memory in the name of a quantum enhancement to the system, such as a full multi-tasking operating system. When this happens, programs that rely on the medium-level interface may not work anymore. However, it seems likely that Apple will give the world plenty of notice before making a change this big.

Usability

For a system's high-level interface to be usable, it has to have several important qualities. First, it must provide powerful services. If the hardware is capable of, let's say, drawing in 4000 colors, then a graphics package that only offers a choice of 16 colors is not powerful enough for many developers; they will go around it and invent their own way of doing things.

A second measure of a high-level interface is flexibility or generality for the programmer. If the system forces you to do things in only one way and that one way doesn't fit the need, you have no choice but to roll your own. For example, if you want to create a menu that's shaped like Malaysia instead of a rectangle, the Menu Manager allows you to write your own menu definition function to do it. You still get the benefit of the Menu Manager's services, such as drawing the menu bar and pulling down the menu. Because of that flexibility, more programs can implement special kinds of menus and still use the Menu Manager. Of course, if you want to create a radically different menu, like a menu that somehow allows multiple items to be selected at once, you'll probably have to abandon the Menu Manager.

The third important usability aspect of a high-level programmer's interface is speed. The system software can provide lots of neat services with tremendous flexibility, but if they don't work fast, they won't be used. All of the great features built into QuickDraw, such as drawing lines, polygons, regions, text, filling with patterns, recording and playing back pictures, and everything else, would be generally ignored by developers if they weren't fast. The basic illusion of the Macintosh user interface—that windows on your computer screen are documents stacked on top of each other—would fail if QuickDraw weren't quick. The speed at which system software works is just as important as the services it provides. If the software is too slow, programmers will be forced to invent their own, even if it blows their compatibility with future systems.

Medium-level Interface

We've talked about the medium-level interface as a way to gain performance over the high-level interface without all the risks of going directly to the hardware ("programming to the bare metal," as some folks say). We've also said that this level is a little dangerous—it's not as stable as the high level. Let's define the medium level a little more clearly. In general, **the medium-level interface to the system consists of the features and capabilities of the Macintosh system that are not available simply by calling the ROM or system software, but do not require operating directly on the hardware.**

Just like several of the Ten Commandments, this statement defines things in terms of *nots*. This is because the range of things that fit into this category is very broad. Note that this definition implicitly refers to system calls made specifically by your program; obviously, every system call eventually operates directly on the hardware. If you call FrameRect, it eventually bangs the hardware, but the banging is not done by your application. This makes it OK: for each new Macintosh, the ROM is revised to make sure that hardware-specific things work.

We can use this definition as a basis for two others. First, **the high-level interface consists of the features and capabilities of the Macintosh system that are available simply by calling the ROM or system software.** It includes all the system calls listed in *Inside Macintosh* and all the features of those calls that are available by passing parameters to those calls. All calls to the Toolbox, operating system, and Quickdraw fall into this category.

Second, **the hardware-level interface consists of the features and capabilities of the Macintosh system that require operating directly on the hardware.** Items in this category include setting the speaker volume by storing a value into the Versatile Interface Adapter (VIA) chip, programming the Small Computer System Interface (SCSI) controller chip directly, or manipulating the control registers on the Macintosh II video interface card. All these things work fine if the right hardware is attached and fail catastrophically if not.

Now that we've semi-formally defined these three levels of interface, let's explore the interesting middle one. It's really a catch-all for whatever falls between the high and low levels, but what specifically does it catch? Let's look at several categories: global variables, trap patching, definition functions, QuickDraw bottlenecks, and assorted miscellaneous things.

Global Variables

The chunk of memory below the system heap contains global variables, also known as low-memory globals or just globals. These globals are used for a wide variety of purposes, mostly as data storage for various Toolbox and operating system routines. Although you might assume these globals would be private and their contents understood only by the routines that maintain them, that's not the case. In fact, many of these variables are intentionally designed to allow programmers to subtly modify or play with the way things work. A lot of the magic of Macintosh applications would be impossible without globals.

There are several hundred of these globals and many of them are officially documented in *Inside Macintosh.* Some of them contain information that's available to you; for example, location $A26, called TheMenu, contains the menu ID of the currently pulled down menu after a menu selection has been made. Some enterprising desk accessory that needs to know about menu selections may be able to use the information provided here. Other globals contain values that can be manipulated by programmers to make things happen. An example of this is ScrDmpEnb, a byte at $2F8, which can be set to 0 to disable Command-Shift-number key combinations normally used to perform functions such as printing the screen.

Another type of global is a **hook**. This is the address of a routine that will be called at certain well-defined times and that's used to modify the behavior of some system call. Most hooks are normally set to 0 (nil), meaning that no routine is implemented. When you want to install a routine into a hook, you just put the routine's address into the hook.

There are lots of hooks that let you customize standard things. A hook called DeskHook (located at $A6C) is called whenever the desktop needs to be repainted or when the user clicks in the desktop (outside of any window). If you want to take some special action in response to these situations, you can write a routine and install a pointer to it in DeskHook.

DeskHook is an example of a hook that's being phased out by Apple as multitasking emerges. Apple has already stated that DeskHook won't be supported by new versions of the Finder and MultiFinder. Unless they change their minds, you need to remember this.

One other kind of useful global variable is available to Macintosh programmers: QuickDraw globals. Because QuickDraw actually predates the rest of the ROM, it does some things a little bit differently than the rest of the system does. Instead of having all its globals in low memory, some QuickDraw global variables are kept somewhere else in memory; their exact location is pointed to by a variable whose address is stored in the 68000's A5 register. For more on exactly how this pointer works, see the QuickDraw chapter of *Inside Macintosh,* or Chapter 5 of *How to Write Macintosh Software.*

The most important of the QuickDraw globals are thePort, a pointer to the current (or active) GrafPort, and screenBits, which we've already mentioned. ScreenBits is a record containing three fields:

* BaseAddr holds the address of the start of video RAM.
* RowBytes, an integer, tells the offset in memory from the start of one row to the start of the next row.
* Bounds, a rectangle, gives the dimensions of the screen in pixels.

  Obviously, screenBits is very important if you want to be compatible with different kinds of screens. By examining its values, a program can figure out the size and location in RAM of the screen.

Where have all the globals gone? How safe from change are these globals? What would happen if their locations ever changed? Almost all the Macintosh software on earth refers to at least one low-memory global variable, especially the Toolbox itself. A lot of software that refers to specific low-memory globals is in assembler and uses symbolic names rather than hard addresses in the source code. Once the source is assembled, the hard addresses are all that remain in the object code; the good old symbolic names are lost. Of course, if any of these globals were moved in future versions of the system, old software would work only if it were reassembled or recompiled with new values for the globals that were moved (the whole process is illustrated in Figure 2-10). Since this would be a pretty painful process for software developers to go through, it's not likely to happen until or unless there's a very compelling reason to do it.

You write an assembly language program
that uses an Apple-defined symbol:

    MOVE.L GrayRgn, (A7)

After you assemble, the symbol is gone
and only the hard address remains:

    MOVE.L $9EE,-(A7)

If Apple changes the location of GrayRgn,
you'd have to reassemble your program.

Figure 2-10.   Symbolic names

What system changes might cause problems for users of low-memory globals? The structure of low memory reflects the Macintosh's original design center of running just one application at a time. Since then, there have been various approaches toward giving the Macintosh the capacity to run more than one application at a time or at least appear to do so. Apple's MultiFinder actually partitions the Macintosh's memory into pieces, one piece for each application. But there's only one low-memory global area: when an application changes a global, the global's address is hard-coded; there's no way to prevent the application from changing it. How does MultiFinder deal with the fact that each application thinks it has the right to molest low memory whenever it likes? Through a simple yet elegant mechanism, naturally.

The first time an application is switched out by the user, a copy of the low-memory global space is saved. The new application then owns low memory; the first time it gets switched out, *its* image of low memory is saved and the saved low-memory area of the application being switched in comes back. Fundamentally, each application has its own copy of low memory. One obvious problem with this scheme is that a switched-out application can't directly access its low-memory globals. The way this is handled is by simply suspending the switched out applications. Only the active application is allowed to run; the others are frozen until they're switched back in.

A dash of multitasking.   MultiFinder was designed to work with most existing applications. However, newly written programs that know about how the system works can do lots of neat tricks, including running things in the background while they're switched out.

Trap Patching

Every call to the Macintosh ROM and RAM-based system software is done by means of a 68000 **unimplemented instruction trap.** System calls show up in object code as a special kind of 68000 instruction. In the 68000 family, all instructions starting with the hex digit $A are called unimplemented. On the 68000, instructions consist of one word (two bytes), so an unimplemented instruction is any four-digit hex number beginning with $A, like $A9F2 or $AC2D.

When the 68000 hits one of these unimplemented instructions (also called **A-traps,** since they always start with $A), it jumps to the routine pointed to by memory location $28. On the Macintosh, this routine is called the **trap dispatcher.** The trap dispatcher takes a look at the other three digits in the instruction and figures out which routine the program is trying to call (for example, $A93D is MenuSelect, and $A851 is SetCursor). The trap dispatcher uses the rest of the instruction to get the address in ROM or RAM of the routine that the program is calling and then goes to that location.

The original Macintosh contained 64K of ROM, which was a large amount at the time. The idea was to put as much of the Toolbox and operating system as would fit into that ROM. Since the idea of shipping 64K of code that's forever cast in silicon can give you nightmares—it makes bug fixes pretty tough—the trap dispatcher design includes an easy way to replace a buggy ROM-based routine with a fixed-up routine in RAM. The table of addresses that the trap dispatcher uses to translate trap numbers into routine addresses is itself in RAM. The operating system even provides a ROM call to change the addresses of system routines (it's called SetTrapAddress). Since all Macintosh Toolbox and operating system calls are implemented as traps, Macintosh programmers have a great opportunity to fool around with the system and customize its behavior, and, if they're careful and not too radical, they still stand a reasonable chance of working on future systems.

One of the problems with doing neat things by patching traps is that somebody else might have another wild idea whose implementation involves patching the same trap as you did. This can lead to the annoying problem of "last one in": the last program that gets to apply its patch has control and has to be really careful to avoid killing anything else. Of course, this is only a problem if the patcher is something other than an application, such as a desk accessory or a persistent piece of code like the Talking Moose. Luckily, these conflicts are pretty rare, but they can happen, so you should watch out if you're not writing an application and you're patching traps.

Smart. When you're using switching and multitasking systems like Switcher or MultiFinder, do different applications have to be careful of patching the same traps? No. The switching mechanism takes care of making sure that every application's patches are used only when that application is active.

Trap patching is a fairly fragile process for another reason: when the system is changed, either with a new system file release or a new ROM, what a trap does can be subtly different. It might tweak a global in a slightly different way or it might do things in a different order—just different enough to break your application. When you patch traps, you're definitely on the hairy edge of compatibility. You must retest your software with each new system file and ROM release (they don't happen all that often, usually every several months). Of course, testing with new system releases is a good idea even if you use only the high-level interface to the system. As Joaquin Andujar says, you never know!

Definition Functions

One of the best ways the Macintosh system software implements its generality is through the use of definition functions. These let you create your own kinds of menus, windows, controls, and lists (for the List Manager), which can be very different from the standard ones. The beauty of creating your own creatures by writing new definition functions (or **defprocs**, as cool Macintosh programmers call them) is that you still get to use the Toolbox to do a lot of your dirty work. If you write your own window definition function, you can slip it into your application fairly easily and still use the tactic of handling events in windows. You can even give your new definition function to your friends to include in their applications.

A word to the wise.   Note that except for the routine that defines a menu, these routines are all functions and not procedures; but no one on this planet uses the term "deffunc." Please be careful here or you may be ostracized from the programming community.

There are several standard definition functions. They define two windows, two controls, one menu, and one list, and are listed in Figure 2-11. The Toolbox Managers that use definition functions—the Window, Menu, Control, and List Managers—don't play favorites when using the standard definition functions. They're called in exactly the same way as custom ones that you create in your own home.

Resource type	ID	Description	In Plus ROM	In SE ROM	In II ROM
CDEF	0	Buttons, check boxes	No	Yes	Yes
CDEF	1	Scroll bars	No	Yes	Yes
LDEF	0	Standard lists	No	No	No
MDEF	0	Standard menus	Yes	Yes	Yes
WDEF	0	Document & dialog windows	Yes	Yes	Yes
WDEF	1	Round-cornered windows	No	Yes	Yes

Figure 2-11.   Standard definition functions

The defprocs are called through a well-defined, Pascal-style interface that's documented in *Inside Macintosh*. When the defproc's manager wants the defproc to do something, it calls it through this interface. Each defproc has to handle the various possible calls—or **messages**—that may come its way. For example, window definition functions must be able to handle seven different messages, including calls to draw the window's frame, draw its grow box, and draw its size box; menu defprocs have to be able to draw the menu they define, highlight the chosen item, and calculate the rectangle that contains the menu; control and list defprocs have to handle other kinds of messages.

Since the interfaces to the defprocs are respected by the Toolbox managers, the interfaces have remained very stable throughout the various incarnations of the ROM. Even though writing your own definition functions has proven to be a pretty stable aspect of the medium-level interface so far, it may be subject to change in the future. The facts that it's so well documented and so commonly used by the Toolbox itself generate lots of momentum for keeping it the same.

QuickDraw Bottlenecks

QuickDraw lets you perform five different kinds of graphic operations on shapes: frame (drawing around the perimeter of an object), paint (filling an object with the pen's pattern and mode), erase (filling an object with the background pattern), invert (changing all the dots in an object from white to black and from black to white), and fill (filling an object with a specified pattern). Each of these operations can be done to six different kinds of shapes: rectangle, rounded-corner rectangle (*roundrect*, for you jargon seekers), oval, arc, polygon, and region. A matrix representing these operations is given in Figure 2-12. QuickDraw also lets you draw text and lines, perform bit transfers, and record and play back pictures. All these capabilities are available through high-level QuickDraw calls corresponding to standard trap calls to the Macintosh ROM, which you can patch with the normal SetTrapAddress mechanism we discussed earlier.

As well as defining each of these calls as traps, QuickDraw provides an additional level of interface for folks who want to customize their operation. All the trap calls that do shape drawing, text drawing, text measuring, bit transfer, picture recording, and picture playback are eventually piped through one of 13 special hooks associated with each grafport. These special hooks are called Quick-Draw bottleneck routines or just **bottlenecks**. They're called bottle-

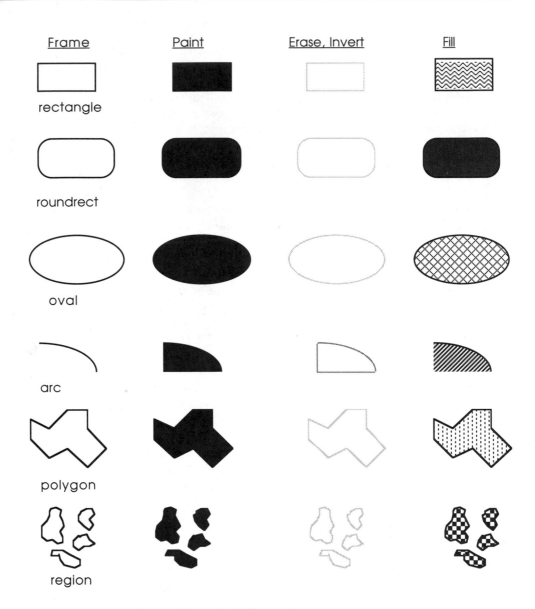

Figure 2-12.   QuickDraw shapes and operations

necks because almost all the QuickDraw routines have to pass through them in order to do their work. You'll find a list of the 13 bottlenecks and a brief description of what they do in Figure 2-13.

Name	Description
textProc	Draws all text characters
lineProc	Draws lines for Line, LineTo, etc.
rectProc	Draws rectangles for all grafverbs
rRectProc	Draws round-corner rectangles
ovalProc	Draws ovals for all grafverbs
arcProc	Draws arcs and wedges
polyProc	Draws pre-recorded polygons
rgnProc	Draws regions
bitsProc	Handles requests from CopyBits
commentProc	Processes picture comments
lxMeasProc	Called to measure chunks of text
getPicProc	Gets information from recorded pictures
putPicProc	Puts new information into pictures

Figure 2-13. QuickDraw bottlenecks

Every grafport includes a field called grafProcs. This field contains a pointer to a record whose type is QDProcs. The QDProcs record consists of 13 more pointers, which hold the addresses of the bottleneck routines. If you want to customize the operation of any of the bottlenecks, you can do so by writing your custom routine and then putting its address in the appropriate pointer.

The advantage to hooking into the bottlenecks is that you can customize all the drawing relating to a particular object without having to patch multiple traps. If you want to implement your own technique for drawing ovals, for example, you'd have to patch all five of the oval-drawing traps, but you can hook in more easily by setting up ovalProc, the field in the QDProcs record that gets control whenever an oval is drawn. This sounds like an interesting capability, but what would you ever want to use it for? In practice, most bottlenecks aren't used very often. Some programs, especially text editors and word processors, hook into the text drawing and text measuring routines to customize their drawing of text on the screen.

Another bottleneck some programs use is the one that processes picture comments. These are a mechanism that allows a picture-recording program to put additional, non-QuickDraw information into a picture when it's created. The assumption is that some piece of software that will be playing back the picture (maybe the same program) will understand the comments and will do something intelligent with them. For example, MacDraw uses picture comments to record additional, non-QuickDraw information about its documents, such as groups of objects, smoothed polygons, and arrows.

The most common use for the bottlenecks is in Apple's implementation of printing. When you print through the Printing Manager, one of your first steps (usually) is to call PrOpenDoc, which sets up a grafport to be used for printing. When this happens, special values are inserted into the printing port's bottleneck pointers. These customized versions of the bottlenecks then take care of QuickDraw calls the application makes when printing a document.

Since both QuickDraw and the Macintosh's printing architecture are based on the bottlenecks, it seems that this interface is pretty safe from future change, but as with all of the medium-level interface stuff, pay close attention to information coming out of Apple, just in case.

Customizing Standard File

Anyone who has had to use an old-fashioned computer knows the incredible rage and frustration that results from forgetting the name of a file that you want to open. You type the name that you remember and the computer says "File not found." You try a different spelling and you get "File not found." A third spelling—"File not found." You throw the computer through the window. You give up on computers and become a yak herder.

To experienced computer users, one of the most wonderful things about the Macintosh user interface is the Standard File Package. This is that wonderful piece of software that magically allows the user to choose a file without having to bother typing in its name. Standard File probably does more user-interfacey things with one trap call than any other part of the system.

The Standard File call that allows the user to open a file by choosing from an existing list of file names is SFGetFile. Consider all the processing you get for this one little call: the system puts up a dialog box that shows a scrolling list of files and folders at the top level or **root directory** of the current disk. The programmer gets to choose which file types will be listed; for example, MacWrite lists all MacWrite documents and all text files. The user can open a file or folder by double-clicking on it. If the user opens a folder, the list of files changes to show the contents of the folder. Controls let the user look at a different disk, eject a disk, move back up through the folder hierarchy, or cancel the whole operation. All of this messing around is handled by SFGetFile.

When the user, at long last, finally opens a file or cancels the dialog, SFGetFile returns and informs the caller which file was selected. The system also remembers the last folder the user opened and the next time Standard File is called, that folder is the one displayed. A lot of value for one little call.

A corresponding call, SFPutFile, is used when the user wants to save a file and it does even more. Like SFGetFile, it also displays a scrolling list of file and folder names, but the file names are there for reference only: Standard File draws them in gray to show that they can't be selected. The folders, of course, can be opened to indicate where the file should be saved.

As in SFGetFile, there are controls for moving between disks, ejecting a disk, traversing the folders, or canceling. There are a couple of other neat features, too. If the user tries to save a file with the same name as an existing file, the system will put up an alert asking the user to confirm the save since it will mean writing over the old file. Also, if the user inserts a new, blank disk while Standard File is in control, it will present the disk initialization dialog and allow the user to format the disk. Once again, you get an awful lot of stuff for just one system call.

As usual, the Macintosh system software designers have gone out of their way to allow for flexibility in the use of Standard File. The operations of Standard File can be customized in several ways to allow for specialized performance. The most common way is through the use of hooks in the SFPutFile and SFGetFile calls.

There is one hook available in SFPutFile. When you call SFPut-File, the fourth parameter is called dlgHook. This is a pointer to a function that gets called every time SFPutFile receives an event. The hook function can use this call to perform any kind of special handling when a particular event takes place. In fact, you can even add new things to the dialog item list resource (DITL) that contains the items for the SFPutFile dialog and then handle these new items by using the dlgHook parameter to SFPutFile. This allows you to add new functionality on top of the standard already provided.

The SFGetFile call contains two hooks. The first one, fileFilter, gives you more control over which files will be shown in the list of file names. If you pass a pointer to a function in fileFilter, SFGetFile will call your function with the name of every file it encounters. You can then use whatever criteria you like to determine whether the file should be displayed. Maybe you only want to list files that start with the letter G, or maybe you want to prevent a certain specific file from being listed. You can use the fileFilter hook to accomplish this special discrimination.

The other hook that SFGetFile uses is called dlgHook, which is similar in function to the dlgHook parameter that we already talked about in the SFPutFile call. If you want to perform some special handling of any of the dialog's items or to add your own items that will require special handling, you can us dlgHook.

In addition to these two calls, which do the work in most applications and provide lots of flexibility, two alternate calls allow you to do even more bizarre and obnoxious things. They're called SFPGetFile and SFPPutFile. Note the letter P in the names after the letters SF: it stands for *programmer*, I think. These special versions of the Standard File calls provide all the parameters the regular versions take plus two additional ones. The first, called dlgID, is the resource ID of the dialog template (DLOG resource) that will be used for the dialog displayed by the call. This gives you a chance to invent your own custom dialog with a new ID rather than messing with the standard ID.

The second new parameter in the "P" calls is filterProc, and it's another hook that increases your flexibility. This parameter is used in the same way as the filterProc parameter that you pass to ModalDialog. In fact, since the SF calls use ModalDialog to handle events, that's exactly what this parameter is for. This gives you a chance to perform any special event filtering or changing of events to look like other events. For example, you might want to define a special Command-key combination as equivalent to a button click.

If you take advantage of any or all of these clever tricks, how likely are you to be compatible with future releases of the system software? When Apple converted from the Macintosh's original flat file system to the current hierarchical system, many changes had to be made to Standard File, of course. Because of thoughful planning, testing, and compassion, many applications stayed compatible with the new, hierarchical, Standard File even if they had made extensive use of its customization capabilities.

In general, there's certainly no problem with using the fileFilter hook in SFGetFile, and it's probably OK if you use the filterProc and dlgHook routines to modify or enhance the behavior of the standard items in the dialogs. You might stay compatible if you add your own items to the dialogs, but be warned: *Inside Macintosh* says clearly that "Future compatibility is *not* guaranteed if you don't use the standard dialogs." The ability to modify the Standard File dialogs is one of the more volatile features of the medium-level interface, so avoid changing the dialogs if you can.

Customizing the Print Manager Dialogs

The Printing Manager provides two dialogs that are the user's interface to printing in most applications. The first one, the **style dialog,** is usually associated with the Page Setup item in the File menu. This dialog asks the user about the paper type, whether the page should be in tall or wide (sideways) format, and other questions that depend on the kind of printer being used. The second dialog is the **job dialog.** This one asks the user to choose the range of pages to be printed, the number of copies, and other stuff that's printer-type dependent, such as the paper source for the LaserWriter or the print quality for the ImageWriter.

Programmers want to customize things that are standard, so many developers were interested in adding things to these **print dialogs.** Developers of word processors wanted to add margin information to the style dialog, for example, and others wanted to disable certain buttons that weren't appropriate to their applications.

For almost three years after the Macintosh was shipped, the print dialogs were available only in the standard forms issued by Apple; they could not be modified by programmers. Actually, a more correct statement would be that there was no "official" or recommended way they could be modified. Enterprising programmers found various ways to do it, often causing problems for themselves as the system software was updated. In late 1986, Apple issued Macintosh Technical Note #95, which describes a method for messing around with the print dialogs. It lists several warnings and makes no promises about future compatibility for any brave souls who use its techniques. This sounds exactly like another feature of the medium-level interface, so it's listed here.

What's your outlook for compatibility if you customize the print dialogs? Since Apple has provided a recommended method for doing this, you should assume they'll make an effort to protect the interface described in the technical note, but given the warnings in that note, it's quite possible changes will come in the future that will invalidate the techniques shown there. Of course, if you do something that goes against the principles of the technical note, you should definitely expect to have your application fail miserably on future printing software.

File System Information

When Apple upgraded to the Hierarchical File System (HFS) in 1985, one of the most important features of the new system was its compatibility with existing software. A key design goal of HFS was for it to cause a minimum number of headaches to software that already worked. This meant that all the calls and features of the original file system had to be supported in the new world.

Of course, any change as major as adding hierarchy to a file system is bound to cause some incompatibilities and HFS certainly caused a few. However, the problems that cropped up were more frequently the result of something unavoidable: the fact that the files on the disk were no longer all at the same level but were now organized into directories or folders. The creators of HFS were very careful to minimize the weirdnesses that can result from making this transition.

There are two important features that are at the heart of HFS's high degree of compatibility with the original flat file system. The first is the emulation of all flat system calls under HFS. The second and more clever feature is the **working directory,** which we'll talk about now.

When you make a call such as PBOpen, the file system can only "see" files that are in one directory. Under the flat file system, all the files on a disk volume could be seen at once, since they were all at the same level. To see all the files on a hierarchical disk, the programmer has to look into all the folders. Also, a file in one folder can have the same name as a file in another folder. Folders have many of the same characteristics as separate volumes did under the flat file system.

On the flat file system, a **volume reference number** is a way of uniquely identifying a volume. No two volumes that are mounted can have the same volume reference number (also called the vrefnum, pronounced "vee-ref-num"), so it's the best way to refer to a volume when making a system call. HFS implements a similar concept for folders: the working directory reference number. When a program wants to work with a directory, it can use the PBOpenWD call to create a **working directory reference number** (or WDrefnum, as you may have guessed) for that directory. This WDrefnum can then be used to identify that directory uniquely in file system calls. The program doesn't ever have to worry about reconstructing the chain of folder names that lead to the folder, since the WDrefnum will identify it. Figure 2-14 shows the process of using a working directory.

err:=PBOpenWD (paramBlock, false);   Opens a working directory

You can now use the working directory ID when calling the File Manager.

Figure 2-14.   Working directory

> **Working for a living.** Note that calling PBOpenWD to get a WDrefnum doesn't really create a directory; it just creates a WDrefnum that can be used to refer to a directory that already exists on a disk. Opening a working directory simply creates a data structure called a **working directory control block,** which specifies the WDrefnum and the directory itself. It doesn't create anything at all on the disk.

The real magic of the WDrefnum is that it's treated exactly like a vrefnum when you make a system call. In other words, all the old (flat file system) calls that expect a vrefnum and a file name will work fine if they're given a WDrefnum instead of the vrefnum. So, if you call PBOpen and you put a WDrefnum in the vrefnum field, the file will be opened from the specified directory.

Many applications only use the file system for opening and saving their documents, and most Macintosh applications ask their users for the names of documents by using Standard File. The usual sequence of calls for opening a document looks like this:

```
SFGetFile (where, prompt, fileFilter, numTypes, typeList, dlgHook, reply);
     { this call asks the user which file to open }
errorcode := FSOpen (reply.fName, reply.vRefNum, fileRefNum);
     { reply.fName and reply.vRefNum came from the SFGetFile call }
```

The call to Standard File returns two important pieces of information in the reply record: the file name selected and its vrefnum. The application then calls FSOpen (or sometimes PBOpen) with the chosen file name and vrefnum, and the file is opened. On the hierarchical version of SFGetFile, Standard File gets a WDrefnum for the folder that holds the selected file and then returns that WDrefnum in the vrefnum field of the reply record. Since the application will simply take this value and use it in its FSOpen call, it will open the file it wants, as illustrated in Figure 2-15. This little invention, a WDrefnum that can be used as a vrefnum in file system calls, is the reason many applications were instantly compatible with HFS.

Flat file system (MFS):
    User selects a file
    File name is returned in SFReply.fName
    Vrefnum is returned in SFReply.vRefNum
    Application calls FSOpen with this file name and vrefnum

Hierarchical file system (HFS):
    User selects a file
    File name is returned in SFReply.fName
    WDRefNum is returned in SFReply.vRefNum
    Application calls FSOpen with this file name and with WDRefNum used
      as a vrefnum; the application doesn't have to know if an MFS or
      HFS volume was used

Figure 2-15.   Standard File process

Names and numbers.   Before you can use a working directory reference number to refer to a directory, of course, you have to call OpenWD—Standard File calls it for you. How do you specify which directory you want? There are several techniques you can use. Every directory has a name, and you can specify the directory you want by using a **full pathname**, which is a list of directory names, starting with the volume name, or **root**, that leads you down a path to the directory that you want. You use a colon to separate each pair of directory names in the pathname. For example, you can specify a directory with "Beethoven 9 Symphonien:disc 4:Symphonie Nr. 6." You can also use a combination of the volume reference number and a **partial pathname,** which specifies everything but the root. Note that *everything but the root* means the file name on a flat volume, since there are no other directories. In addition to its name, every directory has a **directory ID** that can also be used to identify it. Every directory on a volume has a different directory ID, but IDs can be the same across different volumes, so you need to use a volume reference number with the directory ID. These techniques can be used whenever you need to specify a name on an HFS volumes, and you can see them all in Figure 2-16.

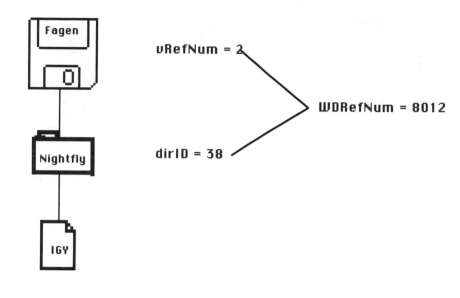

Figure 2-16. Specifying a file

These features are elements of the high-level interface of HFS and programs that used them were rewarded with compatibility when HFS was released. The file system also provides lots of opportunities for the medium-level interface we've been discussing. Let's look at some of those now.

Like any other file system, HFS organizes things in a certain way on its disks. It likes to put its **boot blocks** (or **system startup information,** as *Inside Macintosh* more stuffily calls it) in a certain place; it has to know where its directories are; and so on. These things don't matter to most applications but they do to some, particularly things like disk editors and data recovery programs. Of course, system startup information changed completely when HFS was implemented, but that was absolutely unavoidable.

It's two...two...two mints in one! The hierarchical file system is now widely used, since it's in the ROM of every Macintosh Plus, 512K Enhanced, upgraded Macintosh 512K, II, and SE. Programmers sometimes forget that there are still volumes that have a flat file structure. When 400K (single-sided) disks are initialized, even under HFS, they contain the original, classic, non-hierarchical file structure. Of course, HFS has no problem dealing with these disks, but you must remember not to assume that every volume you encounter is hierarchical, even if you know that HFS is present.

The file system uses several important data structures to keep track of what's going on. If you use these guys, you may run into some interesting compatibility issues, which we will now cover. The **volume information block,** which is kept in block 2 of the disk, contains some interesting stuff like the size of an **allocation block** (the minimum amount of space than can be allocated at one time), the number of unused allocation blocks, and the volume name itself.

In the interest of compatibility, the volume information block on a hierarchical volume contains all the information that a flat volume does and in the same place. For example, the drFreeBlocks field, which contains the number of unused allocation blocks on a disk, is located in bytes 34 and 35 of the volume information block on both flat and hierarchical volumes. Obviously, this was done to give applications the best possible shot at working with the hierarchical file system. The volume information block for a hierarchical volume contains a lot more information than a flat volume. Most of the additional fields are used to maintain HFS's sophisticated system of catalogs and disk space allocation. This additional information is placed right after the original information on a hierarchical volume.

Another important file system data structure is the **volume control block,** usually called a VCB. Every mounted volume has a VCB that's maintained by the file system. It includes information that's a lot like the stuff in the volume information block. In fact, most of the things in the VCB are read from the volume information block and are updated when they change. In addition to this information, the VCB includes some other goodies, including the volume's drive number and the reference number of the driver that handles this volume. As with volume information blocks, a VCB for a hierarchical volume contains all the information that a flat volume does, in the same places, plus additional information that's valid for hierarchical volumes only.

There's an easy, high-level way to get most of the information that's found in the VCB. A File Manager call named PBGetVInfo will tell you most of the information in the VCB, and this call is very likely to stay supported on future systems. If you need information that's not returned by the PBGetVInfo call, you can use an extended version called PBHGetVInfo if you can guarantee that HFS is available. For example, the reference number of the driver that reads and writes to this volume can be found by calling this hierarchical version. If you really need to know one of the few values in the VCB not available by calling PBHGetVInfo, you can look directly in the VCB, if you're careful.

All the VCBs are chained together in a queue. To find the start of the queue, you can call GetVCBQHdr from most high-level languages or you can examine the global called VCBQHdr at location $356. To get from one VCB to the next one in the chain, you can simply look at the first field in the VCB, called qLink, which is a pointer to the next entry. When this field is nil, you're looking at the last VCB.

When Apple went from the flat file system to HFS, the hierarchical version of the VCB was made a superset of the flat one. All the fields in the flat version of the VCB that still make sense in a hierarchical system are found in the same location; the new fields are tacked onto the end. It seems likely, though it's not guaranteed (how's that for building your confidence?), that Apple would continue this strategy in the future, only adding new things at the end of the VCB.

The file system creates another data structure, called a **file control block** (FCB), for every access path to an open file. The FCB includes information about the file's physical and logical end of file, and about the directory that contains the file.

Just like with the VCB, Apple was very smart about extending the structure of the FCB for the hierarchical file system. The extended version is a superset of the flat one, containing all the same information in the same locations, with the new stuff added at the end. As with volume control blocks, you can usually stick to a high-level interface to find out things about a file. Some of the information in a file's FCB can be found by calling PBGetFInfo and more can be discovered by calling PBGetFCBInfo, which is available only under the hierarchical system.

Another use for PBGetFInfo. You can also use PBGetFInfo to find out about a file that's not open. Of course, if a file isn't open, it does not have a file control block, so there's no other way to find out about it (unless, of course, you want to read the directory yourself, but we won't get into that right now).

There's some information that you can get only in the file control block itself; no File Manager call returns it. In this case, you have to go slogging around in the FCB yourself. Unlike volume control blocks, the FCBs are not linked together in a queue. Instead, all the FCBs are jammed together into one big nonrelocatable block in the system heap. This structure is called the **file control block buffer.** The first word of this buffer contains the total length of the entire buffer. On a Macintosh Plus running System 3.2, there's enough space for 40 files in the FCB buffer, and each file uses 94 bytes, so the size of the FCB buffer is 40 times 94 or 3760, plus the two-byte length field at the start, for a total size of 3762 bytes.

To find the FCB buffer, you can use the global at $34E, called FCBSPtr (file control block size pointer). It holds the address of the start of the FCB buffer, which is the FCB buffer's length word, as discussed in the preceding paragraph. The FCB for the first file begins right after the length word. You got all that, system detectives?

If you want to look through all the entries in the FCB buffer, you have to be able to get from one entry to the next. To make this possible, HFS keeps a global at $3F6 (FSFCBLen) that tells the length of a file control block. To get from one entry to the next, you should add this value to your pointer. If you hard-code the FCB size to 94, which is the right value for now, you stand a good chance of getting clobbered in the future, especially since *Inside Macintosh* warns, "The size and structure of a file control block may be different in future versions of Macintosh system software." Hmmm. Seems like *Inside Macintosh* is saying, "Read my lips." Peeking directly into the FCBs is a dangerous enough way to live; you should take all the precautions you can, like using FSFCBLen to find out the size of an FCB.

The structure of a file control block was extended for HFS in much the same way as volume control blocks. All the flat file system information is maintained in the same locations and the new stuff for HFS is glued onto the end. It seems reasonable to expect that in the future Apple will add any new fields at the end of the FCB and leave the current ones intact if at all possible.

In addition to the volume control blocks and file control blocks, the File Manager defines a few other interesting data structures that we won't go into here, just to maintain a little sanity. These include the **drive queue**, which has information on all the disk drives attached to the system, and a bunch of data structures that are used to maintain a volume's hierarchical file catalog and disk space allocation.

Medium-level Summary

This list of things that belong to the medium-level interface may not be complete but it should give you a flavor of the kinds of things that are possible in this realm of Macintosh programming, and it also may have given you some ideas for great features that you can add to your programs.

When you use these features, remember that many of them are only semi-documented or even disclaimed by Apple. You should always be careful to use any extra hints that are around. For example, when you see a global like FSFCBLen that gives you the length of a file control block, you should use it and you shouldn't be surprised if the value changes in the future. As long as you're using the global's value and not hard-coding for the current correct value, you have a much better chance of surviving a change.

Another fact that's important to remember is that Apple is much more likely to stick to a feature that's documented in *Inside Macintosh* than one that's been discovered and never mentioned. Macintosh Technical Notes are another good source of official stuff from Apple. Although they don't seem to carry the cast-in-stone gravity of *Inside Macintosh*, they present amendments and updates to the documentation as well as techniques of the medium-level interface that are likely to be supported in the future. They even have jokes in them now and then.

When changes are made to the system software, Apple knows it's a real good idea to make sure that there's a high degree of software compatibility. When there are changes that cause applications to break, they're usually made to provide some major extension or necessary enhancement to the system. It's very rare that you'll find something changed just for a minor performance enhancement or for no apparent reason. Compatibility is always high on the list of design goals for any new Macintosh system software that Apple produces.

The last thing to remember about the medium-level interface is this: even if you follow the rules and don't do anything overtly anti-compatibility, you may find that something will change on you one day and you'll have to modify your code. To make the best of this possibility, always be sure to test your applications with each new release of system software and especially with new machines. Although Apple does some testing of third-party applications, there's no way they can do it all, so it's up to you. Be careful with the medium-level interface, be creative, and have fun.

Things to Remember

Apple is interested in helping outside developers, so lots of things in the Macintosh are designed to make their lives easier. Compatibility with existing software, for example, is a high priority when new computers are designed.

You should use the high-level interface whenever possible and avoid the low-level. A lot of Macintosh features are accessible through a medium-level interface, but you should be cautious about using them.

Intermission

Did you ever wonder what really goes on in your Macintosh? Well, this is your chance to find out. Come closer . . . closer still . . . right up inside your Macintosh! We're about to embark on an amazing journey.

A mouse is clicked!   A button highlited!   Power surges!
What *REALLY* happens when a mouseDown event occurs inside a Macintosh?
Find out in...

Click!
(a second story)

Our
story
begins as
darkness
is invaded
by Ron,
Macintosh
user.

by Bill Dawson

*R*on has been awakened by the pizza he had for dinner.

*G*roping his way down the hall in search of the bathroom he wanders into his office.

A Macintosh is on the desk.

"BING"

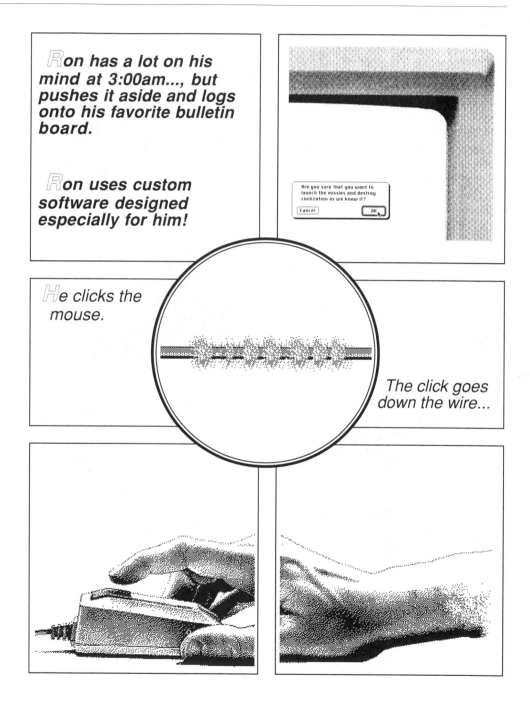

*R*on has a lot on his mind at 3:00am..., but pushes it aside and logs onto his favorite bulletin board.

*R*on uses custom software designed especially for him!

Are you sure that you want to launch the missles and destroy civilization as we know it?

Cancel   OK

*H*e clicks the mouse.

The click goes down the wire...

The Vertical Retrace Manager, **always on the lookout for things like mouse movement and clicks checks the VIA and discovers a click!**

He has to post a mouseDown event and tell the Application about the click.

STACK

HEAP

mouseDown event
To: Event Queue, PostEvent, c/o Event Manager, Macintosh ROM *RUSH*

This end up ↑

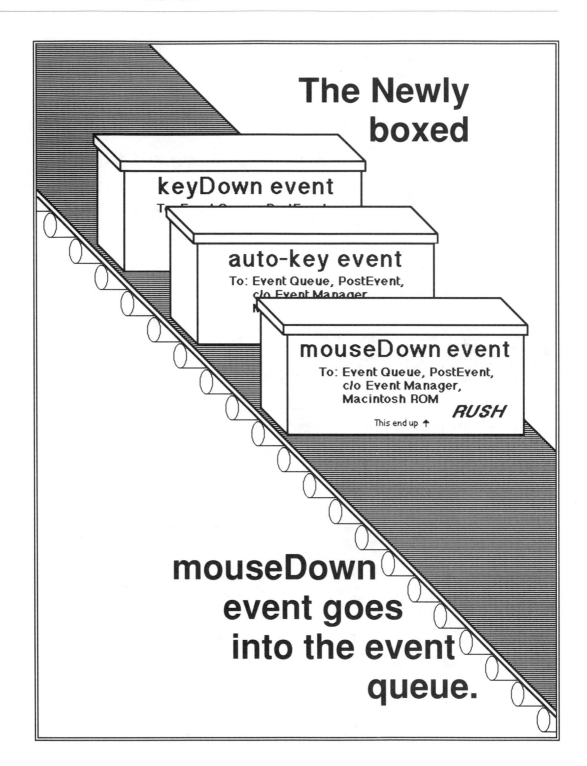

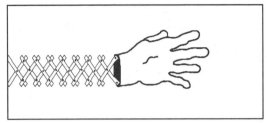

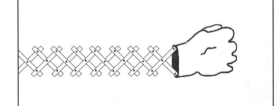
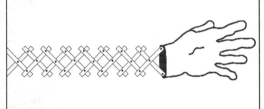
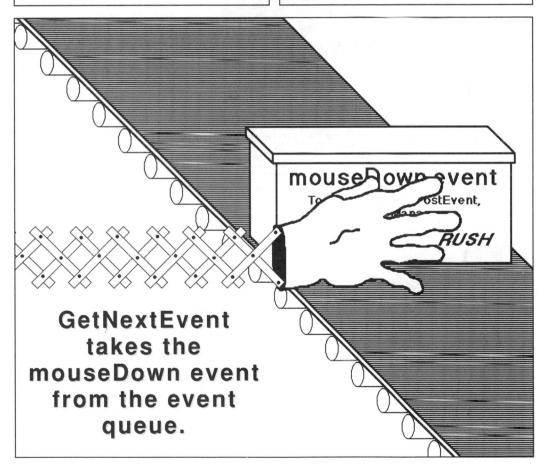

GetNextEvent takes the mouseDown event from the event queue.

The Application gets the event.

He calls the Control Manager to find out if a control was hit.

The Control Manager consults his map of the screen and sees that the click occured in the OK button.

The Application gets a letter back from the Control Manager telling him the OK button was hit! So he gets ready to send back another message addressed to "TrackControl c/o Control Manager, Macintosh ROM".

The Control Manager reads the note from the Application and gets ready to tell QuickDraw to light up the OK button.

QuickDraw will call the screen and ask the bits to invert themselves.

QuickDraw inverts the bits.

The button is highlited.

 *Click!*

The End

P A R T T W O

Technical Adventures

Almost every Macintosh application follows Apple's user interface guidelines, which means there's a lot of friendly, easy-to-use software out in the world. If you use a lot of Macintosh software, though, you'll find that some companies and programmers have really done a great job of adding little tricks and features that make their programs fast, easy, and interesting to use.

In this part of the book, we'll look at some of the most interesting and clever techniques that can make programs slicker and easier to use. Most of these techniques are not officially part of Apple's user interface guidelines and they're not in Inside Macintosh, *so only the smartest developers have put them into their software. In this part, we'll discuss some of the most interesting and convenient of these tricks. Since compatibility with future members of the Macintosh product family is very important, we'll address compatibility issues for these features. For some of the features, we'll look at a little bit of code that will help you implement the tricks, and for others, we'll just talk about how you might go about it, leaving the actual implementation as an exercise for the reader (as the old saying goes).*

C H A P T E R 3

Color

The transformation of QuickDraw into color. The old and new models of color drawing. A vast array of new data structures that convey color information. How pixel maps will change the world. Colorizing pictures in a way Ted Turner never thought of.

The Macintosh II has color! Apple spent a lot of the first three years of the Macintosh's existence explaining why there was no color monitor for the system and denying rumors of the imminent release of one. Finally, in March 1987, the Macintosh II was announced and full color support was built-in.

Most of the changes in the Macintosh II ROM were done to support color video. These new capabilities have added a bunch of pages to *Inside Macintosh,* Volume V, and this section isn't designed to cover all of them. Instead, we'll get an overview of the color capabilites and how they work, discuss what you have to do to get color in your programs, and talk about some of the color data structures. The first section will concentrate on how QuickDraw implements the guts of the color features that you'll have to deal with when you're programming. In addition to QuickDraw, many of the Toolbox managers have been enhanced to support color. There's a lot of information about how they work in Appendix A.

About Color QuickDraw

There's so much new stuff in QuickDraw to support color that it's been renamed Color QuickDraw. Color QuickDraw lets you do everything you could do with the original classic QuickDraw, plus the following new fun features.

- You can draw anything in 16 million different colors, give or take a few hundred thousand, and you can display up to 256 different colors at a time using standard Apple hardware.
- The user can choose how much color, if any, is displayed. If the monitor isn't color, gray scales will be shown automatically.
- There are new transfer modes to do fancy new things with colors, like blending them together.

There are actually several pieces of hardware and software that work together closely to give you what you see on the screen. When you program, you usually call one of the Toolbox managers or QuickDraw, asking for the colors you want. QuickDraw then calls on a new piece of the Operating System called the Color Manager, which knows how to translate what QuickDraw wants into what the monitor can actually provide.

The Color Manager then communicates with the monitor by making calls to its driver, which is usually supplied on a ROM on the video card that runs it. On the Macintosh II, there's no built-in video, so every monitor is connected to a card that's in one of the six

NuBus slots inside the box. The driver actually turns on the little bitty lights that form the images you see on the monitor.

This new version of QuickDraw is present in the Macintosh II ROM only, for two reasons. First, this is the only Macintosh that has an Apple-supplied color monitor. Second, Color QuickDraw uses 68020 code heavily and the Macintosh II is the only Macintosh that comes with a 68020 built-in.

Color Basics

In the original version of QuickDraw, every bit in the RAM that's dedicated to the screen controls one pixel. Since a single bit can have two values, 0 and 1, every pixel can show two things, white or black. On Macintoshes with a 512 by 342 pixel black and white screen, there are exactly 175,104 pixels (multiply it yourself if you don't believe me); at eight bits per byte, that means that there's exactly 21,888 bytes of RAM devoted to the video screen.

In Color QuickDraw, every pixel must be able to show more than just black and white. This means that one bit is no longer enough to hold the contents of a pixel. The number of different colors that a single pixel can display is determined by the number of bits in memory dedicated to that pixel. For example, with two bits per pixel, we can have four different bit patterns, representing four different colors. Eight bits per pixel produces 256 different colors, the maximum that Apple's color monitor will allow.

On the Macintosh II, the actual colors that will be displayed on the screen are determined by the monitor's driver and the hardware itself. As a programmer, you don't have to know anything about the video capabilities to work well with different kinds of screens. When you draw in color, you specify each color by giving an intensity value for the red, green, and blue components of the color. The three numbers that you get when you specify a color like this are called the **RGB value** of the color, named after Reinhardt G. Barnsfarfle, the inventor of the puce scroll bar.

The red, green, and blue components are each 16 bits, which means that you get to use three different numbers ranging from 0 to 65535. For each value, 0 indicates that none of that color will be used and the maximum value of 65535 means that the full intensity of that color will be added to produce the final result. This means that you can specify an intense green with an RGB value of 65535 for the green component and 0 for the blue and red parts. An RGB with a red value of 65535 and blue and green settings of 0 will create a rich, full-bodied red, with a fine flavor and a good bouquet.

> **True colors**. If you're a fan of combinations and permutations, you may have figured out that if the red, green, and blue components of an RGB can each range from 0 to 65535, there are 65536 times 65536 times 65536, or 281,474,976,710,656 (that's 281 *trillion*, sports fans) different combinations of RGB values. Does this mean that QuickDraw can display all those different colors? Yes and no. Yes, you can specify any of the 281 trillion colors when you draw. No, the current combination of QuickDraw and the available color hardware can't handle it. For example, colors on the Apple color monitor are mapped according to the upper eight bits only of each RGB component; this means that colors are limited to a much more narrow selection of just 16,777,216 different values, which is enough to give a different color to every person in Czechoslovakia.

Before pixels are displayed on the screen, the colors are determined on the basis of the RGB values that you ask for. Since you can specify 281 trillion different RGB values and only 256 different colors can be displayed at once on most color monitors, there's obviously some mapping taking place. It works like this: when you draw, you ask QuickDraw to use your favorite RGB values; QuickDraw asks the Color Manager for the available color that comes closest to the one you asked for and then draws in that color.

How are the available colors determined? Most of the monitors that work with a Macintosh II have the ability to match RGB values to colors by using a **color lookup device**, which lets you change which colors are available for use on a monitor at any given time. On the video card that controls Apple's color monitor, there's a color lookup device that allows any 256 of the 16 million colors to be used at once. Usually, this color choosing is done by the system, but if you want to get tricky, you can change it by using the Palette Manager, a new part of the Toolbox that controls color usage.

When you write your application, you have no way of knowing the specific color environment that your user will have. Not only are there zillions of different monitors available, but the user can change the number of bits of color information per pixel by using the Control Panel. If you had to worry about all of this when you were programming, you'd go nuts.

Luckily, the system handles all this for you. When your application draws, QuickDraw and the Color Manager will find the best match for the colors you want based on the current monitor, video card, and user settings. If you try to draw in 256 different colors while the user has the monitor set for four-bit color, QuickDraw and the Color Manager will map each of your 256 requested colors into the nearest match from a color lookup table that has 16 colors (the maximum number you can specify with four-bit values). The same thing will happen if the user has set the monitor for gray scales. The worst case is one-bit mode, in which all colors except white will be displayed as black.

Color Drawing Models

The original version of QuickDraw actually supported color output; it must have been pretty interesting trying to test it. In this version, you could specify that you wanted to draw in any of eight different colors, including black and white. The idea was that for black and white (one bit per pixel) devices, all the non-white colors would just become black, but for devices that could use color information, eight different ones could be specified. Color QuickDraw in the Macintosh II supports this technique, which is doomed to be known forever as the old model of color drawing.

To draw using the old model, a programmer can choose from the eight colors by using the ForeColor and BackColor procedures. These procedures let you decide which colors you want selected for foreground and background drawing operations. They're very simple to use: for example, to draw a blue rectangle, just call ForeColor (blueColor), then PaintRect.

A few clever applications actually started using this technique to draw as early as 1984, anticipating the day when QuickDraw would really be able to draw in color. If they did it right, these programmers had the thrill of seeing things work in color on the Macintosh II.

For the nifty color hardware of the Macintosh II, eight colors just aren't enough, of course. As we just discussed, Color QuickDraw lets you specify an amazing number of different colors with RGB values. These colors are matched with available ones from a lookup table to decide what to show on the screen, and the number of available colors varies depending on the color hardware and the user's settings.

This technique of choosing colors by using RGB values is called the new model. For programs that want to take full advantage of Color QuickDraw, the new model is obviously the only way to go. When you're using the new model, you choose colors by calling RGBForeColor and RGBBackColor. These work like their relatives from the old country, ForeColor and BackColor, in letting you set up foreground and background colors, but they take full RGB values as parameters.

When you write your application, you have a choice to make about compatibility. If you use routines that are in Color QuickDraw only, your application will crash if it's run on anything but a Macintosh II. So, you have to decide whether you want to take full advantage of Color QuickDraw, which will limit your application to just Macintosh II, or whether you should stick with the eight old-model colors and remain compatible with the black and white Macintoshes, since all versions of QuickDraw understand ForeColor and BackColor. You can also choose to write code that handles each case separately. The choice depends on how much you want your program to do and who you expect to use it. The right choice is the one that fits your situation.

Color Structures

QuickDraw uses a whole bunch of new data structures to implement its new color features. Most of them have counterparts that serve similar functions in the original version of QuickDraw. In this section, we'll show each data structure, discuss its fields, gossip about it, and find out what the heck it does.

The basic color data structure in the Macintosh II is the RGB record. This is simply a record composed of red, green, and blue values. It looks like this:

```
type RGBColor = Record
                    red: Integer;
                    green: Integer;
                    blue: Integer;
                end;
```

Each field in the RGB record simply defines the magnitude of that color. As we said earlier, setting all three integers to 0 produces black, while the maximum value for each will create white.

The color stuff on the Macintosh II uses lookup tables extensively to translate various kinds of index values into RGB values. For example, the values for each pixel you draw are mapped into their RGB values through a lookup table associated with the image. To create these lookup tables, QuickDraw defines a **color specification** record, which combines an RGB with an integer that's used as an index or other reference value. The color specification record is declared this way:

```
type ColorSpec = Record
                    value:  Integer;
                    rgb:  RGBColor;
              end;
```

A color table is built by gluing together a bunch of color specification records, plus a couple of new fields:

```
type ColorTable = Record
                    ctSeed: Longint; {usually not used}
                    transIndex: Integer; {usually not used}
                    ctSize: Integer; {entries minus 1}
                    ctTable: array [0..0] of ColorSpec;
              end;
```

CTSeed provides a color table with a unique identifier. Usually, color tables you use will be attached to some other data structure, such as a window or pixel map, and the ctSeed field will not be used. The transIndex field can be used with some Color Manager calls to set a "transparent" pixel in each color table.

The heart of the color table is in the last two fields. CTSize tells how many colors are mapped by this table, minus one (the Color Manager starts counting at zero), and ctTable contains the actual color specifications, each one including an index value and an RGB.

These color tables are used all over the place in the Macintosh II. Virtually every manager in the Toolbox uses a color table to map parts of its structures to RGB colors; for example, the Control Manager has one that tells how to colorize each part of a control. You can find out more about how color tables are used by the Toolbox in Appendix A.

Pixel Maps and Pixel Patterns

The next new concept we'll talk about is the **pixel image**. In the original QuickDraw, a bit image is defined as a bunch of bits that represent an image enclosed by a rectangle. Color QuickDraw extends this definition to create the concept of a pixel image, which is a collection of bits that represent an image that may have more than one bit of information per pixel.

Color QuickDraw defines a data structure called a **pixel map,** which describes a pixel image and associated information in the coordinate plane. The original QuickDraw bit map, a direct ancestor of the pixel map, was a pretty simple structure, containing just three fields. The pixel map tells a lot more: its first three fields are similar to the ones in a bit map, but there are 12 additional fields filled with information.

Here's the structure of a pixel map:

```
type PixMap = Record
        baseAddr:Ptr; {pointer to pixel image}
        rowBytes:Integer; {offset between rows}
        bounds:Rect; {boundary rectangle}
        pmVersion:Integer; {version ID, currently 0}
        packType:Intger; {packing format, currently 0}
        packSize:Longint; {size of packed image}
        hRes:Fixed; {horizontal pixels per inch}
        vRes:Fixed; {vertical pixels per inch}
        pixelType:Integer; {currently 0}
        pixelSize:Integer; {number of bits per pixel}
        cmpCount:Integer; {currently 1}
        cmpSize:Integer; {bits used per RGB}
        planeBytes:Longint; {currently 0}
        pmTable:CTabHandle; {handle to color table}
        pmReserved:Longint; {currently 0}
     end;
```

There's a lot of new stuff in there. BaseAddr is a pointer to the start of the pixel image in memory, just as in a bit map. RowBytes defines the number of bytes in RAM needed to get from one row to the same pixel position in the next row.

The first three fields of a pixel map look just like a bit map and you can substitute one for the other in various places, so Color Quick-Draw uses a flag to indicate that you've got a pixel map: it sets the high bit in the rowBytes field. Since this field is an integer, this is the same as adding 32768 (or $8000 hex) to the value of rowBytes.

The bounds field, just like in a bit map, encloses the pixel map and also defines its coordinate system. The pmVersion field tells which version of QuickDraw created this pixel map; for the first version of Color QuickDraw, this is 0. Note that "currently" in the pixel map declaration above means that this is how it works in the first version of Color QuickDraw.

PackType and packSize are used if the pixel image is packed. Currently, pixel maps are unpacked, so both of these fields are set to

0. The hRes and vRes tell the horizontal and vertical number of pixels per inch. Usually, these values are both 72. PixelType is used to indicate how the pixel image is arranged in memory. Color QuickDraw always uses adjacent bits in memory to form each pixel; this is called the **chunky** format and is indicated by a zero in pixelType. Other formats may be supported in the future that separate the pixel image into planes with each plane containing one bit of information per pixel, an arrangment called **planar**.

The pixelSize field is used to tell how many bits per pixel are in the pixel image. This is called the **depth** of the image. CmpCount tells how many RGB values, or components, are used to make up each pixel. Although QuickDraw currently provides one RGB per pixel, future versions could allow more to provide greater resolution and cmpCount will show how many are being used.

CmpSize indicates how many bits of RGB information are used to draw this pixel map. Since one bit of depth is needed for each bit of RGB information, this field is the same as pixelSize. PlaneBytes isn't used now; if QuickDraw ever supports planar pixel images, it promises to give the offset from one plane to the next.

PmTable contains a handle to a table of colors that's used by this pixel map. It matches pixel values to RGB colors. The last field, pmReserved, isn't used by the current version of Color QuickDraw and it should always be set to 0.

The Macintosh II version of CopyBits can be used to manipulate pixel maps as well as bit maps. This is where that handy flag in the high bit of rowBytes comes in. When you call CopyBits, it can tell whether it's dealing with a bit map or a pixel map by checking this bit. If it's a pixel map, it learns the depth from the pixelSize field; bit maps always have a depth of 1, of course.

When you use CopyBits, it will examine the depth of the source and destination bit maps (or pixel maps). If they're not the same depth, it will automatically adjust the source's depth to the destination's. So, you can copy from pixel maps to bit maps and the other way around. Of course, if you go from a multibit pixel map to a bit map, you'll lose all the color information since there's nowhere to keep it. CopyBits will make sure the image remains intact, in black and white anyway.

The next new idea is a new kind of pattern. In the original version of QuickDraw, a pattern is an 8 by 8 bit image that defines a design or texture that's repeated to fill an area on the screen. Color QuickDraw defines a **pixel pattern** as a pixel image of virtually any size, and containing color information, which can be repeated to fill screen areas. Pixel patterns can also simulate old-version patterns, if necessary.

This is the definition for a pixel pattern:

```
type PixPat = Record
                patType: Integer; {indicates b & w or color}
                patMap: PixMapHandle; {handle to pixel map}
                patData: Handle; {handle to pixel image}
                patXData: Handle; {used internally}
                patXValid: Integer; {valid pattern flag}
                patXMap: Handle; {used internally}
                pat1Data: Pattern; {old-version pattern}
              end;
```

The patType field tells what kind of pattern this is. There are three possibilities: 0 specifies an old-version, black and white pattern; 1 indicates a full color pattern, which can have a wide mix of colors; and 2 is for an RGB pattern, which is a pattern based on a single RGB value.

Creating RGB patterns is especially useful for simulating more colors than you actually have. By using a technique which alternates colors in adjacent pixels, your screen can appear to have a new color. This is called **dithering**. For example, by dithering blue and green, you can simulate a single blue-green color. Of course, this only works when you're drawing more than one line, which is why it can be used with patterns. If you draw just one line or just one pixel, it will appear in just one color.

PatMap contains a handle to a pixel map. All the fields in this pixel map are used to define the characteristics of type 1 (full color) patterns, except for baseAddr. Instead of using baseAddr to point to the pixel image, patData is a handle to the pixels, for easy access. The other fields of the pixel map in patMap give other information about the pattern's pixel image, such as its size, depth, color table, and so on.

The pattern can be used with screens of any depth, so it must be expanded or contracted when a screen with a new depth is encountered. To speed up drawing with the pattern, QuickDraw will keep a copy of the pattern in the current screen's depth in the patXData field. Whenever the current screen's depth is changed, patXData has to be rebuilt. PatXValid indicates whether the current patXData has to be rebuilt; it's −1 if it does and 0 if it already has the right pattern.

PatXMap is used internally by QuickDraw. The last field, pat1Data, contains a copy of the pixel pattern represented as an old-version bit pattern. This is used by QuickDraw for fast pattern drawing when bit patterns are needed.

You can use the patXValid field if you want to change the pattern or its colors. After you make the change, just set patXValid to −1. This will make QuickDraw rebuild the patXData before it draws with the pattern, just as if the screen depth had changed.

Color Grafports

All drawing in QuickDraw is done in grafports, which define the rules and environment for the drawing. Color QuickDraw adds a new kind, a color grafport, that lets you take full advantage of the Macintosh II's color capabilities. If you're using the old model of color drawing (eight colors), you can use an old-version grafport. To draw using RGB colors, you'll need a color grafport.

When you create a window, a grafport is contained in the window record, and all drawing in the window is done with this grafport. The Window Manager in the Macintosh II lets you open a new window with either an old-version grafport or a color grafport (see Appendix A). This choice determines which color model you can use, since old-version grafports can only support the eight old-model colors.

Here's the structure of a color grafport:

```
type CGrafPort = Record
                   device: Integer;
                   portPixMap: PixMapHandle;
                   portVersion: Integer; {QuickDraw version}
                   grafVars: Handle; {more fields}
                   chExtra: Integer; {fractional spacing}
                   pnLocHFrac: Integer; {for fractional text}
                   portRect: Rect; {usable rectangle}
                   visRgn: RgnHandle; {same as in GrafPort}
                   clipRgn: RgnHandle; {same as in GrafPort}
                   bkPixPat:PixPatHandle; {background pixPat}
                   RGBFgColor: RGBColor; {foreground color}
                   RGBBkColor: RGBColor; {background color}
                   pnLoc: Point; {old stuff follows}
                   pnSize: Point;
                   pnMode: Integer;
                   pnPixPat: PixPatHandle; {pen pattern}
                   fillPixPat: PixPatHandle; {fill pattern}
                   {remaining fields same as GrafPort}
                 end;
```

Lots of the fields in a color grafport are the same as they were in the original so we'll just talk about what's new. It's interesting to note that a color grafport is exactly the same size as an old-version grafport. How can this be, if it has to hold all this new color information? The answer is that several fields that were found directly in the grafport are now stashed in relocatable objects and handles to them are stored in the color grafport.

Specifically, the portBits, bkPat, fillPat, and pnPat fields have been replaced by handles: portPixMap, bkPixPat, fillPixPat, and pnPixPat. Handles take up four bytes each, so these four handles use up a total of 16 bytes. Bit maps consume 14 bytes, and patterns take up eight, so these four fields in old-version grafports use 38 bytes. That leaves 38 minus 16, or 22 bytes for new stuff and all of them are used.

The portPixMap field replaces the portBits field in an old-version grafport. It's a handle to the pixel map associated with this grafport. PortVersion is used to tell Color QuickDraw if this grafport is color or not. If it's a color grafport, this field should have its high two bits set, which is decimal 49152 and hex $C000. For old-version ports, this is the rowBytes field of the portBits record, which should always have its high two bits clear. This is how Color QuickDraw determines whether to treat the grafport as a new one or not, so it's very important that it be set correctly.

To cram more stuff into the color grafport, the grafVars field was invented. It contains a handle to seven more fields that didn't fit into the main part of the grafport. We'll look at these additional things right after we're done examining the grafport itself.

The next two fields, chExtra and pnLocHFrac, are used when drawing characters with fractional pixel widths. ChExtra is used to specify the amount to add to the width of each non-space character, which allows you to simulate proportionally spaced text on the screen. PnLocHFrac contains the fractional component of the horizontal pen position for drawing text.

The next three fields are the same as in an old-version grafport, so we won't talk about them here. BkPixPat is a handle to a pixel pattern that's used for background filling operations in the grafport, such as EraseRect. RGBForeColor and RGBBackColor contain the RGB values for the foreground and background colors in the grafport. They're the modern version of the fgColor and bkColor fields in an old-version port.

After the RGB colors, there are three more fields that do the same thing as in a non-color grafport. The remaining two new fields are pnPixPat, which holds a handle to the pattern used for drawing in the grafport, and fillPixPat, which holds the pattern used when you make one of the new calls that fill an object with a pattern, such as FillCOval or FillCPoly. In addition, when you make one of the old filling calls that work with bit image patterns, like FillRgn or FillOval, the pattern is stored in the pixPat record at the end of the fillPixPat handle.

Now let's talk about the additional things in the grafVars field:

```
type GrafVars = Record
               rgbOpColor: RGBColor; {for transfer modes}
               rgbHiliteColor: RGBColor; {for hilite mode}
               pmFgColor: Handle; {Palette Mgr foreground}
               pmFgIndex: Integer; {foreground index}
               pmBkColor: Handle; {Palette Mgr background}
               pmBkIndex: Integer; {background index}
               pmFlags: Integer; {Palette Mgr flags}
          end;
```

The rgbOpColor field is used by Color QuickDraw's new arithmetic transfer modes, which allow you to combine colors in very interesting ways such as adding and blending. RGBHiliteColor is used to highlight an object by drawing it on a colored background so that it looks as if it were colored with a highlighting marker. This method of highlighting can be set when you use the invert calls (InvertRect, InvertArc, and so on). To use it, you have to clear the high bit of the low memory global HiLiteMode; there's no easy-to-use trap call that will clear this bit for you.

The last five fields of the grafVars record are used by the Palette Manager, a Macintosh II invention. On most Macintosh II color monitors, the current set of colors is determined by a color table and at any one time a comparatively small number of colors are available from a huge possible number (on Apple's monitor, it's 256 out of 16 million). With MultiFinder, lots of different programs can be sharing the screen.

If each program went around blasting the color table whenever it wanted a new color, there could be chaos. The Palette Manager was created to provide a central clearinghouse for all applications and desk accessories that want to use a specific color. The Palette Manager provides a higher level of access to colors. You can specify the colors you want in your application and the Palette Manager will try to provide them with a minimum of disruption to the other applications using the screen. You even get to attach a priority to your color request, and you can be as courteous or as demanding as you like when asking for your colors.

Color Cursors and Pictures

The original QuickDraw definition of a cursor allowed for a 16 by 16 bit image, in black and white. In Color QuickDraw, a cursor is still the same size, but a pixel image is used to define it, so it can have color information. This is the declaration for a color cursor:

```
type CCrsr = Record
          crsrType: Integer; {color or b&w cursor}
          crsrMap: PixMapHandle; {handle to pixel map}
          crsrData: Handle; {handle to pixel image}
          crsrXData: Handle; {used internally}
          crsrXValid: Integer; {valid cursor flag}
          crsrXHandle: Handle; {future}
          crsr1Data: Bits16; {old-version cursor}
          crsrMask: Bits16; {mask for drawing cursor}
          crsrHotSpot: Point; {point aligned with mouse}
          crsrXTable: Longint; {used internally}
          crsrID: Longint; {used internally}
       end;
```

The crsrType field tells what kind of cursor it is: 32768 is used for a bit image cursor, –32767 indicates a color cursor. CrsrMap contains a handle to a pixel map and the cursor uses all the pixel map's field except baseAddr, just as pixel patterns do. The main use for this is to define the cursor's color table.

The next few fields are also used like their counterparts in a pixel pattern. CrsrData is a handle to the pixel image for the cursor; crsrXData contains the cursor image refitted to match the current's screen's depth; crsrXValid tells if the crsrXData field is correct; crsr1Data contains an bit map cursor that can be used with old-version grafports.

CrsrMask does the same thing as the mask field in an old-version cursor: it defines what happens under the cursor as it moves over the screen. CrsrHotSpot anchors the cursor to the mouse point, just as with old-version cursors.

QuickDraw's definition of a picture has been extended so that color stuff can be recorded. In the original version of QuickDraw, each operation was represented by an operation code or opcode that's one byte long. To allow for a greater number of opcodes, this field has been expanded to two bytes in Color QuickDraw.

To distinguish between these two versions of pictures, there's a handy version opcode that should be the first thing in all pictures.

The version opcode is hex $11, so all old-version pictures start with
$11 01, which indicates version 1. New-version pictures start with a
new opcode that flags them to QuickDraw. QuickDraw is very flexible in dealing with color in pictures. Old-version pictures can use the
old model calls, ForeColor and BackColor, and new pictures can use
the full range of color calls. An old-version picture with color can be
drawn in either kind of grafport with no problems. A new-version
picture, which can have RGB colors, pixel maps, pixel patterns, and
other color things, can also be drawn into a old-version grafport. The
new version of DrawPicture automatically best-cases Color Quick-
Draw operations in an old-version grafport. Here's what it does:

- Pixel patterns are replaced by bit patterns that simulate the intended effect as closely as possible.
- RGB colors are mapped to the old-model eight colors, again as
  closely as possible.
- Pixel maps are drawn by CopyBits, which adjusts to the appropriate screen depth.

Because of the smart new version of DrawPicture, new-version
pictures that were recorded in full RGB colors on color grafports can
be drawn into old grafports. If they're running on a Macintosh Plus or
SE, they'll be in black and white; on a Macintosh II, they can show
colors.

Things To Remember

Color QuickDraw is a clever new implementation of the classic
Macintosh drawing system that supports both the old ways of doing
things and new techniques for adding color to your life. You can mix
old-version grafports, bit maps, patterns, and pictures with new
ones. You have to be careful about using new Color QuickDraw calls,
since they'll only work on a Macintosh II, but in general QuickDraw
is pretty good about allowing you to mix old and new.

Color QuickDraw decides which colors to draw in by using lookup tables. These tables attach an RGB color value to every set of bits
that describes a pixel. Ultimately, the actual color displayed on the
screen comes from a color lookup device, which is usually on the monitor's interface card.

The RGB model, as implemented by QuickDraw, allows you to
specify 48 bits of color information, or more than 281 trillion different colors. The current version of QuickDraw, used in conjunction with

Apple's monitor, can display 16 million of those colors; any 256 of them can be on the screen at the same time.

The current implementation of QuickDraw uses the chunky bit arrangement, which groups all of a pixel's bits together in memory. Future versions may include support for the planar model, which separates the pixel image into a set of one-bit-deep planes.

You can write general-purpose color drawing code that will work correctly on all Macintoshes, if you stick to the old model of color drawing. To use the full features of the Macintosh II's color capabilities, you either have to write special-case code or sacrifice compatibility.

You'll find Listing 3-1 next. This program provides a simple example of how you can use the old model and get eight colors but still be compatible with non-color systems without having to write special code.

```
program ColorIt;

{Listing 3-1  Example of old-model color drawing that works with
 all Macintoshes}

  uses
     {$U HD:MPW:Interfaces.p:MemTypes.p } MemTypes,
     {$U HD:MPW:Interfaces.p:QuickDraw.p} QuickDraw,
     {$U HD:MPW:Interfaces.p:OSIntf.p   } OSIntf,
     {$U HD:MPW:Interfaces.p:ToolIntf.p } ToolIntf,
     {$U HD:MPW:Interfaces.p:PackIntf.p } PackIntf;

  const
     appleID = 128; {resource IDs/menu IDs for Apple, File and Edit menus}
     fileID  = 129;
     editID  = 130;
     colorID = 131;

     appleM = 1; {index for each menu in myMenus (array of menu handles)}
     fileM  = 2;
     editM  = 3;
     colorM = 4;

     menuCount = 4;     {total number of menus}

     aboutItem = 1;     {item in Apple menu}

     undoItem  = 1;     {Items in Edit menu}
     cutItem   = 3;
     copyItem  = 4;
     pasteItem = 5;
     clearitem = 6;
```

Listing 3-1 continued

```
        newItem = 1;      {items in File menu}
        closeItem = 3;
        quitItem = 5;

        blackItem = 1;
        whiteItem = 2;
        redItem = 3;
        greenItem = 4;
        blueItem = 5;
        cyanItem = 6;
        magentaItem = 7;
        yellowItem = 8;

        wName = 'Window '; {prefix for window names}

        windDX = 25;      {distance to move for new windows}
        windDY = 25;

        leftEdge = 10;    {initial dimensions of window}
        topEdge = 42;
        rightEdge = 210;
        botEdge = 175;

    var
        myMenus: array [1..menuCount] OF MenuHandle; {handles to the menus}
        dragRect: Rect;            {rectangle used to mark boundaries for dragging window}
        txRect: Rect;              {rectangle for text in application window}
        textH: TEHandle;           {handle to Textedit record}
        theChar: char;             {typed character}
        extended: boolean;         {true if user is Shift-clicking}
        doneFlag: boolean;         {true if user has chosen Quit Item}
        myEvent: EventRecord;      {information about an event}
        wRecord: WindowRecord;     {information about the application window}
        myWindow: WindowPtr;       {pointer to wRecord}
        myWinPeek : WindowPeek;    {another pointer to wRecord}
        whichWindow: WindowPtr;    {window in which mouse button was pressed}
        nextWRect: Rect;           {portRect for next window to be opended}
        nextWTitle: Str255;        {title of next window to be opened}
        nextWNum: Longint;         {number of next window (for title)}
        savedPort: GrafPtr;        {pointer to preserve GrafPort}
        menusOK: boolean;          {for disabling menu items}
        scrapErr: Longint;
        scrCopyErr: Integer;

procedure SetUpMenus;
{ set up menus and menu bar }

    var
        i: Integer;
```

Listing 3-1 continued

```
  begin
    myMenus[appleM] := GetMenu(appleID); {read Apple menu}
    AddResMenu(myMenus[appleM],'DRVR'); {add desk accessory names}
    myMenus[fileM] := GetMenu(fileID);  {read file menu }
    myMenus[editM] := GetMenu(editID);  {read Edit menu }
    myMenus[colorM] := GetMenu(colorID);

    for i:=1 to menuCount do
      InsertMenu(myMenus[i],0);  {install menus in menu bar }
    DrawMenuBar; { and draw menu bar}
  end; {SetUpMenus}


procedure OpenWindow;
{ Open a new window }

  begin
    NumToString (nextWNum, nextWTitle); {prepare number for title}
    nextWTitle := concat (wName, nextWTitle); {add to prefix}
    myWindow := NewWindow (Nil, nextWRect, nextWTitle, True, noGrowDocProc,
    Pointer (-1), True, 0);    {open the window}
    SetPort (myWindow);        {make it the current port}
    txRect := thePort^.portRect;{prepare TERecord for new window}
    InsetRect (txRect, 4, 0);
    textH := TENew (txRect, txRect);
    myWinPeek := WindowPeek (myWindow);
    myWinPeek^.refcon := Longint (textH); {keep TEHandle in refcon!}
    OffsetRect (nextWRect, windDX, windDY);{move window down and right}
    if nextWRect.right > dragRect.right {move back if it's too far over}
    then OffsetRect (nextWRect, -nextWRect.left + leftEdge, 0);
    if nextWRect.bottom > dragRect.bottom
    then OffsetRect (nextWRect, 0, -nextWRect.top + topEdge);
    nextWNum := nextWNum + 1; {bump number for next window}
    menusOK := false;
    EnableItem (myMenus [editM],0); {in case this is the only window}
  end; {OpenWindow}


procedure KillWindow (theWindow: WindowPtr);
{Close a window and throw everything away}

  begin
    TEDispose (TEHandle (WindowPeek (theWindow)^.refcon));
                          {throw away TERecord}
    DisposeWindow (theWindow); {throw away WindowRecord}
    textH := NIL;            {for TEIdle in main event loop}
    if FrontWindow = NIL    {if no more windows, disable Close}
      then DisableItem (myMenus[fileM], closeItem);
    if WindowPeek (FrontWindow)^.windowKind < 0
                          {if a desk acc is coming up, enable undo}
      then EnableItem (myMenus[editM], undoItem)
      else DisableItem (myMenus[editM], undoItem);

  end; {KillWindow}
```

Listing 3-1 continued

```
function MyFilter (theDialog: DialogPtr; var theEvent: EventRecord;
    var itemHit: Integer): Boolean;

  var
    theType: Integer;
    theItem: Handle;
    theBox: Rect;
    finalTicks: Longint;

  begin
    if (BitAnd(theEvent.message,charCodeMask) = 13) {carriage return}
      or (BitAnd(theEvent.message,charCodeMask) = 3) {enter}
      then
        begin
          GetDItem (theDialog, 1, theType, theItem, theBox);
          HiliteControl (ControlHandle (theItem), 1);
          Delay (8, finalTicks);
          HiliteControl (ControlHandle (theItem), 0);
          itemHit := 1;
          MyFilter := True;
        end {if BitAnd...then begin}
      else MyFilter := False;
  end; {function MyFilter}


procedure DoAboutBox;

  var
    itemHit: Integer;

  begin
    myWindow := GetNewDialog (1000, Nil, pointer (-1));
    repeat
      ModalDialog (@MyFilter, itemHit)
    until itemHit = 1;
    DisposDialog (myWindow);
  end; {procedure DoAboutBox}

procedure ColorMe (color: Integer);

  begin
    myWindow := FrontWindow;
    SetPort (myWindow);
    BackColor (color);
    InvalRect (thePort^.portBits.bounds);
  end;

procedure DoCommand (mResult: LONGINT);

  var
    itemString: STR255;

{Execute Item specified by mResult, the result of MenuSelect}
```

Listing 3-1 continued

```
var
   theItem: Integer; {menu item number from mResult low-order word}
   theMenu: Integer; {menu number from mResult high-order word}
   name: Str255;     {desk accessory name}
   temp: Integer;


begin
   theItem := LoWord(mResult); {call Toolbox Utility routines to set }
   theMenu := HiWord(mResult);      { menu item number and menu number}

   case theMenu of              {case on menu ID}

      appleID:
        if theItem = aboutItem
          then DoAboutBox
          else
            begin
              GetItem(myMenus[appleM],theItem,name);
              {GetPort (savedPort);}
              scrapErr := ZeroScrap;
              scrCopyErr := TEToScrap;
              temp := OpenDeskAcc(name);
           EnableItem (myMenus [editM],0);
           {SetPort (savedPort);}
           if FrontWindow <> NIL
             then
               begin
                  EnableItem (myMenus [fileM], closeItem);
                  EnableItem (myMenus [editM], undoItem);
                end; {if FrontWindow then begin}
           menusOK := false;
         end;    {if theItem...else begin}
fileID:
   case theItem of

      newItem:
        OpenWindow;

      closeItem:
        if WindowPeek (FrontWindow)^.windowKind < 0
        then CloseDeskAcc (windowPeek (FrontWindow)^.windowKind)
        {if desk acc window, close it}
        else KillWindow (FrontWindow);
        {if it's one of mine, blow it away}

      quitItem:
        doneFlag := TRUE; {quit}

end; {case theItem}
```

Listing 3-1 continued

```
      editID:
        begin
          if not SystemEdit(theItem-1)
            then
              case theItem of {case on menu item number}

                cutItem:
                  TECut(textH); {call TextEdit to handle Item}

                copyItem:
                  TECopy(textH);

                pasteItem:
                  TEPaste(textH);

                clearItem:
                  TEDelete(textH);

            end;     {case theItem}
        end;     {editID begin}

      colorID:
        begin
          GetItem (myMenus[colorM],theItem,itemString);
          myWindow := FrontWindow;
          SetWTitle (myWindow, itemString);
          case theItem of
            blackItem: ColorMe (blackColor);
            whiteItem: ColorMe (whiteColor);
            redItem: ColorMe (redColor);
            greenItem: ColorMe (greenColor);
            blueItem: ColorMe (blueColor);
            cyanItem: ColorMe (cyanColor);
            magentaItem: ColorMe (magentaColor);
            yellowItem: ColorMe (yellowColor);
          end; {case theItem}
        end; {colorID begin}
    end;     {case theMenu}
    HiliteMenu(0);
  end; {DoCommand}


procedure FixCursor;
   var
     mouseLoc: point;

 begin
   GetMouse (mouseLoc);
   if PtInRect (mouseLoc, thePort^.portRect)
     then SetCursor (GetCursor (iBeamCursor)^^)
     else SetCursor (arrow);
 end; {procedure FixCursor}
```

Listing 3-1 continued

```
begin          {main program}

    InitGraf(@thePort);
    InitFonts;
    FlushEvents(everyEvent,0);
    InitWindows;
    InitMenus;
    TEInit;
    InitDialogs(NIL);
    InitCursor;

    SetUpMenus;
       with screenBits.bounds do
    SetRect(dragRect,4,24,right-4,bottom-4);
    doneFlag := false;

  menusOK := false;
  nextWNum := 1;   {initialize window number}
  SetRect (nextWRect,leftEdge,topEdge,rightEdge,botEdge);
                   {initialize window rectangle}
  OpenWindow;        {start with one open window}
{ Main event loop }
  repeat
    SystemTask;
    if FrontWindow <> NIL
     then
        if WindowPeek (FrontWindow)^.windowKind >= 0
          then FixCursor;
    if not menusOK and (FrontWindow = NIL)
     then
       begin
         DisableItem (myMenus [fileM], closeItem);
         DisableItem (myMenus [editM], 0);
         menusOK := true;
       end; {if FrontWindow...then begin}
    if textH <> Nil
     then TEIdle(textH);

    if GetNextEvent(everyEvent,myEvent)
     then
     case myEvent.what of

       mouseDown:
         case FindWindow(myEvent.where,whichWindow) of

             inSysWindow:
               SystemClick(myEvent,whichWindow);
```

Listing 3-1 continued

```
                inMenuBar:
                  DoCommand(MenuSelect(myEvent.where));

                inDrag:
                  DragWindow(whichWindow,myEvent.where,dragRect);

                inContent:
                  begin
                    if whichWindow <> FrontWindow
                      then SelectWindow(whichWindow)
                      else
                        begin

                    GlobalToLocal(myEvent.where);
                    extended := BitAnd(myEvent.modifiers,shiftKey) <> 0;
                    TEClick(myEvent.where,extended,textH);
                  end;    {else}
            end;   {inContent}

        inGoAway:
          if TrackGoAway (whichWindow, myEvent.where)
            then KillWindow (whichWindow);

      end;     {case FindWindow}

  keyDown, autoKey:
    begin
      theChar := CHR(BitAnd(myEvent.message,charCodeMask));
      if BitAnd(myEvent.modifiers,cmdKey) <> 0
        then DoCommand(MenuKey(theChar))
        else TEKey(theChar,textH);
    end;   {keyDown, autoKey begin}

  activateEvt:
    begin
    if BitAnd(myEvent.modifiers,activeFlag) <> 0
      then {application window is becoming active}
        begin
          SetPort (GrafPtr (myEvent.message));
          textH := TEHandle (WindowPeek (myEvent.message)^.refcon);
          TEActivate(textH);
          EnableItem (myMenus[fileM],closeItem);
          DisableItem(myMenus[editM],undoItem);
          if WindowPeek (FrontWindow)^.nextWindow^.windowKind < 0
            then scrCopyErr := TEFromScrap;
        end   {if BitAnd...then begin}
```

Listing 3-1 continued

```
        else   {application window is becoming inactive}
          begin
          TEDeactivate(TEHandle(WindowPeek(myEvent.message)^.refcon));
          if WindowPeek (FrontWindow)^.windowKind < 0
            then
              begin
                EnableItem (myMenus[editM], undoItem);
                scrapErr := ZeroScrap;
                scrCopyErr := TEToScrap;
              end {if WindowPeek...then begin}
            else DisableItem (myMenus[editM], undoItem);
          end; {else begin}
      end;   {activateEvt begin}

    updateEvt:
        begin
          GetPort (savedPort);
          SetPort (GrafPtr (myEvent.message));
          BeginUpdate(WindowPtr(myEvent.message));
          EraseRect(WindowPtr(myEvent.message)^.portRect);
          TEUpdate(WindowPtr(myEvent.message)^.portRect,
          TEHandle(WindowPeek(myEvent.message)^.refcon));
          EndUpdate(WindowPtr(myEvent.message));
          SetPort (savedPort);
        end;  {updateEvt begin}

   end;          {case myEvent.what}

  until doneFlag;
end.
```

Listing 3-1 continued

```
resource 'BNDL' (128) {
    'Scot',
    0,
    {   /* array TypeArray: 2 elements */
        /* [1] */
        'ICN#',
        {   /* array IDArray: 2 elements */
            /* [1] */
            0, 128,
            /* [2] */
            1, 129
        },
        /* [2] */
        'FREF',
        {   /* array IDArray: 2 elements */
            /* [1] */
            0, 128,
            /* [2] */
            1, 129
        }
    }
};

resource 'DITL' (1000, "About box") {
    { /* array DITLarray: 2 elements */
        /* [1] */
        {61, 191, 81, 251},
        Button {
            enabled,
            "OK"
        },
        /* [2] */
        {8, 24, 56, 272},
        StaticText {
            disabled,
            "ColorMe example program\nby Scott Knaster"
            "\nversion 1.0  12:31 AM  7/11/87"
        }
    }
};

resource 'DLOG' (1000, "About box") {
    {62, 100, 148, 412},
    dBoxProc,
    visible,
    goAway,
    0x0,
    1000,
    "New Dialog"
};
```

Listing 3-1 continued

```
resource 'FREF' (128) {
    'APPL',
    0,
    ""
};

resource 'FREF' (129) {
    'TEXT',
    1,
    ""
};

resource 'ICN#' (128) {
    {  /* array: 2 elements */
        /* [1] */
        $"FFFF FFFF 8000 0005 FD00 0005 9100 0005"
        $"9100 0005 91EF 0005 9129 0005 912F 0005"
        $"9128 0005 912F 0005 8000 0805 8F00 0805"
        $"8880 0805 8898 C905 8F25 2A05 88A5 2C05"
        $"88A5 2A05 8F18 C905 8000 0005 8000 0005"
        $"9000 0005 9000 E485 9001 0505 9001 0605"
        $"9C90 C405 9290 2605 9290 2505 9CF1 C485"
        $"8010 0005 8010 0005 80F0 0005 FFFF FFFF",
        /* [2] */
        $"FFFF FFFF FFFF FFFF FFFF FFFF FFFF FFFF"
        $"FFFF FFFF FFFF FFFF FFFF FFFF FFFF FFFF"
        $"FFFF FFFF FFFF FFFF FFFF FFFF FFFF FFFF"
        $"FFFF FFFF FFFF FFFF FFFF FFFF FFFF FFFF"
        $"FFFF FFFF FFFF FFFF FFFF FFFF FFFF FFFF"
        $"FFFF FFFF FFFF FFFF FFFF FFFF FFFF FFFF"
        $"FFFF FFFF FFFF FFFF FFFF FFFF FFFF FFFF"
        $"FFFF FFFF FFFF FFFF FFFF FFFF FFFF FFFF"
    }
};

resource 'ICN#' (129) {
    {  /* array: 2 elements */
        /* [1] */
        $"0FFF FE00 0800 0300 09D0 0280 09D0 0240"
        $"09D0 0220 09D0 0210 09D0 03F8 09D0 0008"
        $"09D0 0008 09D0 0008 09D0 0008 09D0 0008"
        $"09F0 0008 0910 0008 0910 0008 0910 0008"
        $"0910 0008 0910 0008 08E0 0008 09F0 0008"
        $"09F0 0008 09F8 0008 09F8 0008 09E8 5FE8"
        $"09F8 0BE8 08D0 3FE8 08F0 FFE8 0870 3FE8"
        $"0819 FFE8 0800 0008 0800 0008 0FFF FFF8",
```

Listing 3-1 continued

```
                /* [2] */
                $"0FFF FE00 0FFF FF00 0FFF FF80 0FFF FFC0"
                $"0FFF FFE0 0FFF FFF0 0FFF FFF8 0FFF FFF8"
                $"0FFF FFF8 0FFF FFF8 0FFF FFF8 0FFF FFF8"
                $"0FFF FFF8 0FFF FFF8 0FFF FFF8 0FFF FFF8"
                $"0FFF FFF8 0FFF FFF8 0FFF FFF8 0FFF FFF8"
                $"0FFF FFF8 0FFF FFF8 0FFF FFF8 0FFF FFF8"
                $"0FFF FFF8 0FFF FFF8 0FFF FFF8 0FFF FFF8"
                $"0FFF FFF8 0FFF FFF8 0FFF FFF8 0FFF FFF8"
        }
};

resource 'MENU' (128) {
        128,
        textMenuProc,
        0x7FFFFFFD,
        enabled,
        apple,
        {   /* array: 2 elements */
            /* [1] */
            "About ColorMe...", noIcon, "", "", plain,
            /* [2] */
            "-", noIcon, "", "", plain
        }
};

resource 'MENU' (129) {
        129,
        textMenuProc,
        0x7FFFFFF5,
        enabled,
        "File",
        {   /* array: 5 elements */
            /* [1] */
            "New", noIcon, "N", "", plain,
            /* [2] */
            "-", noIcon, "", "", plain,
            /* [3] */
            "Close", noIcon, "W", "", plain,
            /* [4] */
            "-", noIcon, "", "", plain,
            /* [5] */
            "Quit", noIcon, "Q", "", plain
        }
};
```

Listing 3-1 continued

```
resource 'MENU' (130) {
    130,
    textMenuProc,
    0x7FFFFFFC,
    enabled,
    "Edit",
    {   /* array: 6 elements */
        /* [1] */
        "Undo", noIcon, "Z", "", plain,
        /* [2] */
        "-", noIcon, "", "", plain,
        /* [3] */
        "Cut", noIcon, "X", "", plain,
        /* [4] */
        "Copy", noIcon, "C", "", plain,
        /* [5] */
        "Paste", noIcon, "V", "", plain,
        /* [6] */
        "Clear", noIcon, "", "", plain
    }
};

resource 'MENU' (131) {
    131,
    textMenuProc,
    allEnabled,
    enabled,
    "Color",
    {   /* array: 8 elements */
        /* [1] */
        "Black", noIcon, "", "", plain,
        /* [2] */
        "White", noIcon, "", "", plain,
        /* [3] */
        "Red", noIcon, "", "", plain,
        /* [4] */
        "Green", noIcon, "", "", plain,
        /* [5] */
        "Blue", noIcon, "", "", plain,
        /* [6] */
        "Cyan", noIcon, "", "", plain,
        /* [7] */
        "Magenta (in another dimension...)", noIcon, "", "", plain,
        /* [8] */
        "Yellow", noIcon, "", "", plain
    }
};
```

Listing 3-1 continued

```
data 'Scot' (0) {
    $"1853 686F 776F 6666 2063 7265 6174 6564"          /* .ColorMe created */
    $"2030 372F 3131 2F38 37"                            /*   7/11/87 */
};
```

C H A P T E R   4

Event Manager

The mouse placed in perspective. The keyboard resur-
rected as a way of issuing commands. A look at some
unusual software. A discussion on the enhancement of
the user interface. Some closing tips about ensuring
compatibility with other languages and customizing
Standard File.

Using the Mouse and Keyboard

When the Macintosh was first introduced, there was a popular feeling that the essence of the Macintosh user interface was to put all the functionality of a program into its menu items. By having everything a program could do available through menu items, the application could avoid hidden complexities that might make the user go crazy wondering how to do something.

Although the user interface has always provided for the capability of attaching a Command-key equivalent to any menu item, Command keys weren't heavily used by early Macintosh applications. As real people began to use Macintosh software, though, an interesting thing happened: they discovered that it wasn't necessarily bad to have to memorize that, for example, Command-Shift-E is a shortcut for choosing a new font. If you have to choose new fonts all day, every day, you'll likely remember Command-Shift-E and you'll be grateful that it exists. A truly nice application provides both menu commands and keyboard equivalents for as many features as possible.

Another reason why it's important to provide two ways of getting to commands is because of the way people use software. Fundamentally, it works like this: sometimes you're typing and sometimes you're mousing. Very profound, right? If you're typing a lot of text and your hands are on the keyboard, you'd probably rather type a command (assuming you know what to type) than reach for the mouse and pull down a menu. If you're busy mousing, such as when moving things around with a graphics editor, you probably would rather keep using the mouse to perform commands.

Remember that the idea here is to provide both ways of doing things: menu items (or other things to click on, like buttons) and keyboard commands. If you leave out one or the other, you're shortchanging some of your users. The cleverest applications find a way to allow almost any operation by either typing or clicking.

While you're studying your application to figure out how to give equal time to keyboards, though, don't forget that many things the Macintosh does with a mouse and graphics just can't be simulated by the keyboard and text. It's easy to use the keyboard for binary kinds of functions, like saving a document, left-justifying some text, or printing. It's a lot harder to use the keyboard for more analog acts like dragging the scroll box to the location where you think a certain part of your term paper will be found or resizing a window to exactly the right dimensions. You can't do everything with the keyboard; imagine trying to get MacPaint to draw a picture using only a keyboard.

Have It Both Ways

How can you be sure to provide both mouse and keyboard ways of executing commands? To answer this question, we'll look at several different kinds of mousing commands. We'll talk about each of them and some ideas for implementing keyboard equivalents.

The first and easiest category to deal with is selecting things from pull-down menus. The Menu Manager allows you to specify a Command key to go along with any menu item, and then takes care of much of the work of implementing it for you. All you have to do is set up the Command key in your resource file, for example by specifying it in an MPW Rez source file or by using ResEdit. You can even play around with other people's applications, by editing their menus using ResEdit.

The other categories of keyboard equivalents are a little trickier. We'll take a look at setting up keyboard equivalents for buttons that appear in dialogs. Let's say that you're entering lots of data into a spreadsheet (use your imagination) and you want to bring up a dialog that will allow you to set the font for cells in the spreadsheet. If you power-use that spreadsheet, you probably know the keyboard equivalent for the font command you want, so you type it. The dialog comes up, and it wants you to select from three radio buttons and then click Enter or Cancel. Of course, you can also choose Enter by typing the Return key; wouldn't it be nice if you could select the radio button you wanted by typing, too? That way, your hands wouldn't have to leave the keyboard.

Look at the record. Let's add a dash of controversy to this nice mellow book. Some user interface studies indicate that even though the user's hand must move from the keyboard to the mouse in order to select an item from a menu, this is still a quicker process than typing the keyboard equivalent. Others would suggest that split second timing is not as important as user perceptions, and most users believe that being able to keep their hands on the keyboard when they're typing is faster anyway. The important thing here is to give your users what they really want, not what you or someone else thinks is good for them. The latter attitude leads to serious religious problems and we have enough of those on television without having to find them in software too.

You may have noticed that a few clever applications have a way of letting you do this. Being able to choose the default button (usually, it has a thick outline around it) by pressing the Return or Enter keys is standard and many applications allow you to choose the Cancel button by typing Command-period. Only a few applications go out of their way to provide keyboard equivalents for other standard buttons, check boxes, and radio buttons as described in our scenario.

Putting in keyboard ways of choosing buttons seems like a nice thing to do for users who are in the middle of data entry anyway, since they're busy using the keyboard. How do we do it? The first thing to think about is the user interface. Let's continue with our example of a font dialog in a spreadsheet. Figure 4-1 shows a picture of the dialog.

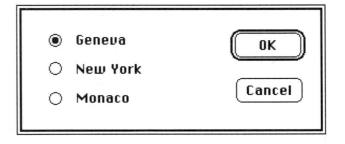

Figure 4-1. Font choice dialog

As you can see, the dialog gives you a choice between three fonts, and it has the standard OK and Cancel buttons with OK set up as the default button. What would be a good way to let users type their choice of font? Normally, of course, keyboard equivalents for commands are typed with the Command key (maybe that's why Apple gave that name to that funny-looking symbol). This distinguishes between regular typing to enter data and special requests to do commands.

Apples on command. On Macintosh models up to and including the Macintosh Plus, the Command key on the keyboard contained the special command symbol (⌘). Starting with the Macintosh SE and Macintosh II keyboards, the Command key has both the ⌘ and the Apple logo. This was done to help move the two Apple product lines, Macintosh and Apple II, to the same keyboard layout. Apple II computers have had two keys with Apple logos on them for a long time. Actually, this move was a compromise. Macintosh users have to get used to the Apple logo instead of the Command symbol; Apple II users lost one of their Apple keys.

So, should we use Command keys to set up keyboard commands for the three radio buttons? We could have Command-G for Geneva, Command-N for New York, and Command-M for Monaco. Is this reasonable? Sure, and it's easy for the frequent flier to memorize. If we wanted to, we could even put little reminders into the dialog, as shown in Figure 4-2.

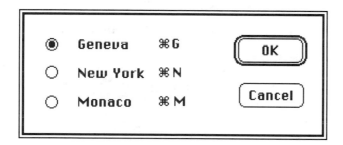

Figure 4-2. Font choice dialog

Streamlining

If we think about this a little more, we can come up with an even classier way to set up keyboard equivalents for these radio buttons. In this dialog and in others like it where there's nothing but buttons, the user normally doesn't have to do any typing at all. Usually, in a dialog like this, anything typed by the user would just be ignored, or would be considered an error and answered with a rude beep.

Well, why not have a single keystroke—a typed letter G, N, or M—turn on the appropriate radio button? There's no conflict with any fields for typing since there's nowhere in the dialog for the user to type. In fact, what we should really do in a case like this is ignore the use of any modifier keys, such as the Command key, and be happy with the keystroke either way. That way, if the user is more comfortable using the Command key for keyboard equivalents, it's perfectly acceptable to have the Command key held down while typing. A real veteran cosmic user, though, need not use the Command key in this case because the letter key will be enough.

This technique is fine for dialogs that don't ask the user to type text, but what about those that do, like the dialog (from the popular baseball manager's program, ConnieMac) in Figure 4-3? In this dialog, there are simple buttons for OK and Cancel, radio buttons for how to pitch to the hitter, and a text field to type in the name of a relief pitcher. We can't let the user just type the letter I for intentional walk, because it might be a letter in the name of the pitcher being typed into the text field. In this case, the only thing we can do is require that the user hold down the Command key while typing the appropriate letter.

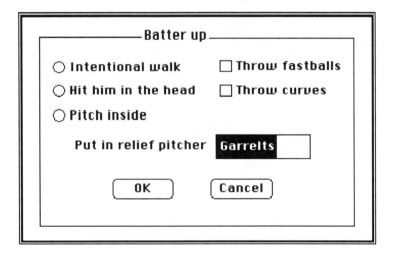

Figure 4-3. Simple common dialog

It seems we've arrived at a reasonable solution here. If there are any text fields in the dialog, the user can "click" a button from the keyboard by using a Command key. If there are no text fields in the dialog, the user can just type a letter key to press a button, but typing with the Command key down will accomplish the same thing.

Now that that's settled, let's throw in one more complication. In both of our examples so far, there have been just a few buttons in each dialog and each choice has started with a different letter, making it easy to figure out what the right Command-key combination would be for each one. What if we've got a much more complex dialog, with lots of buttons to choose from and no easy way to figure out which keys should correspond to which choices? For an example of a dialog like this see Figure 4-4, which is an example of a dialog that might appear for an electronic juke box.

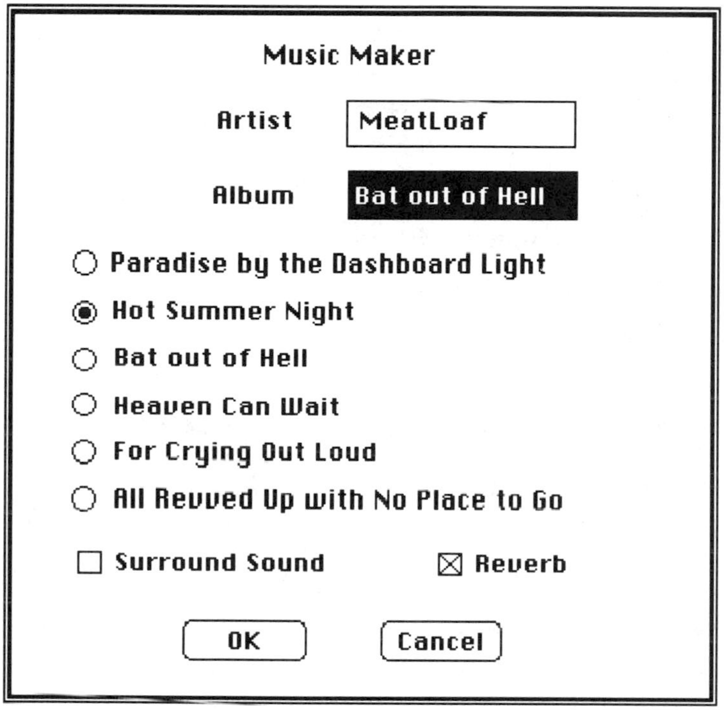

Figure 4-4. Musical dialog

This dialog has zillions of buttons, or at least ten anyway, several of them beginning with the same letter. There's no easy way to assign keyboard equivalents to each of them. What can we do? Let's think about the similar situation that's found in menu items. Not every menu item that has a keyboard equivalent uses a mnemonic one. Eventually you just run out of letters—that happens in Roman languages, you know.

To remind you of the keystrokes that you can use for various menu items, we'll use a very simple strategy: you get to see the Command key listed right in the menu when you pull it down. We can apply this technique to buttons in our big dialog by putting a cheat note for each Command key right in the button text. We've transformed our juke box dialog by adding keyboard equivalents for the buttons and showing them in the buttons themselves, and you can see the result in Figure 4-5.

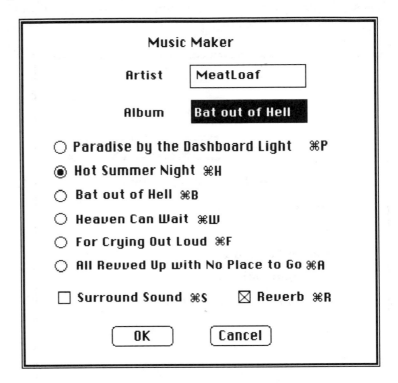

Figure 4-5. Command keys added

Although this looks kind of funny when you're not used to seeing it, it seems like something that you could get used to quickly. Now that we've figured out what the user interface will look like, we can work on the implementation and talk a little about how to write the code to handle the keystrokes.

Command Keys for Buttons

The Menu Manager takes care of mapping keystrokes to menu items for you almost automatically: when the user types a Command key, you call the Menu Manager routine MenuKey and it tells you which menu item was selected. Unfortunately, there's nothing like that available in the Dialog Manager, so we'll have to do most of the work. Since we're at the cutting edge of technology here, we'll have to figure out a good way to get from the keystroke typed by the user to the desired button.

We can use one of the Dialog Manager's best tricks to simplify the processing of button-press keystrokes. Remember that when you call ModalDialog, you get to create a dialog filter function, better known as the filterproc. Whenever the Dialog Manager gets an event, it gives your filterproc a chance to check out the event and do something with it.

In your filterproc, you can decide just what you really want to do with the event before handing it off to the guts of ModalDialog. Generally, you'll do one of three things.

- If you're not interested in the event, you can do nothing and just let ModalDialog handle it normally.
- If the event is a special one you want to respond to, you can do so and not let ModalDialog deal with it at all.
- If you're really sneaky, you can actually change the event record as it's passed to your filterproc, which makes it look like something else by the time ModalDialog gets hold of it.

You can use either the second or third technique to convert keystrokes into simulated button hits. To use the third technique, changing the event record, you have to do a couple of things. First, you have to change a keydown event into a mousedown event and then you have to figure out the right mouse point to put into the event record. To find the right coordinate, you can use GetDItem to find the location of the item, then LocalToGlobal to convert it to global coordinates before stuffing it back into the event record. This way gives you the advantage of having ModalDialog automagically handle the events on controls for you. ModalDialog calls the Control Manager to highlight buttons, so you don't have to.

Popping your buttons. If you use this technique, ModalDialog will call StillDown to see if the mouse button is down after handling the ersatz mousedown event. Since the mouse button was never really clicked at all, it will discover that StillDown is false and it will immediately unhighlight the button. So, the fake button click happens pretty fast, and depending on the monitor and CPU you're using, it sometimes may not even be visible.

The second technique, handling the event yourself in the filter-proc, requires you to highlight the buttons yourself, but you don't have to munge around with the event record to make it appear that a button was clicked. Instead, you use brute force and highlight the button yourself, by calling HiliteControl. You'll actually call HiliteControl twice: once with a hiliteState of 1 to light up the button, then with a value of 0 to turn the button off. In this case, you have total control over what happens in response to the event since you're not relying on ModalDialog to track the buttons. This lets you decide how long you want the button to be lit up—eight ticks seems a pretty good-looking value.

In your filterproc, you can do virtually anything you want except what's prohibited by law. In this case, we'd like to check the event record for Command keys and then use something like a case statement to figure out exactly what to do for each particular keystroke. If we use this technique, we have to tell ModalDialog that we've already taken care of things and that it shouldn't do anything about this particular event. That's easy to do; here's how.

Remember that the filter we're using to examine all the events is a function, and functions get to return values. Specifically, a dialog filterproc always returns a boolean value. If it returns False, Modal-Dialog will handle the event, which might be the real one caused by the user or the doctored one that your filter messed with. If your filterproc returns True, you're telling ModalDialog to leave this event alone and that you've already done everything you wanted to do with it. So in this case, we'll set the filterproc's value to True and ModalDialog will leave it alone.

Localizing

There are a few things to watch out for. One important consideration when setting up keyboard equivalents for your dialog buttons is whether they will make sense when your product is localized into other languages. For dialogs with just a few buttons, you'll probably try to keep the keyboard equivalents mnemonic, as in the examples earlier in this section.

It's important not to hard-code the buttons' keyboard equivalents into your program. Hard-coding makes it much more difficult than it ought to be to change the keystrokes when you convert to other languages. One idea is for each dialog item list to have an associated string list (STR#) resource that contains the keystrokes you're using as shortcuts for each item. Keeping this stuff in resources instead of hard-coding it will make life much easier for your translator and for yourself.

Standard File Dialogs

Two special, very common dialogs that every program uses are the Standard File dialogs for opening and saving, called by SFGetFile and SFPutFile. It's a nice touch to add keyboard equivalents to the buttons that appear there. We'll briefly go over an easy way to accomplish this here.

When you call SFGetFile or SFPutFile, they in turn call on ModalDialog to handle most of the event processing that takes place as the user chooses a file to open or save. ModalDialog takes care of all the list scrolling, typing, and button clicking. However, you don't get to have a filterproc for the calls that Standard File makes to ModalDialog. What can you do?

The trick is to not use SFGetFile or SFPutFile, but instead to use their exotic cousins SFPGetFile and SFPPutFile (note the extra letter P in each call, careful reader: it stands for *programmer*). When you use these versions of the Standard File calls, you get to use a filterproc as one of the parameters.

The P versions of the calls let you use the filterproc to look for special keystrokes and handle them as hits on the buttons. Typically, you'd want to look for the Command key plus O, C, D, and E, and convert them to the Open, Cancel, Drive, and Eject buttons in the getfile dialog, and use the same set for putfile with the change of S for the Save button. If you add any of your own buttons, such as buttons to save in special formats in the putfile box, you can look for those as well. Of course, if you want, you can put the keyboard equivalents right in the button text, as we did earlier.

Things To Remember

Although the Macintosh interface is most famous for its nifty use of pull-down menus and clickable controls, other elements are necessary to successfully support people who use the same piece of software every day—those well-known power users. To really make those users into big fans of your programs, you have to make their lives easier, and a very good way to do that is to let them perform commands both with something mouseable and something typeable.

Command key equivalents for menu items are obvious and easy to do, but don't forget about them. Be sure to implement as many key-

board equivalents for menu items as you can. Since your users can always do things with familiar and friendly pull-down menus, they're never forced to use those mysterious Command keys unless they want to, and after they've become intimate with the program, they'll almost certainly want to.

Using keyboard equivalents for buttons is a more unusual idea and there's less support for it in the Macintosh Toolbox. Still, the principle is the same, and that's never to force the user to dance between the keyboard and the mouse in order to get something done quickly.

Allowing keystrokes as alternatives for buttons is a good way to do this. In fact, supporting keystrokes that do the same thing as standard buttons sounds like something Apple might even implement someday as the Macintosh interface evolves. For now, though, you have to do much of the work yourself. The best way to start is by using the filterproc in your dialogs. With some clever effort, you can help to evolve the interface and make it, like Steve Austin, better than it was.

C H A P T E R 5

Finder

A brief look at living with the Finder. A discussion of the changing world of the Macintosh operating system.

Quitting to Another Application

Many Macintosh applications follow pretty much the same user interface standards, meaning that it's relatively easy for a user to figure out how to work a new application at least a little. Market research (a slightly less exact science than programming) has shown that most Macintosh owners tend to own more software than folks who own other personal computers, and it seems that one reason is that the standard interface makes it easier to play with and learn a new program.

Since most Macintosh owners use a lot of different pieces of software, they like to be able to switch between them quickly. Throughout the history of the Macintosh, inventors have tried to come up with easier ways to make this happen. One idea was Switcher, which let you chop up your Macintosh into pieces and then run an application in each piece.

This made it very easy to switch between applications, but each application took over the whole screen. If you wanted to see windows from your word processor and your drawing program at the same time, you were out of luck. However, you could switch between them very quickly and easily once you had started them up.

The next evolution of this idea was Apple's multitasking version of the Finder, called MultiFinder. With this system, you can have lots of applications open at the same time, but you can share their windows on the screen all at once if you want to. This makes the interface a little more intuitive, since you can just click on a window to make its application come to life.

Both these ideas are great leaps in the power of Macintosh system software. But there are still some little things you can do in your application to give even more power to your friend, the user. One of these is the ability to avoid going back to the Finder when your application quits.

Sometimes, a user wants to quit an application and start another one right away, without going to the Finder. The Macintosh, of course, always wants to return to the Finder as a sort of purgatory between applications. Some folks don't *ever* want to go back to the Finder, so a bunch of Finder replacements have cropped up over the years to take its place. These programs usually provide a different way of doing the Finder's job of managing files and launching applications.

Often imitated. Trying to come up with something to replace the Finder is an intimidating task. You have to replace lots of obvious functions displaying the contents of disks, launching applications, deleting files, creating directories, copying files from disk to disk. In addition, there are other, more subtle things that are very closely related to the evolution of the system. These are tough for someone outside Apple's system software group to keep up with; they include support for the AppleShare file server and compatibility with the multitasking operating system. There are some good Finder-substitutes, but the Finder does things that replacement programs usually don't.

Of course, when you're running MultiFinder, it's very easy to start another application without having to return to the Finder. Under this system, the Finder is always around and so no time is wasted quitting your application and starting the Finder. Still, it's handy to give your users the option of closing up the application and starting another all in one step.

Another way to avoid the Finder when quitting is to give your user a menu option either to exit the normal way and start the Finder or to name another application and just go straight to it. To figure out how we can do this, we should look at the process that takes place when an application runs.

Launching and Quitting

Most of the time when you want to start an application, you double-click it in the Finder. It calls a trap named Launch, which starts the application by opening its resource file, loading in the first couple of CODE resources, and jumping right in. What happens when the application is all done? Is there some sort of "Quit" ROM call that takes place and puts everything back the way it was?

In fact, the ROM does nothing formal when an application ends. It just comes back to the ROM on the "other side" of the application, at which point the system makes another Launch call, this time launching the application called Finder (or whatever other application is pretending it's the Finder at the moment).

Find the Finder.   After your application terminates and the ROM returns to do the post-launching stuff, it isn't hard-coded to launch the application called Finder. Instead, it launches the program whose name is stored in the low-memory global variable called FinderName (a dead giveaway). However, you shouldn't try to put your own application's name here so that it will replace the Finder. Apple has recently defined a new way of making your application into a Finder-replacement, or **shell**, by enhancing the functions of the Launch call. Unfortunately, thanks to the magic of publishing, the details on how this works weren't available at press time, as the saying goes.

Since the system just launches another application, usually the Finder, after it quits your application, you can just call Launch if you want to start up something else when the user quits from yours. A reasonable interface to use here is to present an SFGetFile dialog listing all the files of type APPL, then let the user choose one of them. After one is picked, you can call Launch on it and it will start up as your application quits.

In the first applications that used this technique, the menu item that allowed a user to start another application upon leaving yours was usually labeled Launch. This was a very programmery name to use, since most nontechnical users have absolutely no idea what it means. In fact, most people are more comfortable thinking they're quitting one program (which they are) and starting another instead of the Finder. A better command name, Transfer, started to appear after a while, but an even more appropriate name for this menu option is Quit To, which also looks right when placed next to the standard Quit item in the File menu.

As we said earlier, Apple has recently implemented changes to the way Launch works, in conjunction with the release of Multi-Finder. The time warp between the writing of this book and your reading it means that there's no more information available right now. Before implementing a Quit To feature, or even before calling Launch from your application, you should check the latest documentation and technical notes from Apple to find out about the current state of the art.

Things To Remember

Every application has to live with the Finder, because it's virtually an extension of the Macintosh's operating system. It's been tough to take full advantage of every possible trick, though, because the Finder has been evolving and changing over the last two years. You should watch for Finder technical information from Apple so you can keep up with the state of the art and keep your programs working right.

C H A P T E R 6

Printing Manager

Finding and using the icon of your choice. In which we adventure into the unknown regions of the desktop file. The vital signature resource. A general discussion of the LaserWriter: not so much a printer as a computer with a toner cartridge. Using PostScript tricks to make your LaserWriter get fancy.

The Current Printer

When it comes to having to support a variety of printers, Macintosh programmers definitely have it easy. One of the hardest things for programmers to deal with on many personal computer systems of the past and present are the zillions of different printers and printer interfaces that are available. Printers differ in how they do graphics, how they set tabs, how they do carriage returns and line feeds, and just in their basic interface to the computer. It's not uncommon in non-Macintosh systems to have to deal with dozens of different printers individually with printer drivers or other arcane solutions.

When the Macintosh first appeared, being able to print graphics was an absolutely integral part of the package. Apple had worked hard to come up with a printer that could handle this important requirement, and the result was the original ImageWriter. The Macintosh system software was designed to work with this printer and no other.

So, Apple offered a good quality dot matrix printer at a reasonable price that was really the only option buyers had if they wanted hard copy. Some people predicted that users would revolt at not being able to choose another brand of printer. Interestingly enough, this didn't happen very much. Instead, most Macintosh buyers were happy to find a printer that was as good a value as the ImageWriter and matched the system so well.

In 1985, Apple introduced the now legendary LaserWriter, which started the whole idea of computers being used for desktop this and desktop that. After the release of the LaserWriter (and later models in both the laser and dot matrix lines), the number of Macintoshes with Apple printers attached to them is astonishingly high. More than 90 percent of Macintosh users who are connected to a printer use an Apple printer.

The fact that all those folks are using Apple printers really helps stabilize what software developers have to do for printing. The real key to making printing possible is the Macintosh printing model, which has stayed pretty stable over the years since it was first introduced. Despite vast differences in supported hardware and changes in system software, the way printing works is very much as it was in 1984 when the Macintosh came out. This is pretty good, considering that supported printers range from a 72 by 72 dot-per-inch machine that uses pins to strike a piece of paper through a ribbon, to a 2000 by 2000 dot phototypesetting engine that uses a ROM-based page description language (very different from QuickDraw) to create and image an entire page at once. Just to make it more interesting, both the typesetter and the dot matrix printers will sometimes be connected across a network.

Ch-ch-changes.   When the LaserWriter first appeared, a lot of applications had some trouble printing to it even though Apple's printing interface featured device independence. In fact, a lot of developers had been far enough out on the hairy edge of compatibility that their applications didn't work quite right on the LaserWriter. The interesting thing is that once these applications were modified to work properly with the Laser-Writer, they still remained compatible with the ImageWriter. Even though some situations exist where you want to special-case for one printer or the other, most of the time you only have to deal with one set of printing code.

Since the printing interface on the Macintosh has become so standardized, it's possible to pull off some interesting tricks to make life more fun for your users. Specifically, some applications like information about the currently selected printer, such as its kind or even its icon. There *are* ways of finding out all this stuff or the next section wouldn't be in the book!

The Printer's Type, Name, and Icon

For some applications, it's useful to know what kind of printer is being used—just the type of printer, like ImageWriter or Laser-Writer, and nothing about its capabilities—as well as its icon and its name, if it has one. This kind of stuff is mainly used for decorative purposes, such as displaying the printer's icon while you're printing so that you can "fill 'er up" as the document is printed (see Figure 6-1). You can find out this information by looking in the right places in the system and printer resource files. You can even determine whether the printer that's currently chosen is directly attached to the Macintosh's serial port or has to be shared across an AppleTalk network. With a little more digging, you can find out the icon that's used to show that printer's type in the Chooser. If the printer is an AppleTalk device, you can also find out its name.

The first thing you'll want to do is to learn what type of printer is the currently chosen one. You can do this by looking at resource STR number –8192 in the system file. This resource contains a string that gives the name of the current printer's type; it will say something

DoodahWriter

Figure 6-1. Printer icon filling up

like "LaserWriter" or "AppleTalk ImageWriter," depending on the printer you selected the last time you were in the Chooser.

Getting used.   To find the current printer type, you need to check STR –8192 in the system file, not just any old STR –8192. If you just call GetResource asking for this particular string, there's no guarantee you'll get it from the system file. Remember that the Resource Manager normally searches back through the chain of open resource files, starting with the most recently opened and ending up with the most ancient, which is always System. To get around this and make sure you're pulling the right string, you can call CurResFile to find out the current resource file number and stash it somewhere, then UseResFile (0) to get resources from the system file only, before calling GetResource on STR –8192. After you have the resource, you can set the resource map chain back to normal by calling UseResFile with the value you saved from your first CurResFile call.

Once you know the printer type, you can find out more about the printer itself. The next thing to do is to find out whether it's a local, directly connected printer or if it's sitting on the AppleTalk wire. To do this, you need to know the printer type, which you already got from the system file in the preceding step. This string has another meaning: it also represents the file name of the resource file for that printer. So in other words, if STR –8192 said the current printer type was LaserWriter, then there should be a file called LaserWriter that contains more info about the printer.

Not your type. Even though this resource tells you what kind of printer is currently selected, you shouldn't use this name to make decisions such as assuming that PostScript is in built into the printer or that you can go ahead and send commands that an ImageWriter will understand. There's a better way to figure out what kind of printer is selected. You can look in the print record, at the prStl.wDev field. If this field has the value 256 (hexadecimal $100), the print record is for an ImageWriter; if it's got 768, it's a LaserWriter. Probably, Apple will have new numbers for any other printers that come our way.

Any printer resource file that corresponds to the current printer should be located in the **blessed folder** of the current disk, which is the directory containing the open System file. To find this folder, you can use the SysEnvirons call. The sysVRefNum field of the record returned by SysEnvirons contains the working directory reference number of the folder that has the current printer's resource file in it. So, if the current printer's type is LaserWriter (that is, if the STR –8192 resource in the System file is "LaserWriter"), there's a file in this directory called LaserWriter that will tell us some other interesting stuff.

By looking at this file's type, we can determine whether the printer is directly connected or is an AppleTalk device. A standard for which we can thank the Chooser says that directly connected printers have files of type PRES, while AppleTalk-connected printers' files are type PRER. The Chooser sets up this distinction so that it can know how to deal with each type of device as it encounters them.

We can use PBGetFInfo or GetFInfo to find out the file's type. After making either of these GetFInfo calls, you'll get back a field of type FInfo. The FInfo field includes a field called fdType, and this field contains the file's type, interpreted as four ASCII characters.

Drive defensively. There's a chance of a pretty rare error here. If you pick a printer with the Chooser, then return to the Finder and take that printer's resource file out of the blessed folder or throw it away, the system won't be able to find it when you run the Chooser or when you try to print. If you're mucking through resource files trying to find out about the current printer, you should be sure to check your error results on calls like PBGetFInfo. If it can't find the file, you'll get fnfErr ("file not found"—never pronounced like it's spelled).

After using one of the File Manager's calls to find out the file's type, we'll know whether the printer is directly or remotely connected. If it turns out to be an AppleTalk device, we know something else: it must have a name. We can find out the name by looking at a resource within the file. If the file is type PRER, then it will have a resource of type PAPA and ID −8192, which will contain a string that's the name of the currently selected device of this type. There's more information stored in the PAPA after the printer's name but this is all we're interested in right now. If no printer of this type has been selected, the string will be empty.

Notice that every AppleTalk printer type has a "current" device name, even if it's not the currently selected type of printer. This is so that when you change from one printer type to another and then back to the first, the Chooser can make your life a little easier by reminding you of your previous choice. Of course, if it can't find that choice out on the network (maybe someone has taken it to the beach this weekend), it just doesn't select any printer.

Remember that the printer's resource file has to be open if you want to read the printer's name from it, of course. To make sure it's open, you can call OpenResFile on it. If it's already open, no harm is done since OpenResFile will just return the right reference number to you.

> **PAPA don't preach.**   The obvious question here is this: why on earth is the resource type called PAPA? Is someone expressing a tribute to paternity? Actually, it's much more mundane and less sentimental than that. The package of code that AppleTalk and the Printing Manager use to connect up is called Printer Access Protocol, or PAP for short. The resource type PAPA probably comes from *PAP Address.* Isn't that easier to swallow than some strange Oedipal explanation?

We now know the current printer's type and whether it's an AppleTalk or a local device. If it's AppleTalk, we also know its name. The next interesting thing to discover is its icon. Finding this is easy to explain conceptually but a little trickier to do in code, since it involves unraveling some tightly wound resources.

Finding the Custom Icon: Journey into the Unknown

To find the printer's icon, we have to play with various kinds of resources in the printer's resource file. The types we'll look at are the ones that combine to hook up a file to a custom icon in the Finder's display. The first resource type, FREF, tells which file types should be associated with which icons; for example, it might say that files of type ABCD should have icon number 2000. This means any files that have the same creator as the file itself (for example, LWRT in the case of the LaserWriter), and the type ABCD will be displayed on the desktop with icon 2000 from the LaserWriter resource file. This mapping is pictured in Figure 6-2.

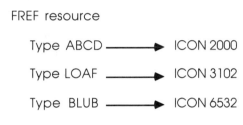

Figure 6-2. FREF file type mapping

So far, this is pretty simple. However, there are a few complexities thrown in which will make it a little harder to follow, so watch closely here as we go through them. The first complication involves icons. As you may know, icons displayed by the Finder aren't just easy little bitmaps. To get really great visual effects, the icons that the Finder displays for files are actually two separate bitmaps.

The first shows what the icon looks like when it's not selected; the second is a **mask** that shows what the icon should look like when it is selected. Each of the two bitmaps is an icon. The two of them together are called an icon list, which is ICN# to the Resource Manager. So, the value in the FREF after the file type is actually an ICN#, an icon list, and not just an icon. We'll modify our diagram to represent this fact as shown in Figure 6-3.

Now comes the interesting part. Let's think about what happens to the FREF and ICN# resources that are stored in your average resource file. The main reason they're there is to allow the Finder to display custom icons for each file type it shows. Since the Chooser also uses icons to display the device types, it can conveniently pick up the icon that's indicated by the FREF and ICN#. Most files have

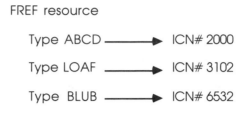

FREF resource

Type ABCD ⟶ ICN# 2000

Type LOAF ⟶ ICN# 3102

Type BLUB ⟶ ICN# 6532

Figure 6-3. FREF to ICN# mapping

nothing to do with the Chooser, though, so their custom icons are only used by the Finder.

The Finder is sort of a collector of icons. Whenever it sees a new file on the disk, it grabs the file's FREF and ICN# information, which tells about the custom icon, and sticks them in a file called Desktop. This Desktop file is a kind of giant dust magnet for information about files on the disk. Every disk that's been seen by the Finder has a Desktop file.

She's not there. You don't usually see a disk's Desktop file because it's marked as invisible. This is a file system flag that tells the Finder not to display a file. The file can be opened, read, and written, but the Finder will hide it from the user. If you want to check it out to learn more about what's in it, you can use a resource editing tool like ResEdit or a file munger like FEdit. The invisible flag is respected only by Apple system software, such as the Finder and the Standard File package.

When the Finder sees a fresh new file, it eagerly checks the file to see whether it has information about custom icons. If it does, the Finder copies the custom icon stuff to the Desktop file. Why does it bother making a copy of these resources when it can always just use the originals? The Finder does this so it will be sure to remember the icon even if the original file is removed from the disk. Remember that the FREF and ICN# are usually only found in one file for each signature, such as an application or a Chooser device file, so if that file goes, there's nowhere else to look for the icon.

When the Finder copies the FREF and ICN# to the Desktop file, a potential conflict arises, which already may have occurred to you. The problem is this: the programmer gets to choose the resource IDs for resources like the FREFs and ICN#s that are in the file. However, what happens if two different applications just happen to choose the same resource ID for an FREF or an ICN#, and the Finder tries to copy these resources into the Desktop file? Sounds like this situation has great potential for disaster, as you can see in Figure 6-4.

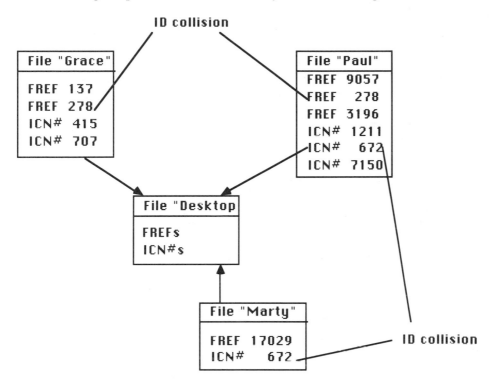

Figure 6-4. Resource ID collisions

One possible solution to this problem would be for the Finder to renumber the resources as it moves them into the Desktop file, just like Font/DA does with font IDs that conflict. This wouldn't work very well, though, because the resources refer to each other. The FREF resource contains the ICN# resource's ID, so changing that ID would completely confuse the FREF (see Figure 6-5).

Since hundreds of thousands of Macintoshes face this problem every day and manage to deal with it, there must be a solution that works. How does the Finder resolve this conflict? It uses an elaborate little indirect numbering scheme that gives each FREF and ICN# resource two different IDs. It works like this: when you create your ICN# resources, each one gets a normal resource ID, but it also gets a special number called a **local ID**. To assign these numbers, you usually just say that your first ICN# is number 0 or number 1 and count up consecutively from there. If you only have one icon list, it's simply assigned a local ID of 0.

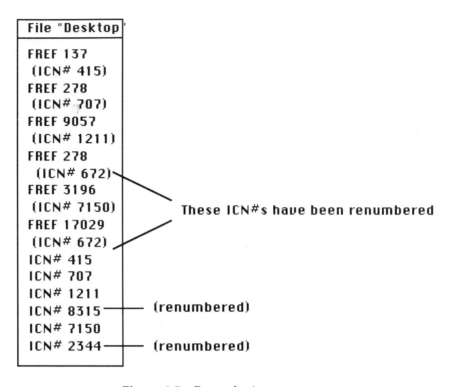

Figure 6-5. Renumbering resources

To tell the Finder how this assignment has been made, you then have to supply some information that maps the local IDs into the regular resource IDs that you set with Rez or ResEdit. The resource that tells about this local to global mapping is a BNDL-type resource (for *bundle*), which is actually constructed as a general-purpose way of mapping local to global IDs, although the Finder only uses it for ICN#s and FREFs. The BNDL resource gets copied into the Desktop file along with the FREFs and ICN#s. Since each application has only one BNDL, its resource ID isn't important; in fact, the Finder will change this ID anyway when it ships the BNDL off to the Desktop so that there are no numbering conflicts.

We can rebuild him. Once a new file has been spotted, the Desktop file grabs its icon and keeps hold of it forever, even if the file is thrown away, on the theory that another file with that signature might be seen someday without its custom icon information. The Desktop file, like an elephant, never forgets. Like an elephant, it can also get very large. There's a hidden Finder command that will wipe out the old Desktop file and force the Finder to rebuild it by checking every file on the disk. This will cause all the icons whose files aren't on the disk any more to be discarded, which can give you back some disk space. To make this happen, you have to hold down Command and Option together as the Finder mounts a volume. On big volumes, rebuilding the desktop can take a few minutes (as an alert will warn you), so be prepared with a cold drink and a newspaper. Also, this action will relieve your files of their Get Info comments, so you shouldn't do it just for kicks to your best friend's two-gigabyte read-write optical drive.

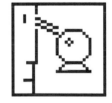

Rebuilding the Desktop file can be useful to cut it down to size, but it's pretty annoying to lose the Get Info comments if you really make use of them. There's a chance Apple will improve this situation with new versions of the Finder; one possibility would be to take the information from an application's signature resource and display it as the Get Info text after rebuilding the Desktop. This feature, or something like it, may already be implemented by the time you read this.

By looking at the BNDL when it copies the custom icon information into the Desktop file, the Finder can renumber the resources without messing anything up. In Figure 6-6 you can see how the Finder uses the information in the BNDL to renumber the resources while keeping the ICN# relationship intact. Since the Finder also has to copy the FREF resources into the Desktop file, it may have to renumber them too, so your BNDL should include a local ID to resource ID mapping for them too.

Now we can see the elaborate copying and renumbering mechanism the Finder has to go through in order to install a custom icon for a file. At a time like this, it's a good idea to step back for a moment and remember what the heck we're doing here. Our objective, you may recall, was this: given the name of a file—in this case the name of the current printer's resource file—get its icon. To do this, we have

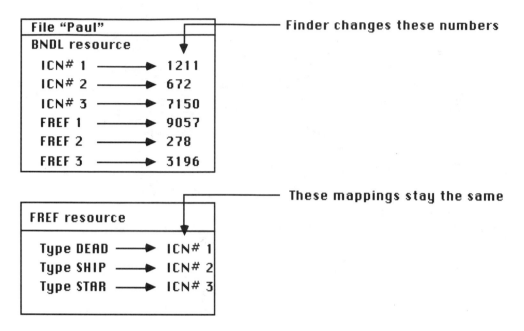

Figure 6-6. Finder renumbers resources

to understand and untangle the bundle of resources that's used to give an icon to a file. With that refresher in mind, we can move forward.

We're almost finished decoding this process so that we can go through it ourselves and find the icon. If you've been following along and trying to develop your own algorithm, you may have noticed that there's still one crucial nugget of information missing. We know that every file with a custom icon will have a corresponding BNDL in the Desktop file, but we don't know the BNDL's resource ID, since the Finder renumbers BNDLs when installing them. How do we find the BNDL we're looking for?

Signature Resource

There's one more thing the file has to provide when it wants a custom icon. There must be a resource called the **signature resource.** This is a resource whose type is the same as the file's signature. For example, the LaserWriter file, which has creator LWRT, also has a resource of type LWRT. It's interesting to know that the Finder absolutely ignores both the resource ID and the contents of this resource; all it cares about is finding the resource itself, although it's conventional to use a resource ID of 0. When it finds the signature resource, it creates a corresponding resource in the Desktop file that's six bytes long and has resource ID 0. The last two bytes of this resource tell, at last, the ID of the BNDL for that file.

That's it. This is the whole process that the Finder runs through in order to install a file's icon into the Desktop and make sure it's unique. Of course, if any file comes along with the same signature as one the Finder's already seen, it will assume that the new file is a later and greater version of the thing it already has and it will toss the old one and put in the new one. This is fine if you've really got a new version of the same old application (or other kind of file). If it's really a different application, though, and it has the bad luck to have to same signature as an application you've already got, the old icon will be lost and both files will now share the same icon. This can look pretty funny if the two files have nothing to do with each other.

If you've ever copied a new application to a hard disk, then found that an old favorite program has suddenly taken on the same icon as the new toy, this is probably what's happened. Also, if you do get two different applications with the same signature, an even more serious problem can happen: when you double-click on a file that's not an application, the Finder uses the signature to figure out which application to launch. This can easily lead to launching the wrong application, which will proceed to try to open a document that doesn't belong to it, resulting in no fun at all.

Register and vote. Having several different kinds of files share the same signature and thus get their icons confused is not exactly desirable, and it's certainly not behavior that you'd normally expect from a major appliance. To prevent this from happening, the venerable Macintosh Technical Support group at Apple has been faithfully collecting signature types from software developers for almost four years now, just like it says on page 9 of *Inside Macintosh*, Volume III. The idea is that developers should check with Apple to be sure they don't come up with a signature that conflicts with anyone else's. In practice, this works pretty well, since many developers take the time to register their file's signatures. Anyway, the odds are on your side; there are more than four billion different signatures possible and there aren't that many different applications yet.

So, if we want to find a file's icon in the Desktop file, like the Finder does, we have to reverse-engineer this process. This means that we begin by finding out the file's signature, which is easy to do

with GetFInfo or PBGetFInfo. Then, we have to get the signature resource from the Desktop file. To accomplish this, we'll have to open
Desktop with OpenResFile, then use the Resource Manager to load
in the appropriate signature resource (remember that the signature
resource's type is the same as the file's signature—LWRT for Laser-
Writer, for example). The signature resource will be six bytes long,
and the last two bytes will contain the resource ID of the BNDL
we're looking for (see Figure 6-7 for the format of the signature resource in the Desktop file).

```
┌─────────────────────────────────┐
│ File "Desktop"                  │
├─────────────────────────────────┤
│ LWRT resource                   │
│ $7723 1199 (4 bytes)            │
│ BNDL ID (2 bytes)               │
│                                 │
│                                 │
└─────────────────────────────────┘
```

Figure 6-7. Signature resource in Desktop

Once we've got the BNDL resource ID from the signature resource, we can take the next step, which is to unlock the secrets in the
BNDL. Specifically, this is where we'll find the mapping between
the local and global FREF and ICN# IDs that will get us the icon
we're looking for.

In the BNDL, the first thing to look at is the list of FREF resource IDs that are used for this signature. A typical BNDL is shown
in Figure 6-8 (it's the one for the LaserWriter file that we've been
using as an example). As you can see from the figure, a BNDL begins
by telling us the signature that owns it, which we can use to double-
check that we're looking in the right place. Following that is a list
of types, and each type contains pairs of numbers. The pairs within
each type match up the local IDs with the resource IDs.

By scanning through the BNDL's list of FREF pairs, we can find
out which FREF resources in the Desktop file belong to this signature. We can then use GetResource to load and examine the FREFs
themselves. Figure 6-9 shows what one looks like when you cut it
open. The FREF is real simple: it has a file type and a local ID for an
ICN# resource. The file type tells which type is being defined by
this FREF and the ICN# local ID gives the icon list that should be
used to display a file of this type.

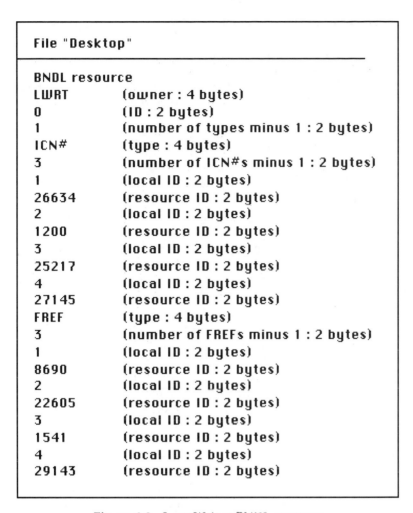

Figure 6-8. LaserWriter BNDL resource

File "LaserWriter"

FREF resource
    PRER (File type: 4 bytes)
        1   (Local ICN# ID : 2 bytes)

Figure 6-9. FREF format

So, using the example BNDL and FREF that we've just seen, we can learn that there are custom icons for four different types of Laser-Writer resource files; we know that because there are four different FREFs. The FREF tells us even more: it says that files of type PRER will be shown with the ICN# that has local ID 1, files of type LROM will get ICN# with local ID 2, and so on.

> **I like icons**.   You may be surprised to discover that there are three different custom file icons owned by the LaserWriter. What are they? There's the standard one you see in the Chooser, of course. There's also the icon used by the LaserPrep file, which holds the PostScript dictionary that gets shipped to the LaserWriter when it's initialized. Then, there are two seldom seen icons that are used for two kinds of files containing downloadable fonts. If you're interested, you can take a look at them with ResEdit.

To translate from these local IDs to the resource IDs, we can take another look at the BNDL, which says that the ICN# with local ID 1 is kept in the ICN# that has the resource ID 26634. We know from our previous discussion that the PRER-type file is the resource file for an AppleTalk-connected printer, like the LaserWriter, so this is the one we want. By calling GetResource on this ICN#, we finally have the LaserWriter's icon.

Let's think for a minute about what we now know how to do. We started out with no information at all about the current printer. We were able to find out what kind of printer it was and, since it was an AppleTalk device, we also got its name. Then, by digging into the Desktop file, we came up with the icon that the Finder displays for the printer's resource file. Great!

Hard luck stories. Resource types like BNDLs and FREFs, which can have variable amounts of data, aren't exactly the easiest thing to deal with in Pascal. In fact, BNDLs are extra hard, since they include recursively defined lists and you don't know how many items are in them until you start walking through. To decode them in Pascal, you'll have to get the resource and use **pointer arithmetic,** which involves dereferencing the handle you get from GetResource and then adding to the pointer to get bytes from the resource. You have to be careful when dealing with a pointer to a relocatable object like a resource. If you execute any commands that can cause memory to be allocated, you should move the resource with MoveHHi and lock the resource in memory by calling HLock, but be sure to HUnlock it when you're done.

You may have realized by now that this technique of extracting an icon from the Desktop file doesn't just apply to printer resource files. You can use it for any file that has a custom icon in the Finder—usually an application. All you have to know to get started is the application's signature. Even if you don't know the signature but do know what folder the file is in on the disk, you can get the signature just by calling PBGetFInfo and looking in the ioFlFndrInfo field.

There must be a better way. So far, we've only talked about locating icons in the Desktop file. This technique is useful for tracking down the icon for any file the Finder has seen and added to its Desktop collection. If you can guarantee that you have access to the original file and not just its Desktop information, the process is a little easier, since you can find the custom icon in the file itself. You can skip the first few steps and go directly to looking at the file's FREFs. You don't need to know their resource IDs; just use GetIndResource to grab them one by one. From that point on, the rest of the process is the same. You'll still need to use the file's BNDL to determine the correspondence of the ICN#'s local ID to its resource ID.

To see how this works for an application's icon, let's go diving into the Desktop file again, this time to try to find the icon for everybody's first program, MacPaint. Before we get started, we'll summarize the steps we have to take to find a file's icon in the Desktop file.

1. If you don't already know it, find the file's signature. You can get the signature from the file itself by calling PBGetFInfo and looking in the fdCreator field of the ioFlFndrInfo parameter, or by calling GetFInfo and examining the fdCreator field of the fndrInfo parameter.

2. In the Desktop file, you should find a resource with the same type as the signature. The ID doesn't matter—you can use GetIIndResource to get whatever resource of this type is there. You'll get a six-byte resource. Pull out the last two bytes and look at them as an integer (a resource ID). If you should find that there's no resource of this type, give up peacefully, as it probably means there's no icon for this file or it's been lost somehow.

3. Using the resource ID that you just acquired, get the BNDL resource that corresponds to it (still looking in the Desktop file). This will be the BNDL that holds the information for the signature we're looking for. Again, if you don't find a BNDL with this resource ID, you should resign gracefully.

4. Get the resource IDs of the FREFs from the BNDL and start loading them in, one by one, until you find the one for the particular file type you're after. If you're looking for an application's icon, you'll want type APPL; if it's an AppleTalk printer, the type is PRER; a directly connected printer will have type PRES; some other kind of Chooser-friendly fellow will be type RDEV. If you're looking for anything else, you'll have to know its type; for example, to find the icon that MacPaint uses for its documents, you'll need to look for type PNTG.

5. When you spot the file type you want in its FREF resource, note the local ID for the ICN# that's also part of the resource (see Figure 6-9 to remember what this looks like). You'll need to map this local ID into the resource ID to find the actual ICN# resource.

6. Look through the BNDL resource at the ICN# mapping information until you find the entry for the local ID you just got out of the FREF. When you see this, get the resource ID that's mapped to the local ID.

7. Get the ICN# resource that has the ID you just found, and that's it.

Now we're all ready to start searching for MacPaint's icon in the Desktop file. The first thing we'll need to know is MacPaint's signature. If we know where it is on the disk, we can use PBGetFInfo to learn the signature, which is MPNT.

The next thing to do is to get the signature resource by calling GetResource for type MPNT and resource ID 0. When we get it, we'll look at the last two bytes of it to find the bundle ID for MacPaint. To make this munge-along a little easier to follow, let's plug in some real numbers. We'll say that the ID we get from the signature resource is 14284, as shown in Figure 6-10. By loading this resource, we can see all the FREFs and ICN#s for MacPaint (also in Figure 6-10).

```
┌─────────────────────────────────────────────────────────────┐
│  File "Desktop"                                              │
├─────────────────────────────────────────────────────────────┤
│  MPNT resource 0                                            │
│  $7723 1100       (always first 4 bytes)                    │
│  14284            (BNDL ID : 2 bytes)                       │
│                                                             │
│                                                             │
│  BNDL resource 14284                                        │
│  MPNT             (owner : 4 bytes)                         │
│  0                (ID : 2 bytes)                            │
│  1                (number of types minus 1 : 2 bytes)      │
│  ICN#             (type : 4 bytes)                         │
│  1                (number of ICN#s minus 1 : 2 bytes)      │
│  1                (local ID : 2 bytes)                      │
│  24927            (resource ID : 2 bytes)                   │
│  2                (local ID : 2 bytes)                      │
│  6965             (resource ID : 2 bytes)                   │
│  FREF             (type : 4 bytes)                         │
│  1                (number of FREFs minus 1 : 2 bytes)      │
│  1                (local ID : 2 bytes)                      │
│  29226            (resource ID : 2 bytes)                   │
│  2                (local ID : 2 bytes)                      │
│  6857             (resource ID : 2 bytes)                   │
│                                                             │
│                                                             │
└─────────────────────────────────────────────────────────────┘
```

Figure 6-10. The larch

The bundle in Figure 6-10 shows that there are apparently two custom icons for files with the MPNT signature. This is pretty consistent with what we would expect for applications, since there's usually a custom icon for the application itself and the documents that the application can produce. In fact, applications that can create several different kinds of files will usually have one FREF and one ICN# for each. The all-time champion of custom Finder icons is probably 4th Dimension, which has 12 different icons for the 12 different types of files it owns.

The next step is to load and look at the FREFs until we find the one we want. In this case we're looking for the application's icon, so we'll search through FREFs until we find the one that tells us about file type APPL (for *application*). The first FREF listed has resource ID 29226 (see Figure 6-10 again), so it's the first one we'll look at. Its contents are shown in Figure 6-11. It looks like we've hit the one we wanted on the first try. This isn't really very surprising, since the FREFs are just listed in the order the developer defined them and the APPL type is almost always the first one defined.

```
┌─────────────────────────────────────────┐
│            File  "Desktop"               │
├─────────────────────────────────────────┤
│  FREF resource 29226                     │
│     APPL (file type : 4 bytes)           │
│     1     (local ID : 2 bytes)           │
│                                          │
│                                          │
└─────────────────────────────────────────┘
```

Figure 6-11. FREF for MacPaint

The important tidbit that the FREF is telling us is that files with type APPL will have the ICN# with local ID 1; in other words, the Finder will use this icon list for the MacPaint application. To figure out this ICN#'s resource ID, we just look back at the BNDL in Figure 6-10, and we can see that this ICN# is stored in the Desktop file with resource ID 24927. All we have to do now is use GetResource to load the icon and we can draw it on the screen or do whatever we want. As Darth Vader said to Luke, "I have you now!"

A lot of the stuff we've done in this section is undocumented and is likely to be subject to great change in the future. Specifically, looking through the Desktop file for things is a technique that might go bad on you as the Finder and the other system software evolves. You can also run into problems when the Desktop file you're spying on happens to belong to an AppleShare file server. Your life will be much, much simpler if you try to find the custom icon resources by looking in the resource file you're interested in, rather than the Desktop file, if you can locate the file in question. That technique has a much longer life expectancy than one based on assumptions about the format of Desktop.

Another compatibility issue to worry about is the method we used to find the current printer. Again, although system 4.1 supports this way of doing things, Apple hasn't promised that it will stay that way forever. In fact, various technical goop out of Apple has hinted at major changes in the way the printing architecture works. If past performance is any indication, this usually means that Apple will try pretty hard not to break any applications that used things documented in *Inside Macintosh* and the Macintosh Technical Notes. However, anything that steps outside those boundaries probably will not be treated as kindly, so be careful.

There are a couple of things you can do to minimize the pain you would feel if Apple makes a system software change that leaves you out to lunch. The first thing to do is document the things you're depending on and understand that they're shaky. If you're counting on an undocumented feature like the current printer's type being in STR –8192 in the system file, make sure you note that fact as a comment in your source code—you do comment your source code, don't you? The other thing to do if you're living dangerously is to minimize your risks. If there's a more compatible road to take, take it. For example, trying to find a file's custom icon resources in the file itself is better than trying to get them out of the Desktop file.

Once you have the current printer's name, what can you do with it that's useful? You can do lots of things to make your users' lives a little easier. We discussed one trick, which is to display the current printer's icon while you're printing, filling it up with black a little at a time to indicate the progress of the document being printed.

Another thing you can do with the printer's icon is to use it in a dialog that gives the user some sort of status report about the document that includes printing information. This could be really useful if you're writing a network utility that tells the user how things are going with any particular printer. Once you know the icon, you have a very convenient way to communicate with the user about the current printer.

Displaying the Document's Name

When you print to a remote, shared printer like a LaserWriter or an ImageWriter with an AppleTalk card installed, the Printing Manager and the associated AppleTalk software get together to display some handy information in a little alert at the top of the screen. This information is useful not only to the person who's printing but also to anyone else who is trying to get to that printer. While the document is printing, the alert displays the name of the document being printed as well as the user who's doing the printing (see Figure 6-12). That lets you know who to yell at when you absolutely have to print your stuff right now.

```
user: Joe J.; document: Beat Crazy; status: printing
```

Figure 6-12. LaserWriter status alert

Where does the information in this alert come from? Every user on an AppleTalk network has a user name, which is usually entered into the Chooser. This name uniquely identifies the user for electronic mail and other network messages. After the name is entered, it's kept in the Macintosh's parameter RAM and also stored in the system file as a resource, specifically STR –16096.

Some clever programs have had fun with the user name by grabbing it and putting it in interesting places. One of the earliest uses was a small patch that ran around inside the Macintosh group at Apple for a while when AppleTalk was first being developed. This patch modified the startup alert (the one that usually says "Welcome to Macintosh") so that it added the user's name onto the end, as in "Welcome to Macintosh, Steve." Cute.

Another trick with the user name can be found in versions of ResEdit that appeared around the beginning of 1986. ResEdit, legendary as a program that was incredibly hard to write, was in its "final" testing at the time. Opening the About dialog presented an address and a request for bug reports. Next to the address was, literally, a bullet with your name on it—a small picture of a bullet with the user name, grabbed from STR –16096, drawn on top of it. This was a very appropriate metaphor for ResEdit at that time.

There are other, more practical things you can do with the user name, of course. We've already mentioned that the user's name appears in the LaserWriter status alert. In addition, AppleShare uses the name as the default entry when you're signing onto a file server. The InterMail electronic mail system from Interactive Network Technologies also takes its default from the user name and even greets the user by name when the system starts up.

In addition to the user name, the LaserWriter status alert also gives the name of the document that's being printed. Where does it find this name? Actually, it has no way of knowing the name of the file that's being printed. So it uses a reasonably clever trick, one any good hacker would be proud of: it looks at the frontmost window and it uses its title. If there are no windows at all when the printing is happening, the status alert just says that the document is "Unspecified," which is not very friendly.

This isn't usually a problem when you're printing, because the frontmost window is almost always the one being printed. However, sometimes this isn't the case. In particular, when the user chooses a document in the Finder and then selects the Print item from the File menu, most applications don't bother opening any windows. They usually just find the document, open the file without creating a window for it, and print.

With this technique, since no windows are open when the printing takes place, the Printing Manager will be reduced to thinking that the name of the document it's printing is "Unspecified." This always makes it look as if the computer and the LaserWriter aren't talking to each other very well and something must be wrong. It's a situation that does not inspire confidence in your users and we should really do something about it.

To tell the LaserWriter the name of the document we're printing, we have to create a window with the desired name and make it frontmost. This presents a dilemma, since we don't really want to have to open a window here. What can we do?

There are actually several choices. When you print, it's a good idea to put up an alert that allows the user to cancel printing by clicking on a Cancel button or typing Command-period. Usually, this alert uses the window type dBoxProc, which doesn't display its title. How convenient! All we have to do is make the window's title whatever we want to appear in the printing status alert and we're all set. Since the window doesn't display its title, we won't be faced with the funny appearance of a cancel printing alert that has the title of the document being printed.

This will work fine if we have a cancel alert, since it provides a window that we can name. What do we do if there is no cancel alert and no place to hang our window name? We still have to come up with a window. One idea would be to open a window with the name we want and then make it invisible. This is a neat idea, but it won't work, since the Printing Manager outsmarts us by making sure that the title it uses comes from a visible window.

On the Macintosh, there's usually more than one way to scam a clever piece of code. In this case, we can make a visible window, but we can stick it way, way out in the QuickDraw coordinate plane, starting at an x,y position of something like 32000,32000, which will put the window just south of Tierra Del Fuego. This will ensure that the window won't be seen, but its title will still be grabbed by the Printing Manager for its alert, which is just what we want.

Oh, say, can you see?   What's the chance that this window, which we're putting at 32000,32000, will actually someday be visible on a large screen monitor? Let's think about that question. The classic Macintosh display has 512 pixels across; a really big screen is one with 1024 pixels in either direction. A typical Macintosh screen packs about 72 pixels into an inch. This means that we would need 32000 divided by 72 inches to see our distant window, which works out to about 444 inches or 37 feet. So, we would need a 37-foot-high monitor to see this window. This seems to be a reasonably safe technique. Of course, with the Macintosh II, the user can have multiple screens, so the window would also be visible with six monitors that were each a mere 6.2 feet high.

It's interesting to note that the Printing Manager actually keeps the name of the document it's printing in the print record. This means that a really clever application that wants to go right to the heart of things can set the document name directly by messing around with the print record. This is a very bad idea if you care about compatibility with future versions of the printing software. Not only is the location of the name not documented, but even more ominously, Apple has warned in technical notes that this field won't be in the same place in the future.

We should talk about one other aspect of the Printing Manager's technique here. The Printing Manager looks for the frontmost window's name when you call PrValidate; then it gets the name and stuffs it into the print record that's passed to PrValidate via a handle. If you're printing more than one document and you want to switch your distant window's title to display the right name, you should do it after you finish printing one document (after you call PrCloseDoc). Then, before you start printing the next document, call PrValidate on the print record to stick the new window's name into the print record.

One last long word of advice about this stuff: be sure you don't call PrValidate while you're in the middle of printing out a document. You'll find that strange things will happen to the print record, and what comes out of the printer may resemble Jeff Goldblum in *The Fly* (a good movie to see after a hard day of writing code, by the way).

General Printing Information

One of the fun and disorienting things that new Macintosh programmers discover is that printing just ain't what it used to be. On a conventional personal computer, printing something involves shooting ASCII characters out the printer port. For example, if you want to print the string "Reconstruction of the Fables," you just send that string to the printer, usually with some kind of standard output statement that your programming language provides.

Things don't work quite that way on the Macintosh, for a number of reasons. The fundamental reason is that users almost never print documents composed purely of text with their Macintoshes. If they'd wanted to do that, they probably would have bought an Intimidating Blue Machine instead of a Macintosh. On a Macintosh, documents that come out of the printer are composed of thousands or millions of pixels—they're **bitmapped.**

Printing with lots of little dots makes it impossible to just send ASCII to tell what to print. Another reason Macintosh printing can't work that way is that when you're printing, you might be working with a printer plugged into a serial port and sitting next to the computer, or you might be dealing with a phototypesetter connected via AppleTalk, an AppleTalk bridge, and a telephone link, which might be sitting in a barn in France for all you know. Since the phototypesetter is really a PostScript-speaking computer that also happens to know how to print, you can't be expected to try to talk to it just by sending plain old ASCII text.

So, in order to be able to talk to the graphic printers the Macintosh demands, you do your printing in the same way as you get things on the screen: by drawing with QuickDraw commands. Before you begin printing, you go through a little ritual, which tells the system that although you're acting as if you were drawing things in a regular grafport, you really want them to appear on a printed page. Specifically, you call PrOpenDoc, which gets you started by creating a grafport set up for printing. Then, for each page, you call PrOpenPage, then whatever QuickDraw stuff you need to draw your image, followed by PrClosePage to tell it when the page is finished.

One of the big ideas of the Printing Manager is generality, something the Macintosh system software really shines at, as we've discussed. For the Printing Manager, this translates to printer independence, which means you should be able to write the part of your program that does the printing and have it work on any printer. Remember that the user gets to decide which printer to use with the Chooser and might even change the selected printer right in front of your nose while your application is running.

You can write printer independent code for your application and have it work properly on any of Apple's supported Macintosh printers, just as you can write programs that open, read, and write files and have them work correctly whether the file is on a floppy disk, a hard disk that has 20, 40, 73, or 119.5 megabytes, or a file server.

Different strokes. Working with different kinds and sizes of storage devices, such as disk drives and file servers, is a well-established procedure that has become an exact science on the Macintosh. As the high-level programmer, you deal with them through HFS, and that's pretty much the whole story. Each device knows how to make itself respond to those HFS commands and so all volumes wind up looking about the same to a program. The situation with printers is not nearly as clean. This is partly because bitmapped printing is a relatively newer technology and partly because the way an ImageWriter makes a page black is so radically different from the way a LaserWriter makes a page black. After all, an ImageWriter is a serial printer that understands some commands; a LaserWriter is a powerful computer that pushes out some paper once in a while as a side effect of its computing.

LaserWriter Specifics

Just as with the different kinds of drives, you may want the flexibility of doing something special for a particular kind of device. For example, you might want to prevent a user from saving certain kinds of files on a file server but allow it if it's a local disk. In the same way, you might want to take advantage of the special capabilities a LaserWriter offers; after all, you paid a lot more for it.

The process that takes place when you print is interesting enough, but the things that happen when you print to the Laser-Writer are downright fascinating. As your program gets ready to print, if the printer that the user has chosen is a LaserWriter, the Printing Manager has to set up communications with the printer across the AppleTalk network.

When you start to print your document, you make things happen by using QuickDraw commands to draw into the printing grafport that PrOpenDoc created for you. The LaserWriter, of course, doesn't know anything about QuickDraw—it has the PostScript page description language in ROM. The LaserWriter must have some way of figuring out how to deal with the mess of QuickDraw commands your program ships out.

The answer is a very slick translation that takes place from QuickDraw to PostScript. You can draw your document's image in QuickDraw, but the LaserWriter driver converts everything to Post-Script so that the LaserWriter knows what to do. This is no mean feat, since QuickDraw and PostScript are very different ways of describing how to put graphics and text onto a page. The LaserWriter driver tries to do as much as it can to turn your QuickDraw doodles into the right PostScript code to make the same doodles.

The basic philosophy behind drawing is quite different in QuickDraw and PostScript, and this presents some of the difficulty in translating from one to the other. QuickDraw was originally designed to be used with memory-mapped screens and so it includes things created with that in mind.

For example, QuickDraw includes the ability to combine bits that are already on the screen with new bits in a variety of different ways called **transfer modes.** You can directly transfer bits to the screen without caring about what was there before (called source copy mode), you can add your image to the ones that were already on (this is source-or mode), or you can combine the pixels in several other ways.

The original version of QuickDraw supports eight fairly straightforward transfer modes that use logical functions on the bits. In Color QuickDraw things are a lot more interesting, since color combinations can be made in so many different ways. To allow more flexibility in combining colors, several new transfer modes for color are available. These include AddOver, which adds the RGB values of the source and destination pixels, and SubOver, which subtracts the destination from the source. If the result of the addition or the subtraction is an overflow or underflow (that is, if the red, green, or blue component is greater than 65535 or less than 0), the value simply wraps around. This means that almost-white colors can wrap around to almost-black colors, which is often not what you want. For this reason, there are the AddPin and SubPin modes, which let you set the highest and lowest RGB values that can be created when combining pixels. For more on how color works, see Chapter 3.

PostScript's basic assumption is that you're drawing on a page that is already white, rather than on a screen that might have some stuff on it already. This means that QuickDraw-style transfer modes, which combine an existing image with a new one, don't make sense in PostScript. In fact, operations that work on existing bits in the grafport, such as EraseRect, usually aren't necessary when you're printing, because the paper starts out blank anyway.

About PostScript

PostScript was designed for devices that typically have a lot more resolution than the Macintosh screen: a LaserWriter has 300 dots per inch, compared to the typical Macintosh screen's 72 dots per inch. PostScript was made to build pages for a printer; QuickDraw's main purpose was to implement the very interactive nature of the Macintosh user interface. These facts combine to give PostScript great features for doing tricks on your output.

PostScript lets you draw several different kinds of things on a page. You can use line- and curve-drawing operators to build different kinds of shapes, simulating QuickDraw's shape-drawing commands. You can also change a curve into a series of lines, fill up an area with a gray tone, change the width of lines that you draw, and rotate things until you're dizzy.

PostScript gives you some very slick ways to deal with text. Each character is stored as an ordered bunch of points that describe an outline of the character, and the character is drawn by connecting the points with curves. The main advantage to this technique is that the characters can be scaled to any size without looking jaggy. This is why any text that's printed in a font stored in the LaserWriter ROM, such as Helvetica or Times, is always nicely scaled, even if it looks bizarre on the screen.

PostScript has a lot more goodies for producing nice images. It can deal with digitized data and bitmaps and do clipping to specified areas. It even contains commands for working with color, if only a color LaserWriter would drop from the heavens.

There's an extensive set of general-purpose programming language things in PostScript that make it easier to do your job when you have to apply some math to your image. PostScript includes commands for the basic four functions, plus a bunch of fancy functions like log, sine, cosine, and square root. Gee, remember back a few years ago when computers were computers and printers were printers? Now we have a printer that knows how to calculate square roots! There must be a really slick hacker-type application there somewhere.

For most applications, the automatic translation from Quick-Draw to PostScript that the LaserWriter driver does for you is enough to make your output beautiful. Sometimes, though, when you really want to produce great printed results and you know you get to print on a LaserWriter, it's nice to take advantage of some of the special tricks that PostScript can do with a printed page. Laser-Writers have become common enough, in fact, that lots of programs work only with a LaserWriter or other PostScript printer. Remember that you can find out whether you have a LaserWriter handy by looking at the prStl.wDev field of the print record.

If you are printing to a LaserWriter, you might want to do all your printing in PostScript. This is kind of similar to choosing to do all your color drawing in the new Color QuickDraw model: you trade the generality of code that works on all systems for some specific advanced features. If you want to have full control of the power in the LaserWriter's PostScript ROM, you can abandon QuickDraw for your drawing and stick with PostScript.

For most applications, though, what you'd really like to do is let the LaserWriter driver translate most of your drawing automatically from QuickDraw into PostScript. Then, in those very special places where you've just gotta have some PostScript action, you can insert it. The Printing Manager and the LaserWriter driver give you a bunch of different ways to do this, and we'll discuss them now.

Using PostScript

When you draw pictures in QuickDraw, you pass a series of operators, like FrameRect, CopyBits, or FillRgn, along with the appropriate data, like the rectangle that you're framing, the bits you're copying, and the region you're filling. In addition to the commands that draw things, QuickDraw allows you to stick comments into your pictures. These **picture comments** can be used to store things that QuickDraw doesn't really care about in the picture.

When you draw a picture, QuickDraw normally just ignores any comments that are stored along with the drawing commands. If you're clever, though, you can set up a hook to receive all the comments as they're processed by QuickDraw's DrawPicture call. Picture comments present an interesting method for communication between programs that create them, such as your application, and programs that install themselves into the hook that sees all the picture comments come flying by. In fact, this is exactly what the LaserWriter driver does when it sets up a printing grafport: it makes sure its comment-processing routine will see all the comments.

> **Send your comments.** If you're interested in how you can get to see picture comments, here's some more information. As we discussed in Part One, every grafport has a set of pointers to routines called bottleneck procedures, stored in the grafProcs field of the grafport. One of these pointers, commentProc, contains the address of the routine that will be called to process any picture comments. Normally, this routine just ignores comments, but you can get in there and see what's going on if you want to, just like the LaserWriter driver does. Of course, you shouldn't mess around with a grafport that's set up for printing, since the LaserWriter will already have grabbed the commentProc hook.

By sticking things into the picture as comments, we can store any kind of special instructions we want to; QuickDraw will leave them alone and just pass them through. It would be really slick if we could put PostScript commands into a picture comment. Then, when Quick-Draw was drawing the picture, it would just pass the comments along to the routine that was hooked in. If that routine were set up to expect PostScript commands, we'd have an easy way of adding Post-Script to our QuickDraw pictures.

Well, this is such a good idea that Apple implemented it. There is a standard set up so that an application can hide PostScript commands in picture comments. When the program calls DrawPicture to print the thing, the LaserWriter driver will recognize the comments as PostScript commands and will execute them. If the printer isn't a PostScript device, no worry—remember that by default QuickDraw simply ignores comments, so nothing will happen when the comments are processed.

How does the LaserWriter know that a particular comment contains PostScript code? It would be pretty closed-minded for the driver to assume that it owned every comment in the picture. In fact, QuickDraw picture comments carry along an integer called the **comment kind,** a convenient number that lets you tell one type of comment from another (after all, they all look alike to us humans).

In addition to the comment kind, every comment carries along some data, which is also used to figure out what to do. The meaning of the data varies from one kind of comment to the next, as we'll see. Putting a comment into a picture is very simple: you just set up the comment kind and the data that you need, then call the QuickDraw procedure PicComment, which adds the comment stuff to the picture, assuming you've already opened a picture by calling OpenPicture and you're recording commands into it.

The PostScript Comments

If you want to send PostScript to the printer with QuickDraw comments, you get to choose from several different ways of doing it. The choices you have involve the source of the PostScript commands, but no matter which technique you choose, you have to start out the same way. You begin with a comment that tells the LaserWriter driver that some PostScript stuff is coming, so it gets ready and flips off its QuickDraw-to-PostScript translator for awhile.

The comment you'll start with is named PostScriptBegin, which has a comment kind of 190. No other data gets sent along with this comment, since it just alerts the driver to the fact that some Post-Script is about to come down the wire—it doesn't actually send any PostScript code itself.

The PicComment procedure actually takes three parameters: the kind of comment (an integer), the size of the data (another integer), and a handle to the data itself. When we want to set the driver up for PostScript, we'll just make a PicComment call with the Post-ScriptBegin comment, which is number 190:

```
PicComment (190, 0, Nil);
```

Since no data has to be sent with this comment, the second parameter, the data size, is 0, and the third parameter, which is usually a handle to the additional data, is Nil here.

Any commands that come next in the picture will be treated differently, since we've placed the LaserWriter driver into PostScript mode. Now we have to decide which of several methods we want to use to draw our masterpiece. The simplest technique, which is especially useful for PostScript one-liners, is the PostScriptHandle comment. This kind of comment lets you put some PostScript code into a relocatable object as a string and then ship it off to the LaserWriter.

The PostScriptHandle comment is comment kind 192 and the data that goes with it is the string of PostScript commands. You can actually have as much PostScript code as you want in the relocatable object, as long as the last character in the string is a carriage return (ASCII 13). The trickiest part of using this method is convincing your programming language to stick the bytes into the relocatable object. One way to do it in Pascal would be to start by putting the PostScript text into a plain old string, like this:

```
{var
p : Str255;}
. . .
p:='/Helvetica findfont 18 scalefont setfont 10 10 moveto (Beam me up)
show'
```

Even if you're not familiar with PostScript, you can probably figure out that this command sets the Helvetica font in 18-point type, moves to a specific location on the coordinate plane, then writes some text. The next thing we have to do is to tack a carriage return onto the end of it.

```
{const
  cr = chr (13);}
  . . .
  p := Concat (p, cr);
```

Now we need to create a new relocatable object that we'll pass on to the picture and then copy the information from the string into the new object:

```
{var
  postParcel : Handle;}
  . . .
  postParcel := NewHandle (length (p)); {should error-check here!}
  BlockMove (pointer (ord (@p)+1), postParcel^, length (p));
    {confusing syntax forced by Pascal: just moving bytes}
```

The weird first parameter to BlockMove is just a way of convincing Pascal to move all the bytes in the string except the first, since the first byte contains the length and isn't really part of the string. Also, note that we don't have to HLock the postParcel handle because there's nothing in the BlockMove call that could cause a heap compaction (that is, no new objects are allocated).

Once we've moved the data into the relocatable object this way, we can go ahead and mail it in:

```
PicComment (192, length (p), postParcel);
```

This PicComment will put the text at the end of the handle into the picture. Then, when the application calls DrawPicture to print to the LaserWriter, the Printing Manager will send it to the printer as PostScript commands.

If this method of sending PostScript to the printer isn't convenient, there are lots of other ways to do it. The next technique we'll look at uses the TextIsPostScript comment kind. This comment allows us to just draw text by using QuickDraw's regular text commands, mainly DrawString. By preceding the text with a TextIsPostScript comment (which is comment kind 194), the text isn't really drawn in the grafport; instead, it's interpreted as PostScript commands.

To make this magic happen, just include a comment number 194 in your picture, then follow it with QuickDraw text drawing commands. The TextIsPostScript comment doesn't require any additional data when you call it since all the PostScript commands appear after it. Make this call to start using this technique:

```
PicComment (194, 0, Nil);{TextIsPostScript, no data needed}
```

Following this comment, we'll send some PostScript off to the printer by using standard QuickDraw text-drawing commands. So, if we want to do the same thing we did in the previous example—write a string of text—we can do it like this:

```
DrawString ('/Helvetica findfont 18 scalefont');
DrawString ('setfont 10 10 moveto (Beam me up) show');
```

This time we've split the command into two lines just to make it a little more readable. Notice that we don't have to care about where the end of the line is and we don't have to add a carriage return at the end as we did with the previous method.

This technique is handy for sending a lot of PostScript commands. It's much more convenient than trying to load everything up into one relocatable object as with the PostScriptHandle comment we used earlier. Whichever technique you choose, remember to start with the PostScriptBegin comment that tells the LaserWriter driver to expect something in PostScript.

The third method of sending PostScript through the Laser-Writer driver is to put the PostScript commands into a disk file. This can be useful for exchanging PostScript information between two applications, although it can be dangerous because the LaserWriter driver expects the file to be there when it prints. Since the user doesn't know when PostScript is being printed from a file, there's no easy way to recover if the file is missing, so the LaserWriter just quits printing if it can't find the file.

There are two ways to include PostScript commands in a file: as resources and as data. The resource format lets you create a new resource that has PostScript commands in it and then add the appropriate comment to your picture. The comment data for this method is the resource type, ID, and an offset into the resource telling where to start looking for the commands. Most folks, including Apple, use resource type POST for PostScript in a file, so you should probably use it too. Also, there seems to be a standard that POST resource IDs should start at 501, although this doesn't seem to be a requirement. Maybe someone is a fan of a particular brand of jeans.

Let's take the same example we've been using and put it into a PostScript resource. Before we can use the PostScript resource, we have to put a little header on the data. The LaserWriter requires two bytes to identify this type of resource, and they should always be $0100. We can build our string like this:

```
p:='/Helvetica findfont 18 scalefont setfont 10 10 moveto (Beam me up)
show'

p := Concat (chr (1), chr (0), p); {add header to string}
```

Before we can make it into a resource, we have to get the Post-Script stuff into a relocatable heap object. If you remember, our first example started by stuffing some PostScript commands into a variable and then used BlockMove to move them into a relocatable object. We'll do the same thing now.

```
postParcel := NewHandle (length (p)); {should error-check here!}
BlockMove (pointer (ord (@p)+1), postParcel^, length (p));
```

Once we've done this, we can make it into a resource pretty easily.

```
AddResource (postParcel, 'POST', 501, '');
```

This makes our PostScript command string into a resource with type POST, ID 501, and no name (that's the empty string in the last parameter). Now that it's a resource, we can use it later in a picture with the right PicComment call. For this method, the comment kind we want is called ResourcePS and its number is 195. As we said, the data for the comment is the type, ID, and index, so we'll have to put those things together first.

```
{var
postData : Record
theType: resType;
theID: Integer;
theIndex: Integer;
       end;}
postData.theType := 'POST';
postData.theID := 501;
postData.theIndex := 2;{start just past the header}
```

Now that we've finally got everything that we need, we can proceed to record the picture comment. Here's how we'd do it:

```
PicComment (195, GetHandleSize (postParcel), postParcel);
```

When this comment is processed as the picture is drawn by the application, the LaserWriter driver will try to find the resource (in this case, it would be POST 501), look into the resource at the index given by the comment, and send the PostScript that it finds.

Resourceful. The technique for sending PostScript as a resource is mainly intended for downloading fonts to the LaserWriter. This is the process the LaserWriter goes through when you need to print a font that it doesn't have in ROM. Some software developers, including Adobe System, the creator of PostScript, use this format to distribute fonts for the LaserWriter to print. If you need more information on how downloadable fonts are constructed or you're just interested in learning about yet another arcane subject, you should consult the *LaserWriter Reference Manual* published by Addison-Wesley.

If you don't want to fool around with resources, or you need to bring in some PostScript code from an application that prefers data files, you can use another comment that lets you put the PostScript into a data file rather than a resource. This comment is called PostScriptFile and it's comment number 193.

When you use the PostScriptFile comment, you just store the PostScript statements in a data file on disk. As with the POST resource, you have to put a two-byte header on the data that tells the LaserWriter what to expect. You should again use $0100 for the header to indicate that you're sending text with PostScript commands in it.

When you make the PicComment call, the data handle should be a handle to a string containing the name of the file with the PostScript in it. The file name should be in Pascal format, with a length byte preceding the characters. Of course, this means that you'd better make sure the file is around when the user tries to print, or the LaserWriter driver will give up, leaving the user pretty confused.

When you're ready to create the comment, it will look something like this:

```
PicComment (193, GetHandleSize (fileNameHdl), fileNameHdl);
```

We've now talked about four different ways of sending PostScript to the printer using picture comments. With these comments, we can print in PostScript without having to give up QuickDraw. In fact, you can be cruising along printing with QuickDraw calls and switch to PostScript using the comments we've discussed.

One more thing to know is how to turn the QuickDraw-to-PostScript translator back on in the LaserWriter driver. As you might expect, you do this with another comment, one named Post-

ScriptEnd. This comment is number 191 and it doesn't take any additional data, so it should look like this when you call it:

```
PicComment (191, 0, Nil); {Turn off PostScript mode in driver}
```

Remember to put one of these in your picture after you're through drawing in PostScript, or you'll find some very strange results.

Fixing the Coordinate System

There's another little trick that you'll need to know if you're going to do PostScript tricks from QuickDraw picture comments. One of the differences between PostScript and QuickDraw is the way the coordinate systems are set up. In QuickDraw, the x-coordinates increase as you move to the right and the y-coordinates get larger as you move down on the screen or page. PostScript is set up like a conventional coordinate plane, with the y values increasing as you move from the bottom of the page to the top.

This means that when you try to print some PostScript from the middle of your QuickDraw picture, you'll get a surprise: the image will be upside down and mirrored! This is probably not what you want. Luckily, PostScript is flexible enough to allow you to redefine the coordinate system to work the same way as QuickDraw's. To do this, you have to issue two PostScript commands to the printer: one to move the origin and one to change the direction of the y-axis.

The PostScript commands you need are these:

```
0 730 translate      % This operation moves the origin
1 -1 scale           % This says to reverse the y-axis
```

The things on each line following the percent signs are comments, and they're ignored by the PostScript interpreter. The effect of these two commands is to turn the coordinate system into approximately the same one that QuickDraw uses. After sending these two commands, you can use QuickDraw comments to draw things and they'll come out right side up. Of course, if you really want them to come out upside down, you can skip changing the coordinate system, but if you're a real PostScript hacker, you can figure out how to rotate or flip anything you want easily.

Escape to PostScript

If you thought you'd already read about a lot of different ways to send PostScript to the printer through the LaserWriter driver, get ready for another one. The driver defines a font, the **PostScript escape font,** which can be used for sending PostScript commands. It works like this: in the LaserWriter resource file, there's a STR resource with ID –8188. If you set this string to the name of a font, then text that's sent to the printer in that font will not be printed but will instead be interpreted as PostScript code.

This is an interesting way to allow PostScript to go to the printer. It means that a user with ResEdit could get into the LaserWriter file and change the STR –8188 resource to a font that never gets used; then, the user could fire up any old word processing program and program in PostScript, just by using the escape font! Talk about power users. This means you can use PostScript directly from MacWrite or anything else that lets you have your choice of fonts.

If you don't change it, STR –8188 is normally set to the string "PostScript Escape," just to remind you of what it does. Note that when you pick a font, you should pick one that you don't want to print in, since anything in that font will be shipped off to the PostScript interpreter and not printed. Another tip is to pick a font that's in the LaserWriter ROM; if the PostScript escape font isn't in the LaserWriter's ROM, the driver will download it to the printer, even though it doesn't really need it.

This little problem of downloading the escape font is present in LaserWriter version 3.1, but it's likely that it will be fixed in the future, and maybe even by the time you read this.

One note of caution about using this trick: if you set the escape font, forget you've done it and then try to print something in that font, you'll have a terrible time. The LaserWriter driver will try to interpret your letter to Aunt Minnie as the next great PostScript masterpiece. If you set the escape font, don't forget you've done it.

Other PostScript Tricks

You can use any of the techniques we've discussed to send PostScript commands directly to the printer. There are some other interesting tricks you can do with the LaserWriter driver that give you access to PostScript at a slightly higher level. We'll talk about a few of those briefly now.

PostScript allows you to define dashed lines to a very great level of detail. You can set a dash pattern for a line and then draw with that pattern. A pair of QuickDraw picture comments, Dashed-Line and DashedStop, allow you to record PostScript dashed line information in a picture. You have to define the parameters for the dash and then tell where to draw it.

One of the neatest things about PostScript is that it allows you to draw at the LaserWriter's full resolution of 300 dots per inch. Usually you have to delve directly into PostScript to draw really tiny dots at LaserWriter resolution; but there's another picture comment that will help you draw very fine lines. This is the SetLineWidth command, which allows you to specify a pen size (height and width) in LaserWriter resolution. When you send this comment, the additional data is an x-y size for LaserWriter line widths. After sending this comment, lines will be drawn in this size.

QuickDraw also has the ability to draw polygons defined by a set of points. You set one up by drawing lines; QuickDraw remembers the point at each corner (or *vertex*, for you geometry fans) and re-draws the polygon by connecting the dots. PostScript includes some more advanced techniques for drawing polygons. The LaserWriter driver gives you access to PostScript's curve-smoothing capabilities by defining polygon comments. These comments use a curve drawing algorithm defined by cubic equations (gee!) to precisely define the curves.

PostScript has the neat capability to rotate things before placing them on the page. There are QuickDraw picture comments that let you rotate things easily. You can rotate any image in general or you can use a special set of comments just to rotate text.

A few other comments give you control over what goes on in the LaserWriter's PostScript brain. The LaserWriter normally plays around with the space between words to make sure that things you print come out where you expect them to. Sometimes, you want to make sure that a block of text comes out exactly centered on the page or pushed up against the right margin, and there are picture comments that you can use to do this.

Sometimes an application will have to print a slight variation of the same page, like a filled-out form, many times in a row. Normally, you have to redraw everything on every page when you print, which takes time and effort in your program and in the printer. There's a picture comment that lets you tell the LaserWriter that you're going to be doing this kind of printing. When you use this comment, the LaserWriter will keep the page definition around in memory after printing it and you just have to draw the stuff that's changed.

These are most of the picture comments that have been defined for the LaserWriter driver as of version 3.1. Apple usually adds capabilities to the driver with each release. If you're interested in taking full advantage of the amazing LaserWriters, you should keep up with the latest technical information by reading Apple's Macintosh Technical Notes and the technical documentation, such as the *Laser-Writer Reference Manual*. By using the power in the LaserWriter you can really add some magic to your printed documents. Just think—you can help desktop publishing live forever.

P.S.

In this section we've talked a lot about how you can get to Post-Script from within your usually QuickDraw-speaking application. Since you'll almost certainly use QuickDraw to draw things on the screen, you'll probably be doing most of your printing that way, too. This makes it most convenient to use the occasional PostScript techniques we've talked about. Sometimes, though, it's fun (and educational too) to mess around with PostScript directly so that you can get a feel for what it can do. There are several ways to do this, and it's worth a few paragraphs to discuss them.

The most direct way to speak PostScript to your LaserWriter is to do it just that way: directly. This means that instead of hooking up to the printer across an AppleTalk network, you just plug right in through the LaserWriter's serial port. To do this, you'll need to adjust the communication-setting knob on the back of the printer. It has four settings: AppleTalk, which is how it's usually set; 1200 baud and 9600 baud serial communication; and Special, which should really be entitled Lobotomy, because it makes the printer forget that it's got PostScript and forces it to emulate a Diablo 630 daisywheel. This is roughly equivalent to making a Macintosh II emulate a four-function calculator. This last setting is mainly for the Big Blue crowd who may not have software that knows how to talk to a printer with a computer inside it.

To send PostScript to the LaserWriter directly, you can set the communication knob to 9600 baud and then just connect your Macintosh directly to either the nine-pin or the 25-pin port on the Laser-Writer. You'll need a run of the mill communications program on the Macintosh, and you should set it for 9600 baud and no parity. To get the printer to say something, you can type a Control-T, which is like asking the LaserWriter how it's doing right now. It should tell you something like its name and the fact that it's idle, and you can go on from there. You'll find the *PostScript Language Reference Manual* very valuable in this endeavor.

Of course, to plug directly into a LaserWriter requires you to have a spare one sitting in a closet somewhere not doing anything; otherwise, the people on the network might get pretty hacked off at you when you disconnect it for your own playing around.

Well, there is a better way. A number of programs let you try out PostScript commands without having to cut off your friends and co-workers. You can find out about these programs by checking out the software ads in any recent issue of your favorite Macintosh magazine.

One program you may not have heard of is called PostHaste, put out by Micro Dynamics, Ltd. of Silver Spring, Maryland. PostHaste implements a very simple idea: you can open windows and edit a PostScript program on the screen, and when it's finished, you can shoot it off to the LaserWriter. The printer is still in its native habitat, an AppleTalk network, and you still behave like a good network citizen when you communicate with it. Of course, since you have access to PostScript directly, you can do nasty things anyway, but PostHaste treats your printing job just like any other on the network.

With PostHaste, you can experiment by typing in PostScript commands directly and then sending them to the LaserWriter to see what they do. You can write your own programs, use the examples that come with PostScript, or try some things from the *PostScript Language Tutorial and Cookbook,* another volume put out by Adobe and published by Addison-Wesley.

As with any computer language, you can learn more about it by looking at some example code. With PostScript, there's an easy way to get lots of example code to study. A special feature of the LaserWriter driver allows you to see the PostScript that would normally be sent to the LaserWriter when you print a document. To use this feature, you hold down the Command and F keys right after clicking the OK button in the print job dialog. Be sure to keep holding the keys down until the alert appears telling you that it's creating a PostScript file.

This trick will make a file called PostScript*n*, where *n* starts at 0 and gets bumped up by one for every new file you create. After making one of these files, you can look at it with any word processor or text editor and learn a little about what PostScript code looks like.

> **Definitions**. If you look through a PostScript file created with Command-F, you'll find a lot of commands that aren't listed in the PostScript reference manual. This is because Apple defines a bunch of additional commands which are used extensively by the LaserWriter driver. The LaserPrep file contains the definitions for these commands. To see the definitions, when you print, hold down Command and K after clicking OK. This will create a text file that you can peruse to help figure out what's going on with your documents.

By using utilities like PostHaste and diligently studying the PostScript and LaserWriter manuals, you can really make the Laser-Writer do some amazing things for you. Remember, though, that if you write PostScript code, you'll only be compatible with printers that have PostScript, so you should be careful about what you implement if you want your program to be used by folks with other kinds of printers.

Creating special effects with PostScript can be really interesting. After working with the LaserWriter in PostScript, you'll begin to appreciate why Apple used to call the LaserWriter "the most powerful computer Apple has ever built," which was absolutely true until the Macintosh II appeared.

C H A P T E R 7

QuickDraw

Behind the scenes with QuickDraw. Meet the bit image, the heart of everything you see on the screen. The world as perverted by color. Drawing on a screen that's not a screen. Pixel images and color tables.

In this chapter, we'll talk about some QuickDraw hints and tips. QuickDraw is vital to virtually every Macintosh application. Anything you can do to increase your knowledge of how it works should lead to better applications and more fun creating software.

Bit Image Updating

Have you ever noticed that some applications seem to update the screen very fast, drawing in one burst, while others seem to take a long time as you actually watch the pieces being drawn on the screen? If you've never noticed this phenomenon, compare the amount of time it takes to draw the newly exposed area of a window that's just been enlarged to the time it takes to redraw the covered-up part of a window when a pulled-down menu is released (see Figure 7-1).

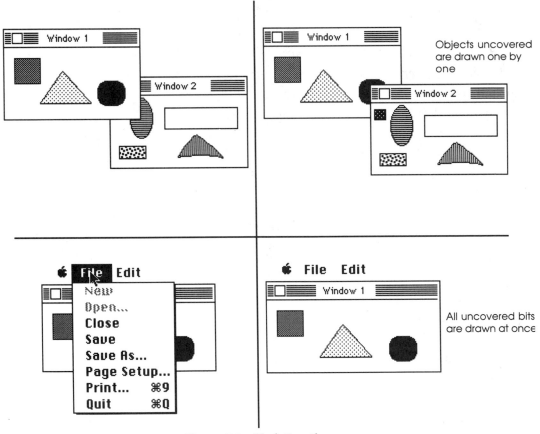

Figure 7-1. Updating the screen

When you let go of the mouse after pulling down a menu, the area "behind" the menu seems to reappear instantly. By comparison, when you make a window larger, most applications take a small but noticeable amount of time to draw into the new part of the window. How do these two drawing operations differ?

These two ways of drawing present a classic case of a tradeoff in computer programming. Consider what happens when you scroll the window. The application draws the newly displayed part of the window by figuring out what should go where and then calling QuickDraw to actually do the drawing. For example, if the application is an object-drawing program like MacDraw, it will go through its data structures to determine what objects (like rectangles, ovals, and so on) should be displayed in the newly opened part of the window. If you've never had the window open to that point before, there will be nothing to draw, of course, but if you have previously been working in that part of the document, it has to show you what's there (see Figure 7-2).

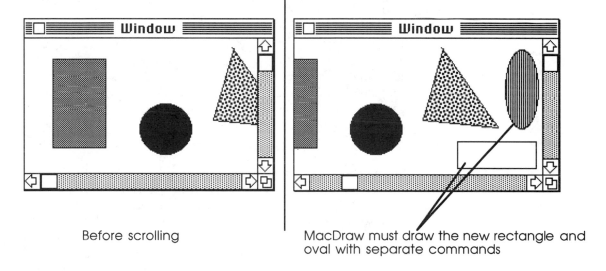

Before scrolling   MacDraw must draw the new rectangle and
                                     oval with separate commands

Figure 7-2. MacDraw redrawing

When the application finds an object that needs to be drawn into the new part of the window, it calls QuickDraw to do the drawing. Let's say that it's MacDraw and it has to draw an oval. MacDraw will call one of QuickDraw's oval-drawing routines, like Frame-Oval, and QuickDraw then determines just what bits to change from white to black on the screen in order to draw the oval. Changing from a FrameOval call into dots on the screen is basically a mathematical operation and it can take some time. But remember that *some time* is a relative term. When the car dealer says it'll be some time before that part you need comes in, he probably means days; we're talking milliseconds here.

Blitting

The Menu Manager uses a different technique to redraw the part of the screen that was behind the menu. Instead of having to redraw everything by calling object-drawing commands (or even text-drawing commands like DrawChar), the Menu Manager simply saves a **bit image** of the rectangle on the screen that will be occupied by the menu before it actually draws the menu. When it wants to restore the image and get rid of the menu, it simply copies the saved bits directly back to the screen location where it saved them from. This operation is pictured in Figure 7-3. This technique of moving data around to change the screen is known by some computer folks as **blitting** (really). On the Macintosh, you can do this with the Copy-Bits call.

> The color version of QuickDraw that's in the Macintosh II includes an enhanced version of CopyBits. This new call knows about the various image depths that are possible with the wondrous new version of QuickDraw. For more about how it works, see Chapter 3.

As you can tell just by watching how quickly a menu is erased, blitting can be incredibly fast. There's no translation that has to take place between a geometric object like an oval and the layout of the Macintosh's screen RAM. Instead, the Menu Manager just calls CopyBits before drawing the menu to save the part of the screen that's about to be written over by the menu and then calls CopyBits again to move the saved bits back onto the screen. It's pretty easy and very fast.

So, the obvious question arises: if zapping the bits around with CopyBits is so fast and easy, why do we need to bother updating the screen in any other way? The answer is the eternal computer tradeoff between speed and size. Redrawing the screen by saving and restoring bits takes a lot of memory: one bit of memory for every screen bit saved (a pretty straightforward calculation). So, for example, to save the bits in a rectangle that's 128 dots wide and 100 rows high, you'd need 128 times 100, or 12,800 bits. There's eight bits in a byte,

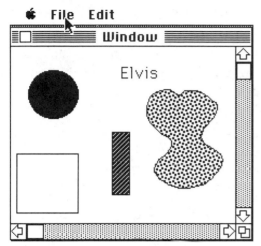

1. User about to pull down menu
Menu Manager computes size of
rectangle where menu will be drawn..

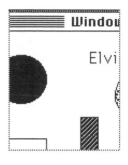

2. Menu Manager saves
bits offscreen. . .

3. . . .draws the menu. . .

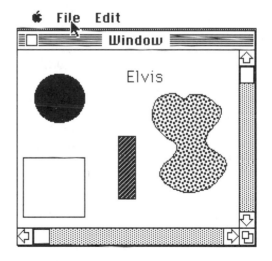

4. . . .and restores the screen
when the mouse button is released.

Figure 7-3. Menu Manager screen action

so you'd have to reserve 1,600 bytes in RAM to save the image in the rectangle.

If your user has a Macintosh II with gray scale or color turned on, the RAM needs are even greater. Every bit of depth in the image is like another layer and the memory requirements are multiplied for every additional bit. For example, if you've got two-bit color, which is pretty cheap, you have to double the memory requirements (in the previous example, that would mean 3,200 bytes). If the Macintosh II is cranked up to eight bits per pixel, your memory requirements really zoom up, all the way to 12,800 bytes for our little bitty rectangle.

If you used the other technique, remembering a description of the objects on the screen rather than the actual bits that comprise the image, how much RAM would it take? Well, it would depend on how many objects were contained in the area you wanted to save, but let's think about it for a minute. Most MacDraw-type objects can be described in just a few bytes. For example, a rectangle of any size can be described in just eight bytes: the top, left, bottom, and right coordinates, each of which takes two bytes.

What if the rectangle were filled with a pattern? A QuickDraw pattern also takes up just eight bytes. So, the definition for a filled rectangle would take only 16 bytes, no matter how big the rectangle. By contrast, we said that a 128 by 100 rectangle would take 1,600 bytes if we saved all its bits! You can see how this works in Figure 7-4. Of course, this is a fairly extreme example, since the rectangle we saved with just 16 bytes can only be filled with a simple pattern; when we save all the bits, the rectangle can be filled with anything and the number of bytes needed will be just the same.

Implementation Choices

This example serves to show the tradeoff between saving object information and saving bit images. When we save object information, we use a lot less memory but it takes longer to redraw, since Quick-Draw has to do more work to draw an object than it does to simply move bits with CopyBits. On the other hand, although CopyBits is pretty fast, it takes a lot more memory to save the image than when using object information. What's a poor programmer to do?

Although using object information rather than bit images saves memory, a lot of people now have Macintoshes with a megabyte or two of RAM, and it's not unusual to see four megabytes (although it still costs big bucks). Of course, this trend will continue in the future: more and more memory will become available. In light of this fact, saving a few thousand bytes here and there is no longer as important

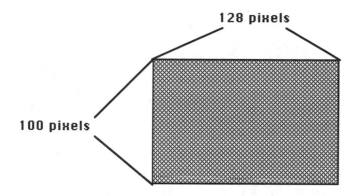

Saving all bits:
  128 pixels x 100 rows =
  12800 pixels =
  1600 bytes

Saving object definition:
top left coordinate = 4 bytes
bottom right coordinate = 4 bytes
QuickDraw pattern = 8 bytes
  16 bytes total

Figure 7-4. Saving rectangle information

as it once was, long, long ago in 1984 and 1985 when machines with 128K RAM were common.

In today's megabitten world, you can really improve your program's performance by using bit images to update the screen. Most applications update their windows by drawing from data structures. For example, a word processor will figure out what text is supposed to be on a newly exposed part of a window and then make Quick-Draw text drawing calls like DrawChar and DrawText to update the screen. If all updates could be done from bit images, everything would be much faster.

The ultimate technique for speed of updating would be to maintain a bit image of all your open documents in a buffer somewhere. If you had this bit image, you could do all your updating, including scrolling and resizing, by copying bits from the bit image buffer. You'd only have to use the QuickDraw object-drawing calls when the user added new things to a document.

To be complete, the bit image would have to include all the bits in the whole document, not just the window and the part that's displayed on the screen. Then, when you had to update the window, you could just CopyBits it back onto the screen and you'd get a very fast update.

Of course, you'd need about a zillion bytes of RAM to use this technique, which is more than the maximum amount of memory supported by the Macintosh Operating System. The reason is this: to save one standard size page (8 1/2 by 11 inches) at the Macintosh's resolution of 72 dots per inch would take about 60K bytes of RAM (you can see how this calculation was made in Figure 7-5). This means that a 20-page word processor document would require an incredible 1.2 megabytes, and that's not even a very big document. Remember, too, that you'd need memory for every one of your open documents. If you've got four documents open on, and each one is about ten pages long, that means that you'd need over two megabytes of space!

$$1 \text{ page} = 8.5 * 11 \text{ inches}$$
$$1 \text{ inch} = 72 \text{ pixels}$$
$$1 \text{ byte} = 8 \text{ pixels}$$

$$1 \text{ page} = (8.5 * 72) * (11 * 72) \text{ pixels}$$
$$= 484704 \text{ pixels}$$
$$= 60588 \text{ bytes}$$

Figure 7-5. Memory required for a page

Finding space for color or gray scale images is even worse. Again, for every additional bit per pixel, you have to multiply the amount of memory you need: a single 8 1/2 by 11 page of eight-bit images would take 480K bytes.

It looks like the idea of keeping a bit image of absolutely everything is impossible for most applications, so let's try to scale down our ambitions. There are several other ways we can use the bit image updating technique to make programs faster.

One idea is to simply keep a bit image copy of the screen, rather than a copy of all the bits in every document. This is a little more reasonable. The idea behind this technique is to save an image of the screen with CopyBits whenever you're finished drawing something. With a bit image of the screen, we can do updates that involve restoring things that were behind other things and then exposed, such as when windows are closed or moved. This technique doesn't help us do any updates that involve displaying information that's newly scrolled onto the screen or parts of windows that are newly seen after the user enlarges the window with the grow box.

How much memory does this take? It depends, of course, on the size of the screen. The classic 9-inch Macintosh screen takes about 22K, which is not an outrageous amount. A Radius Full Page Display has screen dimensions of 640 by 864, so it would require 640 times 864, divided by 8, bytes—about 68K bytes for those of you without a calculator. That much RAM can be a little tougher to find. When you also add the possibility of a really huge (say 1024 by 1024) screen, you can wind up needing 128K of RAM to preserve your bit image.

That's a pretty big chunk to devote to fast screen updating, not to mention the possibility of multiple-bit-per-pixel screens.

One way to solve the problem of finding enough RAM for a bit image for the whole screen is to allocate the memory for the image at the start of the program and use it for updates. Then, if you start to run out of memory, you can get rid of the bit image so that you can use the RAM for something else. One way to do this would be to install a **GrowZone function** that deallocated the bit image buffer with DisposHandle if the program desperately needed memory (see the Memory Manager chapter of *Inside Macintosh* for more information about GrowZone functions). Without the bit image, you'd have to do updates the slow way, by drawing things based on your data structure, but at least you wouldn't run out of memory. You could also monitor available RAM and if enough free memory opened up again, you could get your buffer back and speed things up again.

When you're running with Apple's MultiFinder, the rules change a little bit. Imagine that your application is running and you've taken a snapshot of the screen by CopyBitsing it to a bit image. Meanwhile, some hardy little application has been running in the background and while doing so it's changed something in one of its windows, which is visible on the desktop. If you try to update the screen by just copying the bits you saved previously, a bad thing happens: you copy the old bits back to the screen, thus wiping out whatever changes the hardy little background application had made to its windows. Oops. How can you avoid this problem? When you call CopyBits, you can specify a region (the parameter called maskRgn) which limits the area copied. You can set up maskRgn to be the union of the visRgns of your windows. Then, when you save and update the screen with CopyBits, you won't touch the parts that don't belong to you.

If you don't think you can spare a buffer for the whole screen even some of the time, a compromise is available that's used by several of today's most advanced Macintosh applications. It works like this: whenever the application is about to cover up part of the screen (usually with a modal dialog), it does a CopyBits to save the part of the screen that's about to be obliterated by the dialog. Then when the dialog goes away, the application updates the screen by Copy-Bitsing the saved image back to the screen. This is a lot like the way the Menu Manager does its thing. Here's a list of the steps you could take to implement this technique in your program when you're about to put up a dialog.

1. Determine the size of the dialog's rectangle. You can get this from the DLOG resource of the dialog that will be drawn.
2. Determine the amount of memory you'll need to save the bit image.
3. Get memory for the bit image by calling NewHandle. If the NewHandle call fails due to a lack of memory (it returns memFullError), you can't save the bit image, and you should skip the save/restore trick and just redraw the window when it's time to update it. If this happens, you're probably in deep memory trouble anyway.
4. Save the bit image by calling CopyBits.
5. Put up the dialog and handle it normally.
6. When it's time to return from the dialog, call CopyBits again, this time reversing the procedure by copying from the saved bit image to the screen.

Does this take up much memory? Not really. Most dialogs are small enough that you only need a few thousand bytes to hold the saved bits. Of course, bigger dialogs can approach 20K of bits, which can be a little harder to find. Using this technique of saving and restoring the screen with CopyBits around a dialog is a fairly easy way to make your program faster, both in reality and in your users' perception: it will be faster and it will feel faster, too.

Color

With the introduction of the Macintosh II, Apple now officially supports color and gray scale images. When pixels on the screen can only be in two states, black or white, one bit is enough to represent each pixel, but when you can have color or gray scale, you need more bits per pixel. Two bits can hold four different numbers: 00, 01, 10, and 11. This means you can get four different colors (or shades of gray) if you have two bits per pixel. Four bits per pixel means 16 colors, and eight bits per pixel gives you 256 colors.

Pretzel logic. This discussion of the number of available colors is strictly true, but your eyes can play tricks on you. For example, if you see a pattern of alternating blue and green pixels, your eyes probably won't see blue or green: you'll see a whole new color. This little trick is called **dithering**. The color version of QuickDraw uses dithering to produce more apparent colors on the screen. The tradeoff is that it takes more than one pixel to establish the effect: one blue-green "dot" is really two pixels, for example.

On the Macintosh II, the user is in control of the number of bits per pixel. With the right video hardware, your friendly user can use the Control Panel to run your application with two, four, or eight bits per pixel. What does this mean to you?

If more bits are being used to show what's on the screen, you have to save more bits in your bit image. To save all the possible information on the screen, you have to save the color information, if there is any. Consider this: if the user picks two bits per pixel, there are now twice as many bits required to display the screen. (The number of bits per pixel in an image is called the **depth,** by the way). In memory, adjacent bits are used to construct each pixel (see Figure 7-6). If you only save the number of bits necessary to keep a one-pixel-deep image, what will happen? Let's all find out now.

The color version of QuickDraw defines a new data structure that's like a bit map except that it can have any image depth. This structure is called a pixel map, and you can see what it looks like in Figure 7-7. Color QuickDraw's version of CopyBits is very smart— smart enough to figure out whether you're copying information from the screen to a bit map, for example, which is the technique we've been talking about. When you do this, Color QuickDraw automatically ensures that it copies the complete, black and white (one-bit-deep) image, no matter what the depth of the screen.

When you copy back from the bit image to the screen, CopyBits will again make sure that the proper bit depth is maintained and it will ensure that the one-bit-deep information is copied back correctly. Of course, if you copy into a bit map, you'll lose any color information, since a bit map (as compared to a pixel map) is always one bit deep (see Figure 7-8). How can you make sure that you copy color information, too?

The answer, again, lies in using the new version of CopyBits provided by Color QuickDraw. The new version acts a lot like the old CopyBits, except that it can also be used with pixel maps and so you can use it on images of any depth. In order to make sure you're copy-

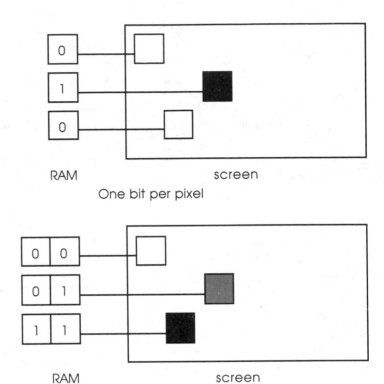

Figure 7-6. Screen mapping

```
PixMap = Record
        baseAddr : Ptr ; {address of pixels}
        rowBytes : Integer ; {offset between lines}
        bounds : Rect ; {boundary of pixMap}
        pmVersion : Integer ; {version number}
        packType : Integer ; {pixMap packing format}
        packSize : Longint ; {packed data size}
        hRes : Fixed ; {horizontal resolution, pixels per inch}
        vRes : Fixed ; {vertical resolution}
        pixelType : Integer ; {always 0 for chunky format}
        pixelSize : Integer ; {bits per pixel}
        CmpCount : Integer ; {always 1 for 1 RGB per pixel}
        cmpSize : Integer ; {bits per component}
        planeBytes : Longint ; {always 0 for chunky}
        pmTable : CTabHandle ; {handle to PixMap's colors}
        pmReserved : Longint ; {must be 0 for now}
                end ;
```

Figure 7-7. PixMap structure

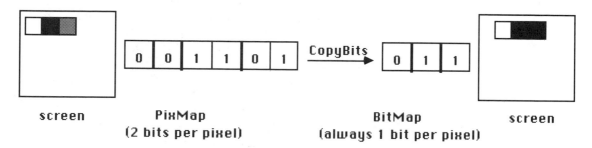

Figure 7-8. BitMap loses color information

ing the right stuff, you can call CopyBits to save and restore the screen image into a pixel map.

There's something else you need to remember if you're using CopyBits to copy a multiple bits per pixel image: your bit image buffer has to be big enough to handle the image depth the user has chosen. For example, if the user is cruising along in four-bit depth, your buffer has to be big enough for four bits per pixel. Obviously, this can make your buffers get pretty big, but since the only Macintoshes that have color also have a lot of RAM, the problem is less serious. If your application doesn't do anything in color, you may want to suggest in your documentation that the user not change the pixel depth, since it'll just cause headaches and use more RAM for your bit image buffers. In general your software should work right in all pixel depths, but if you don't have any special features for color or gray scales, there's no point in the user setting up for it. We'll talk more about using offscreen buffers with multibit images a little later in this section, so please stay tuned.

Using Bit Image Buffers

In addition to using CopyBits to copy things between the screen and a buffer, it's useful sometimes to actually draw into the buffer's image rather than directly to the screen. There are a number of uses for this technique:

- Drawing things that have to be manipulated before they're displayed, such as rotated text.
- Drawing the same image multiple times.
- Updating an image without having to erase and redraw it.
- Making an image appear on the screen all at once, rather than piece by piece.

It's interesting to note that drawing into an image buffer and then using CopyBits to copy it to the screen takes just as long as drawing it directly to the screen; actually, it takes a little longer, since the bits have to be copied to the screen after they're drawn. Even though it takes just as long, a lot of users perceive the process as faster when the whole image appears in one shot, rather than when they watch it draw piece by piece.

The first step in using a bit image buffer is getting the memory to hold it, and before you can do that, you have to figure out how much memory you need. In the previous section, we talked a little about the sizes of bit images. Now we'll get into the grimy facts of figuring out exactly how much memory we need.

Drawing into an Offscreen Buffer

This technique is known variously as drawing into an offscreen buffer, drawing offscreen, and using an offscreen bitmap. Here's the idea: when you draw on the Macintosh screen, you call QuickDraw commands that cause bits to be set to 1 or 0. Because that memory is usu-ally the memory that the Macintosh screen uses to tell it what it should display, this magically causes words and pictures to appear.

What happens if the memory that QuickDraw affects is not the memory that the Macintosh screen is showing? QuickDraw doesn't really care; it still sets the 1s and 0s the same way, just as if it were drawing to the screen's memory. The memory that's drawn into is affected the same way, whether it's actually displayed on a monitor or not.

Bit-o-plenty. How does the Macintosh video hardware interpret the 1s and 0s that QuickDraw sets in memory? Every bit that contains a 0 shows up on the screen as a white dot; the 1s come out black. If you're familiar with monochrome graphics on most other personal computers, you know that this is backwards from the usual scheme: most computers use 0 to represent black and 1 to indicate white. Is this a subtle indicator of the Macintosh's differences from standard computers? Is it a consequence of the Macintosh's black on white, paper-like text display, compared to most computers' white on black? I don't know. This is a software book. Sorry. Thought you'd like to know anyway.

To use an offscreen buffer you have to be able to tell QuickDraw what chunk of memory to use when you draw. Normally, of course, QuickDraw is set up to draw into the screen's memory automatically. If you want to draw into an offscreen buffer, you have to make sure there's memory reserved to receive the drawing. If you're not careful, you risk drawing right on top of anything else in memory, like your program's code or Uncle Elvis's Christmas card list.

There are two ways to set aside memory to be used for an off-screen buffer, and they're the two standard Macintosh ways of allocating memory. Since the offscreen buffer is simply a chunk of memory, you can use ordinary techniques for finding the memory: you can either declare a variable that's large enough to hold the buffer or you can call the Memory Manager to find some memory for you. Let's look at how to do each of these and how to figure out how much memory you need.

Before you allocate memory for the offscreen buffer, you have to know the size of the area you'll be drawing into. Let's say, for example, that you're going to be drawing an image into a rectangle that's 200 pixels on each side. First, we'll set up some constants, like this:

```
drawLeft = 0;
drawTop = 0;
drawRight = 200;
drawBottom = 200;
```

Now that we know the size of the area we're going to draw into, we can figure out how much memory we have to grab for the buffer. Let's see: we know that one pixel on the screen takes up one bit in memory and that a byte contains eight bits; therefore, it seems like the number of bytes required should equal the number of pixels times eight.

Does this work? Well, no. There are a few problems with this simple assumption. The first problem is the way bitmaps are described by QuickDraw. Every QuickDraw bitmap, whether on the screen or not, includes a field called rowBytes that tells the number of bytes in each row of pixels. The first step in computing the number of bytes for the bit image buffer is to figure rowBytes.

More than meets the eye.   Actually, the complete definition of rowBytes is a little more subtle than that. As you may know (and if you don't, you'll learn it as you read on in this section), a QuickDraw bitmap includes a bounding rectangle in addition to the rowBytes field. This seems redundant, and this seems redundant: rowBytes tells you the width of the bit image, so why do you also need a rectangle? The answer is that there may be unused bits at the end of each row, so the bounding rectangle is used to indicate the right edge of the bits that are actually in the image (see Figure 7-9). So, a better definition of rowBytes is that it defines the offset in memory from one row to the next. This definition becomes especially important when you're dealing with the Macintosh II, where you can find multiple bits per pixel.

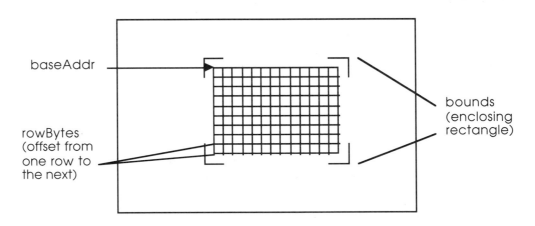

Figure 7-9.   BitMap

There's a non-obvious formula for computing rowBytes based on the width of the image that you're drawing. It goes like this:

```
bitsRowBytes := (((drawRight - drawLeft - 1) div 16) + 1) * 2
```

Now you know why I said this formula was non-obvious. Without going into it so deeply we both go insane, let's talk a little about where the formula came from. The basic ideas are these:

- RowBytes is approximately equal to the width of the bit image in pixels divided by eight. This accounts for subtracting draw-

Left from drawRight, integer-dividing by 16 (that is, divide and throw away the remainder), and multiplying by two.

- RowBytes must always be even. This is why we have to go through the bizarre complication of first subtracting one, integer-dividing by 16, adding one, and then multiplying by two, rather than just dividing by eight.

Let's see what happens after we pump our numbers through this formula.

```
bitsRowBytes := (((200- 0 - 1) div 16) + 1) * 2
             = ((199 div 16) + 1) * 2
             = (12 + 1) * 2
             =  26
```

As a reality check, we can use the fact we discovered above, that rowBytes is approximately equal to the width of the bit image in pixels divided by eight. Does this work here? The width of the image, 200, divided by eight is 25, which is as close as you can get to 26 without going over. This seems a good number for rowBytes. Maybe we can even use this formula to win prizes on "The Price is Right."

Now that we've figured out the size of rowBytes, we can determine how much memory we need for the bit image buffer. Figuring out this number is a lot more intuitive than the convoluted formula for rowBytes. To get the size of the buffer, just subtract the bottom coordinate from the top and multiply by rowBytes. For those of you who speak math, the formula looks like this:

```
bufferSize := (drawBottom - drawTop) * bitsRowBytes
```

This formula is definitely a lot easier to follow than the previous one. We're simply figuring the total number of bytes needed by first computing the number of rows in the image (drawBottom – drawTop) and then multiplying by the number of bytes per row (bitsRowBytes). In the case of our example, this comes out to 200 times 26, or 5200 bytes.

Now that we know how much memory we need, we can use the Memory Manager to find it for us. Normally, we're good Macintosh citizens and we allocate only relocatable blocks. However, Quick-Draw bit images are something special. When you draw into one, QuickDraw wants a pointer to it, not a handle. This means you may as well make it nonrelocatable, since if it were relocatable it would have to be locked anyway.

To get the memory from the Memory Manager, we recite the following incantation:

```
bufferAddr := NewPtr (bufferSize);
```

> **Alternative factor.** As we said earlier, you can use either of the two standard Macintosh ways of getting memory when you need to create a buffer for offscreen bits. Calling NewPtr to get the memory from the Memory Manager is one way, of course; the other is creating a global or local static variable. For example, in Pascal you could simply declare a variable.
>
> ```
> VAR buffer : array [1..2600] of integer;
> ```
>
> This little fellow reserves space for 2600 integers, a total of 5200 bytes, just big enough for our buffer. Why did we ask for 2600 integers? That's not really what we're storing, of course. The answer is that there's no special reason to call the buffer an array of 2600 integers; any other declaration that reserves 5200 bytes would work just as well. Since we're never going to be using array indices to refer to the "array," it doesn't really matter. The important thing here is simply the number of bytes. Is this the best way to reserve space for our bit buffer? No, for a couple of reasons. First, most compilers limit the amount of global storage you can have, and 5200 bytes is a lot to use up all at once. Second, this technique assumes you know how big the buffer will have to be when you write the program, and this isn't always the case. Often, you have to compute the buffer size based on changing factors like the window size, the screen size, or the pixel depth. The bottom line is that you'll usually reserve space for the bit image by calling the Memory Manager.

Now (assuming the NewPtr call succeeded) bufferAddr has the address of a block in memory that's big enough to hold all the bits in our offscreen buffer (in this case, the block is 5200 bytes big). Now that we've got the memory, what do we do with it? We need to let QuickDraw know about it, of course.

To do this, we have to use QuickDraw's bitmap data structure. As you can see in *Inside Macintosh* (or in Figure 7-10, presented here for your convenience), there are three fields in a QuickDraw bitmap. The first, baseAddr, contains the address of the memory that holds the bits for this bitmap. The second field, rowBytes, is the number of bytes per row of the bitmap, as we've already discussed. The third field is called bounds and it contains the boundary rectangle that limits the bit image, as we discussed a little earlier.

```
BitMap = record
        baseAddr : Ptr ; {address of bits}
        rowBytes : Integer ; {row to row offset}
        bounds : Rect ; {enclosing rectangle}
                end ;
```

Figure 7-10. BitMap structure

Before we can draw into our offscreen buffer, we have to allocate a bitmap and then set up its three fields. Once we've got our bitmap all set up, we can proceed to use it for whatever kind of drawing operation we've got in mind.

> **Terminology corner.** Note that while *bitmap* is often used to indicate a collection of bits displayed on the screen or sent to a printer, the QuickDraw data structure called a BitMap is a record consisting of the fields baseAddr, rowBytes, and bounds. It takes up 14 bytes and it does *not* include any image-representing bits; instead, it includes baseAddr, which tells the address of those bits. In this context, the bits themselves are usually called a bit image.

The easiest way to create a bitmap is to simply declare one as a static variable, like this:

```
VAR offMap : bitMap
```

Now that we have a bitmap and a place to store the bits, we can assign the right values to the fields in the bitmap's record:

```
offMap.baseAddr := bufferAddr;
offMap.rowBytes := bitsRowBytes;
SetRect (offMap.bounds, 0, 0, 200, 200);
```

Now we're really rolling. The bitmap is set up and we have the buffer where we're going to store the bits. The next step is to create the image itself in the offscreen buffer.

Just what you do at this point depends on what you want to use your offscreen buffer for. If you're using it to save a copy of part of the screen for fast updating after putting up a dialog, the next thing to do would be to call CopyBits to save bits from the screen before putting up the dialog. For our example, we'll draw some stuff directly into the offscreen buffer and then copy it to the screen all at once.

With the bitmap all set up, only one step remains before we can draw directly into it. We've filled in all the blanks in the bitmap data structure; now we just have to tell QuickDraw that it's the bitmap of choice. How do we do this? Well, remember that QuickDraw always draws into the current grafport. All we have to do is convince QuickDraw that our offscreen friend is attached to the current port. A handy QuickDraw call, SetPortBits, will do exactly what we want. It takes an existing bitmap and makes the current port use it. After using SetPortBits on our offscreen bitmap, we're all set for drawing.

Myth interpretation.   What does SetPortBits do, really? Every grafport has a field called portBits that contains the bitmap used by the grafport. It seems like all you'd have to do to make a port use a different bitmap is change the value in the portBits field. This is exactly what SetPortBits does for you. If that's all it does, why call it? This brings up the old argument about using the high-level interface. If you always call the trap, you'll get the benefit of whatever interesting changes Apple might make to SetPortBits in the future.

After we're done messing around with the offscreen bitmap and we want to set things back to normal, we're probably going to want to restore the previous value of the grafport's portBits field. So, before we blast it by calling SetPortBits, we should save the old value. We can do this by declaring another bitmap and then saving the port's real bitmap by assigning it to this variable:

```
realBits := thePort^.portBits;
```

There's one more thing we might want to do before we actually begin drawing into our bitmap. Remember that the memory we got from the Memory Manager is just a chunk of RAM that's located nowhere in particular. Since this memory may have held anything before we grabbed it, it's probably a jumble of 1s and 0s, which wouldn't look very nice on the screen. So, before drawing, it's a good idea to clear the memory to all white (0s). Since we're treating this area as a rectangle, an easy way to clear it is by filling a rectangle with white pixels, like this:

```
EraseRect (thePort^.portBits.bounds);
```

All right already, enough fooling around. Can we finally draw into this thing? We can now actually draw into our offscreen bitmap, using any old QuickDraw commands you have lying around the room. This includes just about anything: frame, paint, erase, invert, or fill commands; anything involving lines, rectangles, ovals, arcs, regions, or polygons; text-drawing stuff; and bit transfer commands like CopyBits. All of these will affect the undisplayed image in the offscreen bitmap. If you want to apply some sort of mathemagical trick to the bits, such as rotating them, you can do that too.

After you've created the image that you want in the offscreen buffer, the magic moment takes place when you bring it onscreen for your users to see. This is accomplished in two steps. First, we have to tell the current port to go back to using its regular bitmap (the one we saved in realBits, you remember). Then, we use CopyBits to actually blit the bits from their offscreen receptacle onto the screen. Here's what those two lines of code would look like.

```
SetPortBits (realBits);
CopyBits (offMap, thePort^.portBits, offMap.bounds, thePort^.portRect, srcCopy, NIL);
```

In the CopyBits call, we're telling QuickDraw to copy from the offscreen bitmap to the current grafport. The rectangles offMap.bounds and thePort^.portRect allow us to further define the rectangles to use when copying the bits, in case we want to scale the image between rectangles of different sizes. The srcCopy parameter is where we specify the QuickDraw transfer mode, which defines the mathematical rules to use when combining bits from the source with the destination. A transfer mode of srcCopy means that the source bits will completely replace the destination. For some slightly funkier examples, you could invert the source image by using the notSrcCopy mode or you could "punch a hole" in the destination by using the srcBic (source bit clear) mode. Check out Figure 7-11 to see what these would look like.

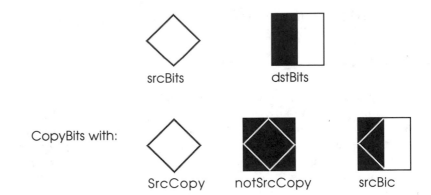

Figure 7-11. QuickDraw transfer modes

That's it. After the CopyBits call, your carefully orchestrated bits should appear on the screen, just as though they were made from scratch. Let's go over the steps necessary to pull this off.

- Compute the value of rowBytes by using the formula, which in case you haven't memorized it already is: rowBytes := (((drawRight − drawLeft − 1) div 16) + 1) * 2.
- Compute the size of the bit buffer by subtracting the top coordinate from the bottom, then multiplying by rowBytes.
- Call NewPtr to get some memory for the bit buffer.
- Prepare the three fields of the bitmap.
- Save the value of the current port's portBits and then use Set-PortBits to set it to our offscreen bitmap.
- Draw like crazy into the bitmap.
- When we're done drawing, use SetPortBits to restore the regular bitmap and then use CopyBits to move the bits onto the screen.

By using offscreen drawing techniques, you can make your window updating faster. If you keep a copy of your data drawn offscreen and then use CopyBits to copy it onto the screen when you need an update, users will really feel like your application is fast. If you play around with offscreen drawing, you can find lots of uses to enhance your fun and profit.

The Multibit Shuffle

The Macintosh II has incredibly flexible video capabilities. It can display both color and black and white, and the black and white can be turned into gray scale display if you don't have a color monitor. To further complicate things, the user is in control of the choice of color, black and white, or gray scale, and can even change it right smack in the middle of an application. After all, in the Macintosh way of doing things, the user is supposed to be in charge. The Macintosh II video capabilities certainly live up to this.

As if multiple user-selectable video modes weren't enough, the Macintosh II applies a coup de grace: the user can configure multiple monitors, which can be set up in any arrangement, with the main screen (the one with the menu bar) also selectable. Since each monitor has individually changeable video settings, this means you can set up an array of, oh, let's say six monitors, three of them color and three monochrome, and arrange them in a T-shape, as shown in Figure 7-12. You can set up each monitor for a different video mode: one of each type, black and white or color, can be set for different pixel depths, such as one bit, four bits, and eight bits. You can even have a single window that spans all six monitors! Figuring out how to finance this system is left as an exercise for the reader.

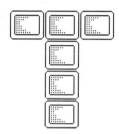

Figure 7-12. Six monitors arrangement

All this flexibility does have a price. Thanks to the beautiful generality of the original QuickDraw model, all these enhancements to QuickDraw for the Macintosh II are possible in the first place, and the enhancements were made while retaining compatibility with many existing Macintosh applications. Some of the new goodies come free: QuickDraw and the Window Manager take care of letting your windows stretch across multiple screens. All you have to do is be smart enough to check the size of your window and take full advantage of it, as most good applications (like yours) do anyway.

Although upward compatibility was a key consideration for Color QuickDraw, some of the new features have caused headaches for programmers. When you write software for the Macintosh product line now, you have a fundamental choice to make about video displays.

- You can ignore color entirely, assuming that your users will run your application only in the plain old ho-hum black and white mode on a Macintosh II.
- You can choose to support QuickDraw's old color model only, which allows for eight different colors without requiring any new QuickDraw calls.
- You can really have fun and support the new color model implemented by Color QuickDraw, which allows you to choose 256 colors to be displayed on a monitor at any one time.

Let's take a look at each of these choices, then discuss them as we run through our familiar example of using an offscreen bitmap.

The easiest choice is simply to ignore the new capabilities of QuickDraw altogether. To do this, just continue to program as if there were no color Macintoshes in the world at all. The applications you create should work OK on color monitors set to display black and white, of course. If users try to get sneaky and run your application in a multibit (color or gray scale) mode, you might be all right as long as nobody tries to paste in a color picture that was created with another application; if that happens, you could be in trouble.

Why would a color picture cause a problem? It depends on how you redraw the screen if you get an update event for the color picture. If the user covers up the color picture and then uncovers it again, you have to redraw it. Depending on your updating technique, you might call DrawPicture with the original picture or you could call Copy-Bits if you've saved the image to an offscreen bitmap. The fun begins if you use CopyBits to try to save multibit information. When you create the offscreen bit image buffer, you're only allowing space for one bit per pixel. If you try to copy, say, a four-bit-per-pixel image, something has to give (see Figure 7-13).

Uh-oh. This looks like it has great potential for disaster. At first glance, it seems like the CopyBits command will try to copy four times the number of bits you have room for, thus (it would seem) really messing up your life by destroying a few thousand bytes of memory, which is probably holding other data of some kind. In reality, though, good old Color QuickDraw is much kinder and wiser than that. If it sees that you're trying to copy a multibit image into a mere one-bit-per-pixel bitmap, it will only copy a one-bit version of the image into the offscreen bitmap, thus saving your other data in RAM.

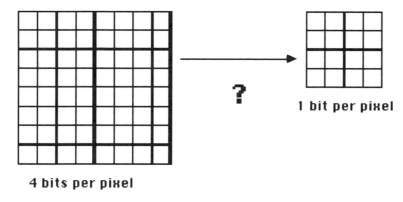

4 bits per pixel

Figure 7-13. Four bit to one bit copying

Of course, this isn't a completely wonderful solution. When the copy of the bitmap is made, there's only one bit of information per pixel, which is only enough room to remember two colors. So, if you use CopyBits to update your windows, and the user sets up a monitor for multiple bits per pixel *and* the user pastes or displays a color picture, then the picture will appear to lose its color information when it's updated. Thanks to Color QuickDraw's smarts, you don't have to worry about overwriting memory by trying to put too much in your offscreen bit buffer. Very soon we'll talk about how to CopyBits to a buffer that will keep track of the screen's color information.

Instead of ignoring color, a more enlightened choice is to support the old color model. Longtime Macintosh aficionados and well-read techies know that QuickDraw has had the capability of supporting color ever since it was first plugged into the original Macintosh. Of course, there were no color output devices at that time, which made it a little tough to see your handiwork if you decided to draw in color, but the software was there and still is.

If you support the old model, you can stick to QuickDraw calls that are available in all Macintoshes. This means you can draw in color by using QuickDraw's old model commands, ForeColor and BackColor, and Macintoshes that don't have color displays (like almost all of them) will display whatever you draw in glorious black and white. The rule it uses is that anything that's not white shows up as black.

The great advantages to using the old model are that you don't have to write any special-case code and that your software works on all Macintoshes. Of course, the limitation is that you only get eight colors. For many applications that don't do a lot of drawing, like word processors, databases, and shrimp-farm management systems, eight colors is plenty. For this reason, many general-purpose applications stick with the old model.

You can also solve the problem of a too small offscreen buffer by being a little more clever when setting up your CopyBits to save the screen. If you're sure Color QuickDraw is present (you can find out by calling SysEnvirons), you can set up a newfangled data structure called a pixel map. This Color QuickDraw structure allows for multiple bits per pixel so that when you save information into one, it will retain all that carefully created color information. We'll get into using pixel maps very soon.

The last choice is the most fun: use the new QuickDraw color model, which gives you access to up to eight bits of color or gray scale information per pixel. With Apple's deluxe video card, you can pick 256 colors at a time from a palette of over 16 million choices. Of course, the big drawback to using the new model is that your program will run only on machines with Color QuickDraw. Still, if you need more color capability than the eight colors of the old model will provide, the new model is for you. You can really produce some spectacular images using the eight-bit depth that Apple's Macintosh II monitors provide. You can find more information on color in Chapter 3.

Pop quiz. As a homework assignment, name the 16 million colors that can be displayed by Apple's video card. Be sure to list them in alphabetical order.

Offscreen Drawing Revisited

Let's take another look at that problem of drawing something offscreen and then using CopyBits to move it into a window in one shot. This time, we'll complicate things severely: we'll say that we're drawing with the new color model on a Macintosh II. This means that we pour in the possibilities of multibit images and multiple screens. Let's see how these new fun features affect our technique.

Before we can do anything at all, we have to make sure that Color QuickDraw is hanging around the computer that our program is running on. If there's no Color QuickDraw when we try to make calls that don't exist in the original version of QuickDraw, our pro-

gram will die horribly, with big nasty pointy teeth. The easiest
way to do this is to use the SysEnvirons call.

```
err := SysEnvirons (1, envRec);
if (envRec.hasColorQD = True)
   then {it's cool, we can go ahead}
   else {give it up, no color QD here}
```

   If there's no Color QuickDraw, we can't use the new model; otherwise, we can move bravely forward. For this example, we'll use a
pixel map instead of a bitmap when we draw offscreen, so that we
can accommodate color stuff. Just like before, we'll begin by setting up
some constants for the rectangle we're going to use.

```
CONST
     drawLeft = 0;
     drawTop = 0;
     drawRight = 200;
     drawBottom = 200;
```

   The next thing to do, as before, is to figure the size of rowBytes
for our offscreen pixel map. The formula we'll use looks a lot like the
one we came up with for figuring rowBytes in a plain old bitmap.
However, this time we have to figure in the pixel depth when doing
the computation, since you need one extra bit per pixel in memory for
each bit per pixel that displays the image. See Figure 7-14 to understand how this works.
   This is great, but how do we find out the pixel depth? We have
another thing to worry about, too: in order to use the new model, we
need a new kind of grafport, a color one. Since the current grafport
may not be a color port, the easiest thing to do is to create a new one
to do our drawing. So, let's back up a bit and begin with that step.
We can use Color QuickDraw's OpenCPort call.

```
VAR colorPort : CGrafPort;
    colorPPtr : CGrafPtr;

    . . .
    colorPPtr := @colorPort;
    OpenCPort (colorPPtr);
```

The variable declarations will allocate space for a new-style grafport and a pointer to the port; the two statements will make the
pointer point to the port and then initialize the port itself so we can
play with it.

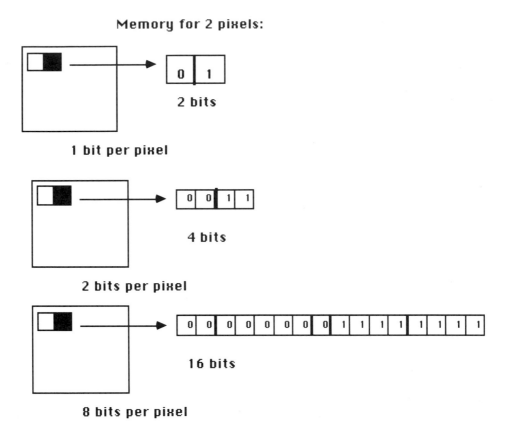

Figure 7-14. Memory for multibit images

Now we're ready to figure out how much memory we need for the offscreen pixel buffer. The first step is to compute rowBytes, but before we can use the rowBytes formula, we have to find out the pixel depth. Think about the issue of pixel depth. Each monitor attached to a Macintosh II can have its own pixel depth setting, as we discussed above when dreaming about our six-monitor fantasy. This means that when you create space for your offscreen pixels, you better make sure there's enough room for the deepest device you've got.

Luckily, Color QuickDraw has once again anticipated this need for us, and provides a handy call for finding out just how deep is deep. The new call GetMaxDevice can be used to find out about the screen that is set for the greatest pixel depth—that is, the monitor that's set to display the most bits per pixel at the time you make the call.

When you call GetMaxDevice, you pass it a rectangle in global coordinates and it gives you back a handle to another new Color

QuickDraw data structure called a graphics device or **gDevice.** The gDevice contains information about a graphics device (usually a monitor) that's being used by Color QuickDraw. One of the fields in the gDevice record, called gdPMap, is a handle to the pixel map being used by the graphics device. Finally, within the pixel map is a field called pixelSize, which will tell us the actual number of bits per pixel being used.

So, we can find out the number of bits per pixel by getting the handle from GetMaxDevice, following it through the device record to look at the pixel map and then pulling out the pixel depth. Since we have to pass GetMaxDevice a global rectangle that indicates where we want it to look, we have to set up this rectangle. First, we'll set up the local rectangle, then convert it to global coordinates.

```
copyRect.left  := drawLeft;
copyRect.top := drawTop;
copyRect.right := drawRight;
copyRect.bottom := drawBottom;
LocalToGlobal (copyRect.topLeft);
LocalToGlobal (copyRect.botRight);
```

After doing this, we can go ahead and find out the pixel depth of the fanciest device. When we're done with calling GetMaxDevice, we can convert our rectangle back to local coordinates for some stuff we'll have to do later.

```
deepDeviceHdl := GetMaxDevice (copyRect);
pixDepth := deepDeviceHdl^^.gdPMap^^.pixelSize;
GlobalToLocal (copyRect.topLeft);
GlobalToLocal (copyRect.botRight);
```

How deep is your love. When you call GetMaxDevice, remember that you get to pass a global rectangle that tells GetMaxDevice where to look when it tries to find the deepest device. In our example, we're converting our rectangle into global coordinates and then passing it to GetMaxDevice. Notice that you can't just call GetMaxDevice once when your program starts up and assume it will never change; the user might mess you up by choosing a new pixel depth with the Control Panel. You have to be careful that you redo the GetMaxDevice call every time the pixel depth might change. To be safe, call it right before you draw offscreen.

Now that we've got the pixel depth, we can use our famous secret formula for computing rowBytes, modified to include the new factor of pixel depth. Since there's basically one set of bits in the buffer for every bit in a pixel, we have to multiply the rowBytes value by the number of bits per pixel. Just in case you've forgotten, here's that formula again.

```
pixRowBytes := ((pixDepth*(drawRight - drawLeft - 1) div 16) + 1) * 2
```

Just for fun, let's use this formula to figure out the value of rowBytes for our example. Let's say that GetMaxDevice found that the device we're using was set for eight bits per pixel. In that case, the numbers for rowBytes would look like this:

```
PixRowBytes := ((8 * (200- 0 - 1) div 16) + 1) * 2
            = (8 * (199 div 16) + 1) * 2
            = (8 * (12 + 1) * 2)
            = 8 * 26
            = 208
```

Now we're ready to figure out the size of the buffer we'll need for our offscreen pixel map. To do this, as you'll recall from back in our black and white days, we need to figure out how many rows there are in the pixel map and then multiply that value by the rowBytes number we just got. That computation looks like this:

```
bufferSize := (drawBottom - drawTop) * pixRowBytes
```

This plain vanilla formula lets us know how much memory we need for the offscreen pixel buffer. Once again, let's fill in the real numbers from our example.

```
bufferSize := (200 - 0) * 208
= 41600
```

That's a pretty good chunk of memory for a little buffer. In fact, you've probably noticed that it's exactly eight times the amount of memory we needed for the black and white example that we did earlier. Well, gosh, that sure seems to make sense, since we've said that the image we're working with now is eight bits per pixel. Even in Color QuickDraw, some things are intuitive.

> **Living color.**   Remember that you don't really care here
> whether the user is set up for color or black and white. The im-
> portant thing is the pixel depth since that's what determines
> how much memory is needed to hold the bits.

Now it's time to get the memory for our offscreen pixel map. Just
like before, we'll get the memory by calling the Memory Manager's
NewPtr routine.

```
bufferAddr := NewPtr (bufferSize);
```

> **To err is human.**   In real life, it would be a very good idea to
> check for a Memory Manager error after this call. As your off-
> screen buffer gets bigger, the amount of memory you need grows
> very quickly for multibit images. You won't regret it if you
> check MemErr after trying to allocate memory. This has been a
> public service announcement.

If the NewPtr call succeeds, we can go ahead and set up our offscreen pixel map so that it's ready for our drawing. Setting up the
pixel map involves the same steps as preparing a bitmap: you have
to initialize the baseAddr, rowBytes, and bounds fields. However, a
pixel map is a much more complicated gizmo than a bitmap and it
has many more fields. We have to do a couple more things before we
can start drawing. First, we have to set the pixelSize field to the
depth that we want. Then, we have to adjust the rowBytes value to
tell QuickDraw that we're creating a pixel map here and not a mere
bitmap. QuickDraw decides whether a pixel map is multibit or not
by looking at the high bit of rowBytes; if it's set, it's a pixel map.
Since this is what we want, we'll have to set the high bit of
rowBytes.

The pixel map we're playing around with here is associated
with the new color grafport we created a ways back with the
OpenCPort command. When we called OpenCPort, it created all the
data structures used by the new port, including the new pixel map,
and that's the pixel map that we'll draw into.

Here's the code for setting up the values we need in our pixel map.

```
with colorPPtr^.portPixMap^^ do
    begin
        baseAddr := bufferAddr;
        rowBytes := pixRowBytes
        BitSet (@rowBytes, 0){turn on high bit}
        bounds := copyRect;
        pixelSize := pixDepth;
    end;
```

Outstanding in their fields.   There are lots of other fields in the pixel map, so why don't we have to worry about setting them up? When we called OpenCPort to initialize the new color grafport, it took care of filling in default values for all the fields of the port. The pixel map that's created takes its values from the current graphics device at the time the call is made. This means that the pixelSize value for our port will be based on whatever device was the current one, not necessarily the deepest device. So, we have to change its value by plugging our pixDepth value into it.

Setting the Table

Now it's time for another color complication. When you're using Color QuickDraw, every pixel map has a **color table** associated with it. This color table helps the system translate between the 256 colors that you have available on the screen and the palette of 16 million that are available. When we created the color grafport with OpenCPort, we got a color table that was a copy of the current device's table.

To be sure that we keep the colors we want, we have to make a new table that's a copy of the one from the deepest device. After we do that, we have to do a slight tweak to the color table, since we're taking it from a color device but we're going to use it with an off-screen pixel map. The tweak involves filling in the indices for each color value and then clearing the high bit in the transIndex field of the color table. QuickDraw uses the distinction so that it can ensure that pictures drawn in color keep the right colors with them.

First, we'll grab the handle to the color table and use the utility routine HandToHand to make a copy of it, and then we'll set up the new color table. As we return to our story, we find that the color table is another field within a pixel map. In this case, we want the one that goes with the deepest device.

```
colorTblHdl := deepDeviceHdl^^.gdPMap^^.pmTable;
err := HandToHand (Handle (colorTblHdl));
    {Makes a copy of the color table; colorTblHdl leads to it}
with colorTblHdl^^ do
    begin
        for index := 0 to ctSize do
            ctTable [index].value := index;
        BitClr (@transIndex, 0); {clear high bit}
    end;
```

Utility players.   The HandToHand function, which sounds like the name of some sort of bizarre marketing campaign, is one of a little used group of utility routines in the Macintosh ROM helpful for various general tasks with pointers and handles. As you've seen, HandToHand lets you make a new relocatable object that's a copy of an existing one. These are the others in the group: PtrToHand, which lets you copy any run of bytes into a new relocatable heap object and returns the handle to it; PtrToXHand, which puts the bytes you specify into an existing relocatable object; HandAndHand, which lets you add the bytes from one relocatable object onto the end of another; and PtrAndHand, which, given a pointer, grabs a chunk of bytes and adds them to a relocatable object. These handy calls are present in every version of the Macintosh ROMs, all the way back to the original.

Before we can start drawing, there's one more thing we have to do. We'll make the deepest device into the current device, so that when we begin drawing QuickDraw can figure out which colors we want to use. While we're at it, we'll also set the current grafport to our offscreen structure. To do this the clean way, we should preserve the old device and grafport first and then set the new ones.

```
savedDevice := GetGDevice; {preserve the graphics device}
SetGDevice (deepDeviceHdl);  {make the deep device current}
GetPort (savedPort); {preserve the grafport, too...}
SetPort (GrafPtr (colorPPtr);  {...and set the new one}
```

Finally, we're ready to start drawing into our offscreen pixel map. We can use any Color QuickDraw commands we want. We should start by setting up a background color with RGBBackColor and then use EraseRect to fill up the rectangle with that color. This will clear out any unwanted stray bits. After doing that, we can set up our own colors and use RGBBackColor and RGBForeColor to draw in them; we can use the color object-filling commands, like FillCRect, FillCRgn, and FillCPoly, to paint shapes with Color QuickDraw patterns (called **pixel patterns**); we can use SetCPixel to set individual pixels to any color; and we can do whatever other neat stuff Color QuickDraw provides.

As we draw offscreen, a buffer will be created that's a replica of the bits necessary to display our image on the screen. Since we were careful to make sure we had a buffer big enough to handle the maximum pixel depth being used and we set up a color table for our image, after we're done drawing we'll be able to copy the whole schmeer to the screen and have it show up just as we drew it offscreen. First, we'll set the graphics device and grafport back to the screen.

```
SetGDevice (savedDevice);  {Back to reality}
SetPort (savedPort);
```

When we're ready to blast everything onto the screen, here's the CopyBits call we'll need.

```
    CopyBits (BitMap(colorPPtr^.portPixMap^^),
thePort^.portBits, copyRect, copyRect, 0, nil);
```

That's it. Now, let's play "what if." What if we copy it back to a screen that's set for a different pixel depth than the one we started with? In our case, we drew assuming eight bits per pixel; what happens if we try to copy back to a screen that's only four bits per pixel? Is it the end of the world, the end of our program, or what? Well, if you don't know the answer, you're probably guessing that Quick-Draw is smart enough to help you out as much as it can, and that's exactly right.

First, it will automatically adjust to the different pixel depths. That means it will have to map every pixel into a maximum of 16 different colors, since four bits of information is enough to represent 16 different things. Since the original pixel map was created with 256 different colors available, it's likely that it will want colors that aren't available in the more restricted four-bit mode. When this happens, Color QuickDraw cleverly tries to find the closest available color to the one requested. This makes the pixel map show up as close as possible to the original.

Things to Remember

Let's compare what we had to do to use offscreen drawing with old and new QuickDraw. Unfortunately, we can't just write one unconditional set of code to handle both cases. Right up front, we have to check to see whether Color QuickDraw is running; if it is, we can then worry about dealing with multibit images.

Color QuickDraw does help out a lot, though, once that initial decision is made. After the test for the existence of Color QuickDraw, our program doesn't have to worry about a lot of other specific tests, such as how many monitors the user has, whether they're set for color or black and white, and whether they're set on one bit per pixel or more. As long as Color QuickDraw is present, we can handle all the other cases with generic code.

There's a slight fly in the ointment that shows up when you draw in color using the old model. If you try to use CopyBits on the part of your image that's in color and you use a bit map (not a pixel map) as the destination of your CopyBitsing, you'll lose the color information. This means you should use the pixel map CopyBits technique if you want your application to work right on a color Macintosh.

Remember that even if you don't allow your users to draw anything in color, you could still get color stuff in your documents. This can happen if your artistic user makes a color picture with another application and then copies and pastes it into your document. Color QuickDraw cleverly allows pasted pictures (PICT resources) to include color information, so you might be getting color stuff into your documents through the back door.

So, the decision of what to support comes back to you. The most inoffensive, middle-of-the-road choice is to do the following.

- Draw in color in the old model only. This allows you to draw in eight colors, which is plenty for most applications, and you don't have to worry about what the colors will look like when used on a Macintosh Plus or SE, since all non-white colors will show up as black.
- Check for Color QuickDraw by calling SysEnvirons and if it's there use pixel maps when CopyBitsing images that might have color in them. This will ensure that you don't lose any color information that might be in a picture or that your users may have drawn with your application.

That's the end of our offscreen color adventure. There's a lot more about the color stuff in QuickDraw in Chapter 3, "Color." You can't miss it—it's printed in black and white.

C H A P T E R   8

Resource Manager

Applying the concepts of neatness and courtesy to your applications. A discussion of what must be remembered to restore the state of a program. A look at a well-done example from a surprising source. Errors to watch for.

In this chapter, we'll talk about what you can do to make your application's environment more consistent for your users. This idea really fits only vaguely under the heading of the Resource Manager; but of all the chapters on Toolbox managers, this one is probably the best place for this discussion.

Restoring the State of Things

One of the Macintosh user interface's best features is the edict that says you should do things in a predictable, familiar way. It may not sound like a virtue to be predictable and familiar, but in software for personal computers, it really is. Most people don't want excitement and surprise when they're trying to write a report, create a database, or design a new bathroom on their computers.

Most Macintosh applications have done a pretty good job of following this rule. In general, things in Macintosh software behave as you would expect them to. Buttons that say "Cancel" usually cancel things; clicking on arrows that point down usually makes something move down; you can operate on something by pointing at it and clicking.

When a user works on an application and then quits, there are lots of settings that the user has made, either consciously or unconsciously (I hope there aren't too many unconscious users out there). Many of these settings automatically become part of the document. Every word processor remembers the settings of margins and tabs for paragraphs, every spreadsheet keeps track of things like column widths and cell entries, and every database remembers the structure and the records that you've entered, of course.

Lots of these applications aren't as friendly as they could be. A really great application ought to keep track of other important settings for its users. When you're using a spreadsheet program, you might have several windows open at once. You may have taken the time to carefully position each one on the screen so that the right information from the different windows is showing in just the right places. Wouldn't it be nice if the spreadsheet program would remember which windows you had open, where you had them, and how big the windows were? Yep, it sure would, and a few of the really cool programs do just that. For example, when you quit Excel, it creates a document called Resume Excel that remembers all this good stuff. If you double-click this document to restart the program, all your windows will come back just as you left them—the way your bedroom looked after your first vacation from college and your parents hadn't cleaned it up yet. If you don't want your previous configuration to come back but want to start with a clean desktop instead, you can just double-click the application instead.

To implement this fun feature, you have to be foresighted enough to save the global state of everything when the user quits your application. Usually, you can do this in a special resource file, which many bright applications like Excel and MORE call the Resume icon. This icon represents a file containing the information the application needs to recreate the world as the user left it.

There are some potential problems that can arise with this scheme. Let's say the user quits the application, then throws away one of the documents that was left open in the application. Then, the poor unsuspecting user double-clicks the Resume icon, causing the application to start up again and making it go looking for a file that doesn't exist any more. What happens?

Well, the application is in complete control of what goes on here, so it can be just as friendly or as nasty as it chooses. When the user restarts the application with the Resume icon, the application is going to try to find all the documents that were open the last time the user quit the application. If one has been thrown away, the application will get an unwanted surprise when it tries to open the ex-file: a "file not found" error code.

At this point, depending on how helpful and clever the application is, three things can happen.

1. After finding out that the file it wants isn't there, the application can just continue starting up without being able to open that document and try to do everything else necessary to restore things to the way they were when the user quit.
2. The application can tell the user that it can't find a file and give the user the option of looking for the file on another disk or in another directory. The easiest way to do this is to call SFGet-File, which will give the user a chance to pick out the file in a very familiar way. This is useful if the file that the application wants to find has been stuck into a different folder by the clever user. Of course, if the file has been thrown away, there's really nothing much to do.
3. The really brain-damaged thing to do is to forget to check the error result when trying to open the files. This can really lead to disaster as the application plows blindly ahead, acting as if the file were open and possibly trashing memory along the way. This would be bad.

Saving Local Information

It's very important to save global information, such as the names of documents and the sizes and locations of windows, when the user quits an application. It's just as important to keep track of local stuff that's specific to each window so that it can be restored when the user wants to get things going again. Local information varies depending on the type of application. If your application is an outline processor, the state information that's saved should tell which headlines' topics were expanded and which were collapsed and should also include remembering which topic was selected when the user quit.

The current selection, or position of the cursor, is a very nice thing to keep track of for each window. You should also save something that tells you the place the user was looking at in the document. Remembering the location of the selection and scrolling right to it really makes it convenient when you go back to working on a document. Users take time to carefully position and resize windows just as they want them (after all, it's a *personal* computer). Restoring the window just exactly as the user left it, including showing the right position and selecting the right thing, makes it easy for your users to get comfortable and start back up in a hurry.

Role model. One of the best models for doing this is the MPW Shell. When you edit a document in MPW and save it, MPW is very careful to save everything that will affect the state of the document. This guarantees that the document will come up just as it was when the user left it.

How to Save the Information

The usual way of saving the state of things when the user quits the application is to create (or modify, if it exists) a file that's often called Resume something (like Resume MORE or Resume Excel). This is the file that should contain all the global state information, like the names of the open documents and any default kinds of settings the user has made that affect the whole application rather than a particular document.

It might seem like a clever idea to save the state information in the application resource file itself, rather than to create a new file just for the state information. One reason you shouldn't do this is that the application might be a **multi-launch** version living on a file server, which means that several users depend on the same copy. If you change the one and only copy of the application, you'll really confuse people as they wind up opening someone else's documents. Another reason not to change resource files on a file server is that resource maps aren't designed to be shared by multiple users. It's a good idea to let the user choose whether stuff from a previous session should be used or not, and creating the Resume icon is a good way to do that.

> **Legal department.** In case you're interested, people may legally use an application from a file server if the license agreement that came with the software expressly permits the user to share the application on a network. Many applications now have a special site license agreement that allows a group of users to pay a set fee for a certain number of users. Other programs, like 4th Dimension, provide a special runtime version of the application, which inexpensively allows lots of users to work with data.

To save the state information, you should create a resource with space for everything you need to save. Usually, all you need to save for global information are the names of the open documents listed in the correct order (or at least remembering which window is frontmost). For each document, you need to save enough information to find it later and open it. One way to do this would be to save the full pathname of the file, which includes all the directory information needed to find the document. It would look something like this:

```
Music:CD:Mister Heartbreak:Sharkey's Day
```

As you probably know, full Macintosh pathnames start with a volume name and include colons to indicate each level of directory that we pass through; so, in this pathname, "Music" is a volume name, "CD" and "Mister Heartbreak" are directory (folder) names, and "Sharkey's Day" is the file's name at last.

There's actually a better way to keep track of files than to record the full pathname. In the Macintosh's legendary Hierarchical Filing System (HFS), every directory has a number that uniquely identifies it. This number, called the directory ID, never changes once it's attached to a directory. The directory ID (also called a dir-ID) sticks with the directory forever (this has been proven), not just until the system is restarted. The directory ID follows the folder around even if it's moved into other folders or brought out to the root level of the disk, or even if the directory's name is changed. This makes it a very reliable way to find a file's directory.

To fully specify the file, you'll also have to save information about the disk it's on. When you have an application running, the best way to refer to a volume is by using a volume reference number. Unfortunately, the vRefNum doesn't stick with a volume once it's been unmounted from the system, so it's pointless to store the vRef-Num and expect it to be valid the next time you want to open a file from that volume.

The only way you can save information about a volume and use it to find the file the next time is to store the volume name along with the dirID and the file name. Then, when you have to reopen the file, you can use the combination of the volume name, the dirID, and the file name.

It's interesting to note that the user can screw things up in various ways. Of all this information, only the dirID is guaranteed to stay the same after the user quits the program. If the user does anything tricky, such as renaming the file or the volume or sticking the file in a different folder, the program won't be able to find it when it comes looking. If this happens, the application's best recourse is to put up an SFGetFile dialog asking the user where the file went.

Usually, a lot more state information needs to be saved about each open document. This includes things like the size and location of the window, the position of the selection or insertion point, and the part of the document that the user was looking at. Although there's more stuff to be saved with each document than there was with for the whole application, the general technique is the same. Figure out everything you need to save for each window, then create a resource with fields for everything and store one of those resources in the document's resource fork.

A good example of the state information to save for a document is what the MPW Shell (version 2.0) keeps track of for each of its documents. Every document created or edited by the MPW Shell has a resource of type MPSR with ID 1005 (don't ask me), which contains the state-saving information for the window. Taking a peek at what MPW keeps in this resource will give us an idea of what we have to save with documents created by all kinds of applications.

Documents created by the MPW Shell use one font and font size for the whole window. This information is stored in the MPSR by MPW. It's valuable to note that the font is stored by its name, not its number. This is because the font number can be a fleeting thing. As fonts are removed and installed, Font/DA Mover will sometimes renumber them to avoid conflicts in the system file. Font names, on the other hand, stay very constant. They never change unless users explicitly change them, and that rarely happens. This makes it safer to keep track of the font's name than its number to ensure the right thing for the user.

The MPW Shell also has a global tab setting for an entire window. It keeps this setting as part of the MPSR resource, too. This is very straightforward: an integer in the MPSR tells how many spaces apart the tabs are set for.

We said that real friendly applications remember the size and location of windows when they're closed. MPW Shell does a good job of this. There are actually two different rectangles to remember, since MPW like most Macintosh applications allows the user to click in the zoom box to grow and shrink the window. The MPSR includes space for two rectangles: one of them gives the size and location of the window when it's zoomed out and the other tells about it when it's zoomed in.

Other fields in the MPSR resource record information about the user's text selection in the window. The values of the starting and ending locations of the selection are stuffed into the MPSR. If there's no selection and just an insertion point, these two values are the same, but in that case they tell where the insertion point belongs, just like TextEdit does.

The next piece of information recorded by the MPW Shell in every document's MPSR resource is the position in the file the user was looking at when the window was closed. This is called the document's display position. Note that this doesn't necessarily have anything to do with the selected text in the document. A user can easily have been looking at a part of the document that's different from the part that contains the selection.

What's the best way to record the display position? You can keep track of the setting of the scroll bar, as MPW does. This lets you set the scroll bar when you open the window and position the text at the right place. If you have both horizontal and vertical scroll bars, this technique will allow you to set the document to exactly the same place it was when the window was closed.

When you're editing a document with the MPW Shell, you can choose to turn automatic indenting on or off, depending on what kinds of things you're editing and whether you like auto-indenting or not. This setting is recorded for each window in its MPSR resource. In the same way, every window can be set to display characters that are normally invisible, like carriage returns and spaces. The window's setting for this feature is also kept in the MPSR.

By saving all this information in the MPSR for each document, the MPW Shell can restore the environment of every window to just the state it was in when it was last closed. This really makes it easy and convenient for the user to remember what was going on the last time the window was open. When you make the document open up right where it was left, you're really doing something nice for your users.

When Something Goes Wrong

You can run into some problems when you're trying to restore the state of things as they were. The problems usually arise from changes in the environment that occur between the last time the user worked on a document and the next time, when everything is supposed to be restored just as it was.

We already discussed what to do in the most common situation of this kind, when a document that's supposed to be opened isn't where it should be. Other things can happen, and you should be prepared for them so that your application doesn't get so confused that it crashes and breaks your user's document.

A simple way to make sure this doesn't happen is to validate the steps you're taking to restore your environment before assuming that everything is working OK. Before you assume that you've opened a document and you're going to do something to it, make sure you were really able to open it by checking the error code returned by PBOpen.

Specifically, when you're trying to restore a window to the way it was, you should realize that someone may have used a different application to modify the document after the last time your application saw it. Of course, the other application isn't as clever as yours, and so it doesn't know how to maintain your carefully designed resource that remembers the document's state. In fact, a heavy-handed hacker playing around with ResEdit could have messed up the saved state.

As you're reopening the window and setting it up according to the saved data, make sure that every setting is reasonable. It it's not, you should set it to some safe default value. For example, be sure that you don't set the window size and position to some nonsensical value. If the rectangles saved for the window seem to be real bizarre, set them back to a nice default value. If you keep a global tab setting, as the MPW Shell does, make sure it's not a ridiculous value (say, anything greater than 50). If it is, reset it to something reasonable.

Another example of a possible problem that you should handle elegantly involves the font name. Let's say the user saves a document in an editor like MPW Shell, which displays an entire window in the same font. Then, at some later date, the user decides that font is just too ugly to be believed and takes it out of the system with Font/DA Mover. What will happen?

You should be prepared for the chance that the font you're looking for may not be there any more. If you try to draw some text in a specific font, you can check first to see whether the font is there by calling GetResource to get a handle to the font. If GetResource returns nil, you'll know it couldn't find the font you want.

If that happens, you should pick another font to use. Obviously, you should try to be sure it's a font that's really there, not a fly-by-night font like the one you've already looked for. There are a couple of things you can do here. You can use font number 0, which is the system font. If any font at all is available, the system font will be, so this is a safe bet. You can also use font 1, which represents the application font (usually Geneva). In extremely tight memory situations, there's a chance the application font won't be around, but this is pretty rare.

You should be aware of some other things that won't cause crashes but will drive your users crazy. One of them is especially important in today's world of lots of different Macintoshes with lots of different-sized screens. You might be using your Macintosh II with 19-inch monitor (we've all got those, right?) to work on a document. Then, you pass a copy of the document along to your poor coworker who uses a good old Macintosh Plus with the classic 9-inch display and your document is nowhere to be found. Why? The application you're using has thoughtfully placed the window exactly where it was when you last had it open; but now, it's about 500 pixels too far south to be seen.

This scenario can even happen to a single Macintosh II user who reconfigures the monitor settings. If the user has two monitors arranged with the main one on the right, puts a window over there, and then rearranges the monitors to put the main screen on the left, the application will put the window out into never-never land if it just sticks it back where it was on the desktop.

The smart way to avoid this situation is to make sure the window is located on the visible part of the desktop before drawing it. One way to do this is to check the window's rectangle against the global variable called GrayRgn, which contains the region that forms the desktop. You can use QuickDraw's RectInRgn call to see whether the window's rectangle is anywhere on the desktop. If RectInRgn returns false, you'll know the window won't show up anywhere on the desktop. If this happens, you should put the window in some default location that you're sure of. Since the upper left corner of the main screen always starts at 0,0, you can use a location that's an offset from that point.

Most of the discussion in this section has been based on the example of a text editor, such as the MPW Shell. A lot of the stuff that we talked about saving, such as the window's location, applies to almost every application, so you'll be able to use it directly. Other things will be specific to your kind of program.

For example, if you're writing a drawing program and each window can optionally have a tool palette and a design palette associated with it, you'll have to keep track of whether these palettes were open when the user saved the document. If you're creating an application that allows split views in a window, your state-saving information should tell about where the window was split and what was going on in each part of the split.

Things to Remember

A great way to win fans for your application is to try to restore the way things were when the user last had each document open. To do this, you'll have to store the state information. A good technique for storing state information is to create a special resource file named Resume followed by your application's name (like Resume Tango). In this resource file, you should put enough information to set things up the way they were when the user quit the application. Usually, you'll need the names of any open documents. To open the documents, you'll have to know the names of the disks they're on as well as the directory IDs of the folders they're in.

To keep track of information that's specific for each document, you should make a saved state resource and stick it in each document. This resource will have settings that affect a whole document, like the size and location of the window, the position of the insertion point or selection, and the display location. You'll also store other stuff in this resource that your application needs to reopen the window and make it just like it was.

While you're busy restoring the world for the user, you should watch out for problems that can occur because some ResEdit junkie was messing around with the documents or because something in the system (like the fonts or the screen configuration) has changed since the last time the document was opened. To be very friendly, you should validate all the information in the saved-state resource before you rely on it to be true. If anything turns out to be unusable, you should substitute a default value.

With just a little thought and some code, you can add this feature as a nice little touch that will really please your users. Putting things back the way you found them is not just good user interface practice. It's the polite thing to do.

C H A P T E R 9

Window Manager

The window population explosion and how you can help. Nice ways of dealing with many windows. Helping your users out by arranging the windows in an orderly fashion. Tiling and stacking. How to browse through the windows with just a keystroke. Multiple screens and what they will do to you.

Managing Your Windows

Among the neatest tricks of the Macintosh is that almost no applications really draw on the screen; instead, they draw into windows. This magic difference is the reason it's really quite easy to change the dimensions of the screen from the classic 512 by 342 to something like 1024 by 1024 and have most applications automatically take advantage of the new real estate. They weren't really limited to the small screen in the first place; they were drawing into QuickDraw's massive imaginary rectangle, with its 65,000 dots on each side. From their point of view, even a million pixels is just a drop in the bit bucket.

Many of the first applications were stuck to a single application window at a time. But as the state of the art evolved and customers got more demanding, folks figured out that it was possible to let the user have more than one document open at a time, each one with its own window. Eventually, Apple made things even more advanced by teaching the Finder to start up other applications without having them take over the computer.

As applications evolved into allowing lots of windows to be open at once, users started to have more trouble figuring out where their windows were when they needed them, especially on the 9-inch classic Macintosh screen. When you've got five or six windows open at the same time, it's easy to lose track of the one you want or to be unable to click on it because it's completely covered up.

In the Macintosh world, when necessity cries out, the invention is born. Many applications started including a menu that listed all the available windows on the screen at any time; when the list of windows changed, so did the menu. This gave users a way of bringing a window to the front without having to seek it out and click on it. Instead, a user could just find the right window title by pulling down a menu and perusing the list. There's even a desk accessory that looks through the window list and builds a menu with a list of all their names and then brings one to the front if the user chooses from the menu.

Freedom of choice.   It's important to note here that letting the user bring a window to the front by using a menu is a sometimes great alternative to just clicking on the window. It works with the Macintosh interface because it could never replace the more obvious and intuitive method of seeing what you want and clicking on it. Once again, you're giving a more experienced user an additional tool to make life easier.

Once you've got a menu built that lists all your application's windows, the biggest trick is keeping it up to date as your user changes things. This is actually pretty easy to do. Every time you open a new window, you can call InsMenuItem to add the new window's name to your menu. When you close a window, you can call (surprise!) DelMenuItem to take it out of the list. You should also use CheckItem to put a check mark next to the window that's currently at the top.

Sometimes you'll have windows that you don't want to appear in the menu's list. This is true, for example, if you have any invisible windows, special "ghost" windows that are never supposed to be selected, or other funky windows the user shouldn't select. Make sure you leave these out of your menu when you're building or updating the list.

The InsMenuItem and DelMenuItem calls are not available in the 64K ROM included in the Macintosh 128K and 512K (that's ROM version $69) or any of the 64K ROM images on the Macintosh XL. If it's vital that your application work on old ROM machines, you'll have to use an alternative technique to mess around with your window-list menu. Here are two suggestions.

1. Completely rebuild the menu every time you open a new window or close an existing one. You can do this by using Delete-Menu to remove the old menu, AppendMenu to construct the new one, then calling InsertMenu to stick it into the menu list. To learn the names of all the windows, you can either maintain a list yourself as part of your global data or you can waltz through the window list by using the nextWindow field of each window record. For each window, this field points at the next window behind it. If you start with the frontmost window, you can see all of them; the last one's nextWindow field is nil.

2. For the thrill-seekers: dive directly into the menu's data structure in memory, which is well-documented in *Inside Macintosh* Volume I, and modify the menu's data directly. You'll find a handle to the current menu list at location $A1C. The menu list consists mainly of handles to the menus. With some tricky munging, you can modify the menu directly in memory; this is the Macintosh equivalent of open-heart surgery, so be careful. If you're sure to do this only on computers with ROM version $69, you'll be OK, since the format of a menu is frozen forever on those machines. There's a small chance that Apple will someday release a new version of the system file that patches in a new Menu Manager in RAM for these old systems, but it's extreeeemely unlikely.

Now that we've built a menu listing all your application's open windows, we can do something else to make the application even easier to use. Sometimes, a user knows the contents but not the name of the window that should be brought to the front. One clever way to help with this dilemma is through a mechanism that quickly zips through the open windows, bringing each to the front, one by one.

A clever way to do this is to attach a Command-key equivalent to the window that's all the way in the back. Just for discussion, let's say it's Command-E. When the window list changes, you can remove the Command-E from its old item and add it to the new one. By pulling down the menu, the user can see which window will be selected with Command-E, and your documentation can say that Command-E always selects the next window. Power users will love this. An even more clever idea might be to use Command-down-arrow to move through the windows from front to back, and Command-up-arrow to take the backmost window and stick it in front.

Another trick for quickly selecting a window is to tie a Command key to every window in the list. This only makes sense if the Command keys follow some logical progression. One idea is to make the first one Command-1, the second Command-2, and so on for up to nine open windows, which should be enough to satisfy most folks.

Segregation. One decision you'll have to make when constructing your list of menus in a window is whether to include windows that belong to desk accessories. Probably the best decision is to leave them out, for at least two good reasons. First, if a user wants to make a desk accessory window frontmost, selecting the accessory's name in the Apple menu will do the trick very nicely, so there's no need to duplicate this. Second, most users think of the windows that make up their documents as separate from the desk accessories. Also, if you're running a multitasking version of the system, desk accessory windows may not even appear in your application's window list.

More Fun with Windows

There are a few other nice tricks you can provide to help users make their multi-windowed lives easier. One of these, making a window fill the screen, is supported by the Macintosh Toolbox in all versions except the first (the 64K ROM, version $69).

The standard way to deal with this window zooming, as it's called, is to draw your windows with a variation code of 8 on the standard window definition function. This variation will draw the familiar zoom box in the upper right corner of your window. You can then use the TrackBox call to watch the user's mousing after a click in the zoom box and ZoomWindow to make the window full-screen or shrink it back down if it's been zoomed already.

Don't forget that users like to be able to accomplish binary kinds of things with the keyboard as well as the mouse and would appreciate having a keyboard way to zoom the windows as well. Window zooming is an interesting situation: most applications not only don't have a keystroke for doing it, they don't have a menu item for it either. It seems like a good idea to have a menu item with a Command-key equivalent for window zooming, both for keyboard fans who want an alternative to clicking the zoom box and for raw beginners who may not even know about the zoom box but might figure out how to zoom if they saw the item in a menu.

There are other important window-twiddling functions that an application should have that aren't as nicely supported by the Toolbox as window zooming. A nice thing to do for users with lots of windows is to **stack** the windows for them; that is, show them all on the screen like a fan of cards, with each window spaced just down and to the right of its neighbor, as in Figure 9-1. This tool makes browsing through the windows more convenient.

To stack the windows, you'll have to resize and reposition them. They're all going to wind up being the same size, so the first thing to do is to figure out what size that will be. A good rule is to take the size of the screen and subtract 100 pixels from the width and the height. You also have to decide how far apart to space the windows as you shuffle them on the screen. Try moving them down and over by 20 pixels and see what you think, then adjust it to whatever you like.

You should definitely not try to stack any windows that belong to desk accessories. Most of them aren't resizeable. You will cause them serious brain damage if you try to mess with them.

To actually move and shrink or grow the windows, you can call MoveWindow and SizeWindow. To avoid messy redrawing, you can make each window invisible by calling ShowHide, move and resize it, and then bring it back to visibility with another call to ShowHide. You should increment variables that hold the coordinates of the window's upper left corner and pass them to Move-

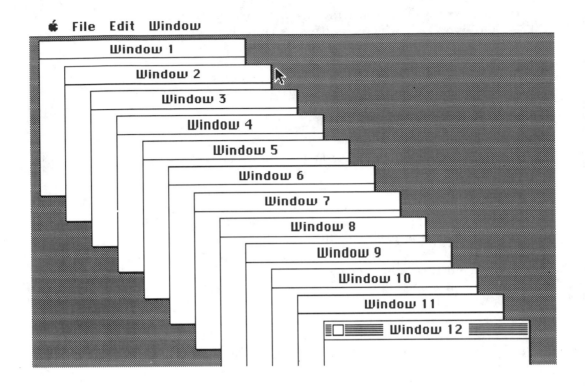

Figure 9-1. Stacked windows

Window. Since you want all the windows to be the same size, you don't have to worry about recalculating the size for each window.

There are a couple of slightly different ways of handling a window-stacking algorithm. One variation is to leave the windows sized as they are and just move their top left corners into a stacked alignment, as in Figure 9-2. This makes things faster and easier, since you don't have to call SizeWindow or bother making the windows invisible.

Another elegant variation is to resize each window so that it extends just to the bottom of the screen.

Which one of these styles should you use? It's not really that big a deal, after all. If you were really fanatical about it, the right thing to do would be to implement them all and then allow the user to switch between them with some sort of "preferences" or customizing technique; but nobody is really that fanatical, right?

Sometimes, a user who has a lot of windows open wants to see them all, as with stacking. Instead of piling them on top of each other with just the title bars showing, though, it might be more in-

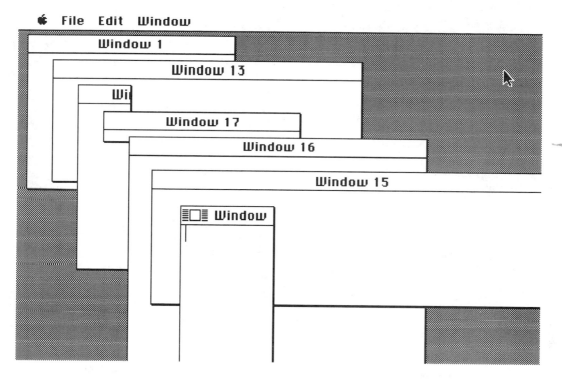

Figure 9-2. Stacked windows, different sizes

teresting to resize them all so they're the same size and share the screen real estate equally. This is usually called **tiling** the windows, and all the really chic applications do it.

Tiling involves trying to evenly divide the screen space among the open windows. An example of four tiled windows is shown in Figure 9-3. Although this may sound easy at first, there are some pretty interesting decisions to make in some cases. Let's consider a few examples and try to build an algorithm for tiling the windows.

Let's say the user has two windows open and chooses to tile them. What should you do? The idea of tiling is to the windows in the most usable configuration with no overlap and with each window the same size. With two windows you have two choices: you can either put the windows side by side or one above the other. Macintosh users are used to seeing most of the width of their documents but not the height; having each window full height and half width probably wouldn't be the most comfortable configuration for them. A better idea is to put them one above the other.

What if the user has a portrait-style screen like the Radius FPD? This screen is much taller than it is wide, but horizontal stacking still seems like a better thing to do. The added screen space of

✎ File Edit Window

Window 19	**▤□▦▦▦▦▦ Window 21 ▦▦▦▦**
Nice Up Dancee, Natural Beauty.	Beat Crazy
	One to One
Do the Dance, Barrington Levy	In Every Dream Home (A
Reggae Ska, Michigan & Smiley	Nightmare)
Springheel Skanking, Don	The Evil Eye
Carlos	Mad at You
Teach Me to Dance, Wayne	Crime Don't Pay
Smith	Someone Up There

Window 20	**Window 22**
I. G. Y.	Alabama Getaway
Green Flower Street	Far From Me
Ruby Baby	Althea
Maxine	Feel Like a Stranger
New Frontier	Lost Sailor
The Nightfly	Saint of Circumstance
The Goodbye Look	Antwerp's Placebo (The
Walk Between Raindrops	Plumber)

Figure 9-3. Four windows tiled

the Radius monitor allows each window to be more reasonably sized. You might want to have your tiling algorithm put two windows side by side if you find a really huge monitor that has room for two full-width pages, but that's up to you and the demands of your users.

Things get a lot more interesting when you have three or more windows to tile. With three, the best course of action is the same as with two: stack them above each other. A third of the screen is really too little to devote to a document's width in most cases.

Stay away from the DA. Just as with stacking, you should not try to do your tiling thing on desk accessory windows. Most of them get very disagreeable if you try to resize them. It's a good idea just to leave them alone and tile your own windows.

As you have to tile more and more windows, you'll reach a point at which it's no longer practical to pile them on top of each other with each one occupying the full width of the screen. On a classic

Macintosh screen, you get about 320 pixels for windows after subtracting space for the menu bar. This means that trying to divide the
screen's vertical space evenly among, say, four windows would allow
just 80 pixels for each.

A mere 80 vertical pixels per window isn't very much when you
figure that the title bar and the bottom scroll bar, if there is one,
take up more than a third of that space. When you get to five windows, the resulting space of 64 pixels per window is downright ludi-
crous (see Figure 9-4). It seems like we should do something else here.

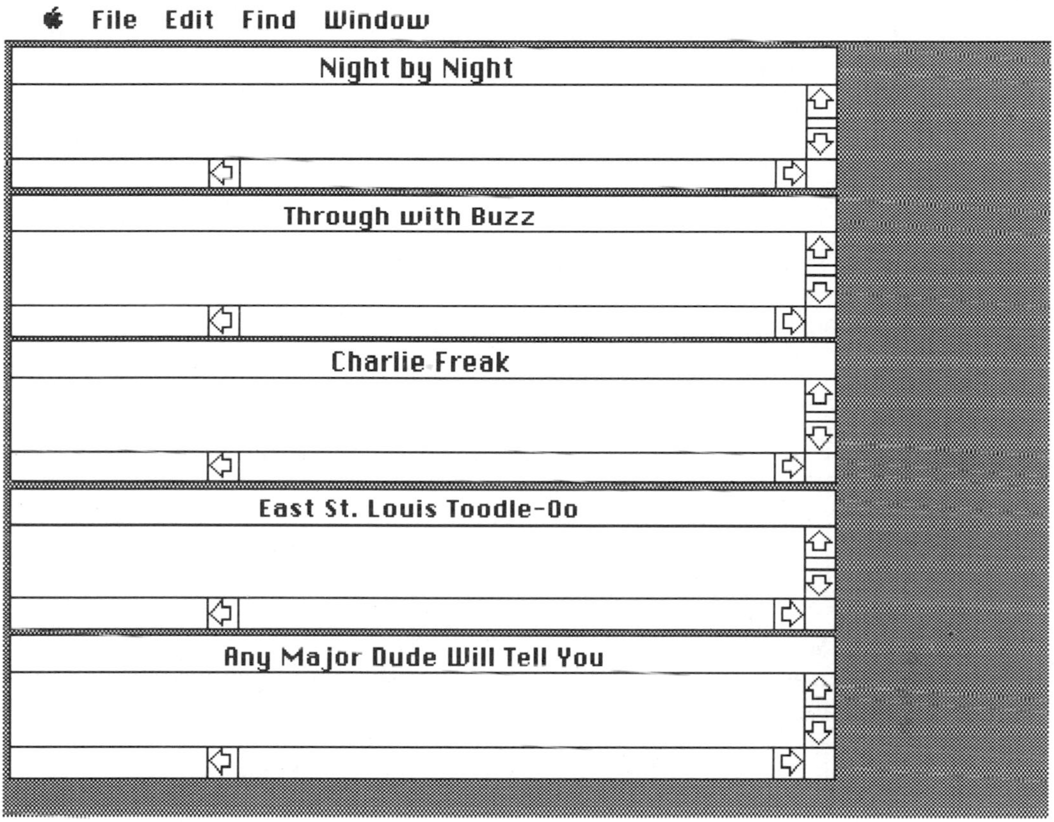

Figure 9-4. Five windows stacked vertically

The obvious change to make is to stop allowing windows to take
up the full width of the screen, and to start making them half-
width instead, as we saw back in Figure 9-3. For our algorithm, we
need to specify when to switch over from full width to half width.
We should do this whenever the resulting full-width windows
would come out sized smaller than some minimum we've decided on,
like 100 pixels.

Fine tuning. The 100-pixel minimum really indicates the space between the tops of adjacent windows, rather than the space in them. Most windows have a title bar that's 16 pixels high, so this leaves only 84 pixels for the window itself, including a scroll bar that may be across the bottom. Remember that when you call MoveWindow, you're positioning the upper left corner of the window's portRect, which does not include the title bar, and when you call SizeWindow to resize it, the new height again excludes the title bar. When you figure the total number of pixels that the window uses up, though, you have to remember to add in that extra 16 pixels.

So, the decision really depends on the vertical size of the screen: if it's a big screen with 900 vertical pixels available and we decide that the minimum horizontal size is 100, we can have (get your calculators out here) nine windows at full width before we have to start worrying about splitting the horizontal dimension. For a more common 342-pixel monitor, we should switch to the new style when there are four windows to tile.

As soon as we figure we have enough windows to start laying them side by side as well as piling them up, we can start dividing up the screen space. Figuring the horizontal dimension (also known in English as the "width") is easy: it's just half the width of the screen. Computing the vertical dimension (colloquially called the "height") is a little trickier, and we'll discuss it now.

Consider, for example, the case of five windows. We can't make them full-width windows because each one would be too small to do anything interesting. So we'll put them side by side and divide the vertical space equally. There's a problem, though, if we divide all the windows into two equal-width columns: two into five doesn't go, as they used to say in third grade. We can't have two equal columns of windows when there are an odd number of windows.

There are two possibilities here: the consistent and the convenient. To be consistent, all tiled windows should be the same size. So, following this logic, we should divide the screen into equal chunks using the number of windows; if there's an odd number of windows, we should divide by the number of windows plus one. For example, with five windows, each of them should occupy one sixth of the screen. The remaining sixth will just be blank, which seems kind of a waste but does follow the rule of tiling that all windows be the same size. This is also the easiest technique to code, since all windows get resized to exactly the same dimensions.

If you just hate to see a chunk of the screen unused and you don't mind straying from absolute consistency, which demands that all the windows be the same size, you can do something a little different. The easiest way to use the whole screen is to choose one window, such as the first or last one you resize and move, to take up the full width of the screen. This alternative is shown in Figure 9-5.

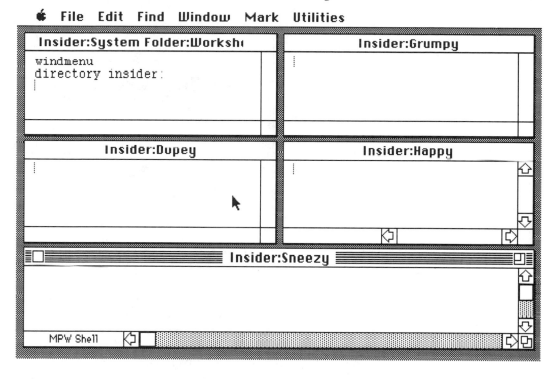

Figure 9-5. Five windows, one full width

Another idea is to size the windows in each column independently, as shown in Figure 9-6. This spreads the wealth of extra screen space evenly among all the windows in one column. To figure the sizes for these windows, compute their heights by dividing the number of vertical pixels by the number of windows in each column. The widths of all the windows are still the same, of course. Before you bother using either of these tricks, though, remember they'll only come into play when the user has five or more windows open. In such a case, most folks would probably zoom up each little window before working on it anyway.

Now we've extended our algorithm to include up to twice as many windows as before, by reducing each one to half the width of the screen. As those of you who are thinking ahead may have al-

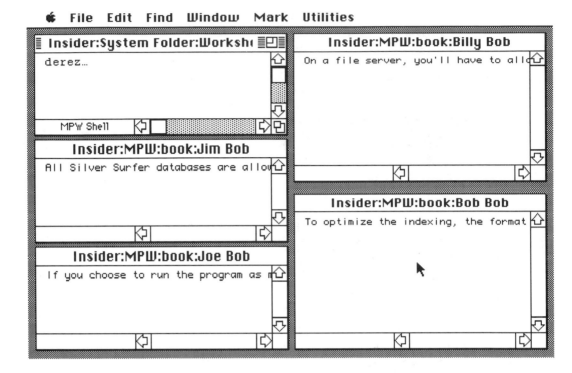

Figure 9-6. Five windows tiled

ready realized, we'll run out of space for this technique too, as soon as we get enough windows. We've said that 100 pixels was the minimum height for each window, so there's room for three windows in each column on our plain vanilla 342-pixel-high screen.

We can obviously accomodate six windows with the scheme, but what should be do when we get to seven? One idea is to add another column to the screen, splitting it into thirds. This would mean three windows in one column and two in each of the others, with each window one third as wide as the screen (Figure 9-7). Earlier we said that a third of the width wasn't enough to work on a document, but with so many windows as in this case, there isn't much else we can do. Even if tiling the windows makes them too small to work with conveniently, it does allow the user to quickly zoom one and have it fill the whole screen.

One other option you may prefer is to continue with two columns of windows, even if each window has to go below the 100-pixel minimum. This is based on the rather arbitrary idea that your users may prefer to avoid anything skinnier than half-width windows, even if it means making them very short. What you wind up doing also depends on your application. It may be that your windows may

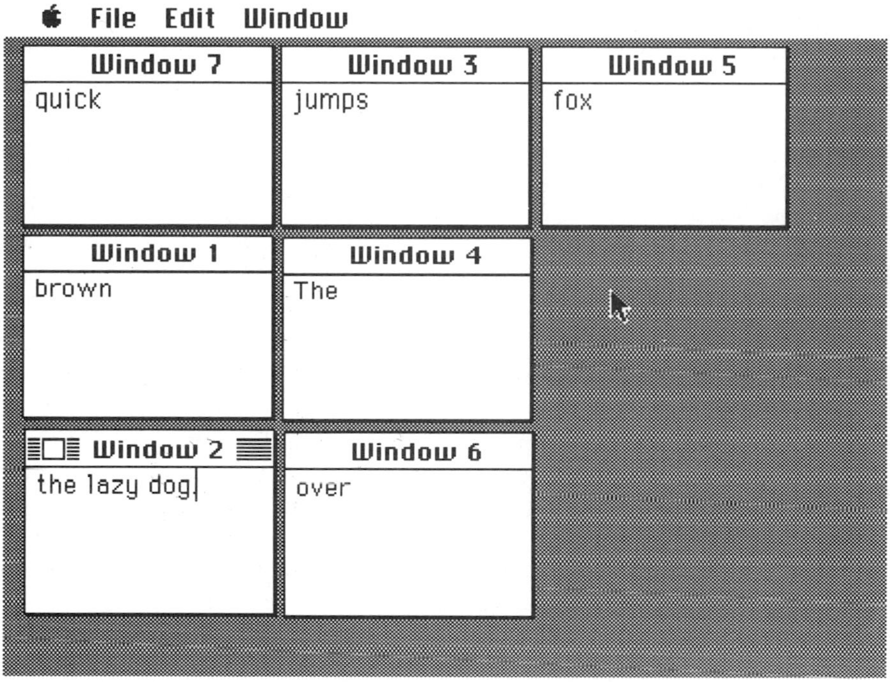

 File   Edit   Window

Window 7	**Window 3**	**Window 5**
quick	jumps	fox

Window 1	**Window 4**
brown	The

Window 2	**Window 6**
the lazy dog|	over

Figure 9-7. Seven equal-size windows

actually show something useful when they're very narrow but may have to be, say, at least 150 pixels high to be meaningful.

If you choose to keep adding another column whenever the windows get shorter than 100 pixels high, you'll be able to put nine windows into three columns on a classic Macintosh screen, then 12 into four columns, which is probably more windows than people should open at once. Just to be complete, though, we should also set a minimum window width that we'll tolerate. When we hit that limit, we should probably just quit trying to tile. For this example, let's use 100 pixels as the minimum allowable width, just as we did for height.

Since the standard Macintosh screen has 512 pixels across and 342 down, we can get up to the fairly ridiculous figure of 15 windows, each one at least 100 pixels on each side, tiled on the screen at once. Of course, with a larger screen, our tiling algorithm would take us down a slightly different path: with 640 by 1024 resolution, we could pile up 10 windows before we had to resort to splitting into columns; then, we could get up to six columns of 10 windows each, which should be enough for even the most demanding fan of spreadsheets, word processing, or computerized knitting applications.

The Tiling Algorithm

Now that we've discussed what will happen when tiling our windows all the way up to running out of screen space, we can summarize what we want to do when the user wants the windows tiled. Each step is shown in words and in code.

1. Determine the available screen space. You can do this by starting with screenBits.bounds, then subtracting the size of the menu bar, which can be found in the global called MBarHeight at location $BAA. If you're not comfortable using low-memory globals, it's a reasonably safe assumption that the menu bar will never be taller than 40 pixels. It's usually only 20 pixels high, but that can change if you're using a non-Roman script like Chinese or Japanese, or something special like a big screen display that causes the menu titles to be drawn in a larger point size. For both the height and the width, you should also subtract a small number of pixels that will give you a tiny buffer against the edge of the screen. A good value to try for this is four pixels each at the top (under the menu bar), bottom, left, and right, which means we subtract eight pixels from both the available height and width. You can compute it like this.

```
availHeight := screenBits.bounds.bottom - 8 - MBarHeight;
availWidth := screenBits.bounds.right - 8;
```

2. Determine the number of windows you're going to tile. The easiest way to do this is to maintain a global count in your application but you can also discover it by going through the window list using the nextWindow field of the window record. We'll call this variable numWindows.

```
numWindows := {However many windows you've got};
```

3. Decide on your minimum acceptable window height and width. We've been using 100 pixels for each dimension, but you might want to adjust that.

```
minHeight := {Your minimum acceptable window height};
minWidth := {The minimum window width};
```

4. Divide the height of the screen by the minimum acceptable height of a window (round down or use integer division, like the "div" operator). The result is the maximum number of spaces for

windows vertically on the screen. We'll keep it in a variable
called maxWindsCol.

```
maxWindsCol := availHeight div minHeight;
```

5. Can we keep each window the full width of the screen? Divide
    the available height by the number of windows and compare the
    result to the minimum height. If the result is too small, we need
    multiple columns.

```
if minHeight > (availHeight div numWindows)
then {we need more than one column}
else {hooray, we can fit everything in one column};
```

6. If everything will fit into one column, things are cool. We know
    that each window will be the available width of the screen. To
    compute the height of each window, we can just divide the
    available height by the number of windows and then subtract 16
    pixels to allow for each window's title bar. Once we've computed
    these numbers, if we're only going to need one column we can skip
    the next two steps and go on to the moving and resizing stuff.

```
newWidth  := availWidth;
newHeight := (availHeight div numWindows) - 16;
```

7. If we need multiple columns, we have to figure out how many.
    We can do that by dividing the number of windows that will fit
    in a column into the number of windows, then rounding up any
    partial columns, which we can check with a remainder function,
    like Pascal's mod. At this time we should also figure out how
    many windows (or blank window-sized spaces) will actually ap-
    pear in each column. This will usually be the same as max-
    WindsCol, but it could be smaller if there aren't very many win-
    dows.

```
numCols := numWindows div maxWindsCol;
if (numWindows mod maxWindsCol) <> 0 {round up # of cols}
then numCols := numCols + 1;
numWindsCol := numWindows div numCols;
if (numWindows mod numCols) <> 0 {round this up too}
then numWindsCol := numWindsCol + 1;
```

8. Compute the size of our windows. If we're going to make them all
    the same size, we can figure out what that size will be using the
    values we got earlier for spaces and numCols. To find out the

width of each window, divide the available screen width by numCols; to get the height of a window, divide the available height by the value we calculated for the number of windows in a column and then subtract 16 for the title bar of each window.

```
newWidth  := availWidth div numCols;
newHeight := (availHeight div numWindsCol) - 16;
```

9. Now we're ready to move and resize all the windows. First, we need to initialize some variables. We'll need a pointer to the frontmost window, which we can easily get from the Window Manager by calling FrontWindow. We should also initialize a variable of type Point that will serve as the destination for the windows we're moving. It should start out as the upper left–most point we'll be moving windows to. Allowing for the four-pixel margin we discussed earlier, this will usually be 4, 24: but to get it just right we should compute the vertical coordinate by starting with the height of the menu bar.

```
tiledWindow := FrontWindow;
newPoint.h  := {value of left margin for windows --- usually 4}
newPoint.v  := MBarHeight + {top margin} + 16 {for title bar}
```

10. Beginning with the frontmost window, we should call ShowHide to make the window invisible, MoveWindow to move it to its new destination, SizeWindow to set it to its new size, and ShowHide to make it reappear. After fixing up each window, we need to update the Point variable that's keeping track of where the next window should go. An easy way to do this is to increment the Point.v value (the y-coordinate) by the value of newHeight plus 16 for the window's title bar and then test it to see whether it runs off the bottom of the screen. If it does, reset it to the top of the screen and increment the value of the horizontal coordinate of the point by adding newWidth. We can get ready to move the next window by going through the window's nextWindow field.

```
repeat
 ShowHide (tiledWindow, false); {hide this guy}
 MoveWindow (tiledWindow, newPoint.h, newPoint.v, false);
 SizeWindow (tiledWindow, newWidth, newHeight, true);
 ShowHide (tiledWindow, true); {bring 'im back alive}
 newPoint.v := newPoint.v + newHeight + 16;
 if (newPoint.v + newHeight) > screenBits.bottom  {too beeg!}
  then begin  {move to top of new column}
         newPoint.v := MBarHeight + {top margin} + 16;
         newPoint.h := newPoint.h + newWidth; {new column}
      end;
 tiledWindow := tiledWindow^.nextWindow; {tiptoe through the windows};
 until tiledWindow := Nil;  {do it for all the windows}
```

We also discussed a couple of possible variations that could change the dimensions of some windows if there were an odd number of them. The first idea was to widen one or more of the windows to avoid leaving any unused screen space. If you do this, you have to figure out how many windows have to be widened. For example, if there are seven windows to be tiled you'll have nine spaces, so two windows get to be wider than the others. The other variation was to make all the windows in a column the same size. Again, to do this be sure you figure out how many windows there are in the odd column.

We don't serve their kind. While we're worrying about things, another thing to worry about is how to avoid tiling desk accessory windows. As we link through the window list by using the nextWindow field of the window record, we're liable to run into desk accessory window records that might be lounging around. How can we avoid them? The best way to detect desk accessory windows is by the windowKind field in their window records: it's negative. To avoid tiling desk accessory windows, we can add a line of code to ensure that the window we're about to tile doesn't have a negative windowKind field and that if it does, the next one will be grabbed instead.

Trying Some Real Numbers

It's always reassuring to check out numerical algorithms by trying actual numbers. This is the time-honored **reality check,** a good way to see whether your brain is reasonably well-aligned. We'll invent some real numbers and run through the tiling algorithm we just summarized. Note that some of the statements here have numbers plugged in as if they were constants. Of course, in the program, they wouldn't look like this; we're doing it here so that we can compute the values for everything.

The first thing to do is to determine the available screen space. For our example, let's say that we're using a standard Macintosh screen, which is 342 by 512 pixels, and that the menu bar is the standard size, which is 20 pixels. This leaves 322 vertical pixels. If we provided a margin of four pixels each at the top and the bottom, we wind up with 314 surviving pixels to work with. For the width, the only thing we have to do to the original size of 512 is to subtract the four-pixel margin from each edge. There will be 504 horizontal pixels available for our windows.

```
availHeight := 342 - 8 - 20 {314 vertical pizzas...}
availWidth := 512 - 8       {...and 504 horizontal ones}
```

How many windows are we going to tile? Let's say arbitrarily that we have four open windows to be tiled. What's our minimum acceptable window width and height? We've been using 100 pixels for each value, so let's stick with that figure.

```
numWindows := 4;{Four windows to be tiled, please}
minHeight := 100;{Make sure they're at least 100 high...}
minWidth := 100;{...and 100 wide, too}
```

Now we'll compute the maxWindsCol variable, which tells us how many windows can appear in a column. We can calculate it by dividing the screen height by the minimum window height.

```
maxWindsCol := 314 div 100;{up to 3 windows per column}
```

Now we need to test to see whether all our windows can fit in one full-width column on the screen. If we've done things right, it should tell us we need two columns, since we know there's not enough room for four 100-pixel high windows in one column.

```
if 100 > (314 div 4){Yep, 100 is greater than 78}
then {we need more than one column}
```

Our algorithm told us we need more than one column, so things seem to be working so far. Now we can move ahead to the calculations for number of columns and number of windows in each column.

```
numCols := 4 div 3;{Integer dividing gives 1}
if (numWindows mod maxWindsCol) <> 0   {1 <> 0}
     then numCols := numCols + 1; {numCols now becomes 2}
numWindsCol := 4 div 2;{2 windows per column}
if (numWindows mod numCols) <> 0 {it divided evenly}
     then numWindsCol := numWindsCol + 1; {remains at 2}
```

This one turned out as we expected, too. We wanted the algorithm to tell us that there should be two columns with two windows
in each, and it behaved perfectly. We can now compute the desired
size of the tiled windows.

```
newWidth := availWidth div numCols; {504 div 2 = 252}
newHeight := (availHeight div numWindsCol) - 16; {157 - 16 = 141}
```

This says that each of our four windows will be 252 pixels across and
141 pixels down. Mapping that out mentally, it seems to make sense.
The width of 252 will give us 504 pixels worth of windows across the
screen and the height of 141, plus two 16-pixel title bars, adds up to
314 pixels down.

The next step is to compute the initial point we'll be moving windows to. You'll remember that we want to set this one to the first position in the upper left corner of the screen.

```
tiledWindow := FrontWindow;   {OK, fine}
newPoint.h := 4;{windows start 4 pixels in from left}
newPoint.v := 40 {menu bar + 4 pixel margin + 16 for title bar}
```

We've made all the computations and we're ready to start the
real dirty work. The next bunch of statements should move and resize
our first window. Fasten your seat belt, and here goes.

```
ShowHide (tiledWindow, false);{Hides the first window}
MoveWindow (tiledWindow, 4, 40); {Move it to 4, 40}
SizeWindow (tiledWindow, 252, 141, true} {Resize 'im}
ShowHide (tiledWindow, true);{Hey! It moved! It shrunk!}
```

At this point, the first window should have been moved and sized to
the upper left quadrant of the screen, with the title bar just below
the menu bar and the left edge just in from the edge of the screen. Of
course, there's no easy way to do a reality check on something like
this. The only way to really find out whether it's working is to see it
on the screen. So, we have to take a little leap of faith here or else
actually sketch out the windows on a piece of paper.

After moving the first window, we now have to set up the values for moving the next window. This involves updating the newPoint value that tells where we're moving it to, jumping over to the next column if we have to, and getting the next window pointer.

```
newPoint.v := 40 + 141 + 16; {new coordinate is 197}
if (197 + 141) > 342{No, 338 is less than 342}
      {room for another window in this column}
```

The "if" statement here is designed to test whether another window would run off the bottom of the screen. The left side of the statement (197 plus 141) will find out where the bottom of the window would fall. Since this statement told us that it wouldn't be below screenBits.bounds, we can put another window here; so we can move ahead.

```
tiledWindow := tiledWindow^.nextWindow; {next, please};
until tiledWindow := Nil;  {Is this the end?}
```

This will set tiledWindow to point at the second to frontmost window. If we've just processed the only window, the "until" clause will take us out of the window-munging loop. In our case, though, we've said that there are four windows, so we know that tiledWindow won't be nil. Time to loop through again and fix up the next window.

```
ShowHide (tiledWindow, false); {don't look}
MoveWindow (tiledWindow, 4, 197, false);
SizeWindow (tiledWindow, 252, 141, true);
ShowHide (tiledWindow, true); {now see what you've done}
newPoint.v := 197 + 141 + 16; {makes it 354. Hmmm...}
if (354 + 141) > 342 {no room at the inn, so move over...}
 then begin  {...to next column}
        newPoint.v := 20 + 4 + 16;  {y-coordinate is 40, again}
        newPoint.h := 4 + 252; {x-coordinate moves over to 256}
     end;
tiledWindow := tiledWindow^.nextWindow;  {all things must pass}
until tiledWindow := Nil; {we're not finished yet}
```

Now, let's quickly go through the loop for the third and fourth windows.

```
ShowHide (tiledWindow, false); {put in closet}
MoveWindow (tiledWindow, 256, 40, false); {top right spot}
SizeWindow (tiledWindow, 252, 141, true); {standard size}
ShowHide (tiledWindow, true); {let's look in now}
newPoint.v := 40 + 141 + 16; {back to 197}
if (197 + 141) > 342 {we can fit another in this column}
 then begin  {the "if" is false, so nothing happens here}
        . . .
     end;
tiledWindow := tiledWindow^.nextWindow;  {yes, there's another}
until tiledWindow := Nil; {so you want more, do you?}
```

And now, the compelling conclusion, with the shocking birth of Robin's baby . . .

```
ShowHide (tiledWindow, false); {close your eyes}
MoveWindow (tiledWindow, 256, 197, false); {last place}
SizeWindow (tiledWindow, 252, 141, true); {same old size here}
ShowHide (tiledWindow, true); {Mr. Window's grinning}
newPoint.v := 197 + 141 + 16; {354}
if (354 + 141) > 342 {this column is full}
 then begin  {we'll move over, but we're done anyway}
        newPoint.v := 40;
        newPoint.h := 408; {new column, if we had one}
     end;
tiledWindow := tiledWindow^.nextWindow;  {now it's nil}
until tiledWindow := nil; {finally, it's nil, and we're done}
```

That's it. We've now successfully moved and resized all four windows. Did our reality check out all right? Everything went pretty much as expected. One weird thing that took place when we played with the fourth window was that even though we were finished moving and shaking all our windows, our algorithm went right ahead and got ready to place another window.

This is because we don't check for the end of the loop, which happens when tiledWindow equals nil, until the bottom of the loop. The "repeat . . . until" statement is Pascal's most convenient way of handling this situation. We could add a test to see whether we've moved all the windows just as soon as we've finished moving one and then jump forward if we have. It's really no big deal either way, though, since the few extra statements that get executed don't take

much time and they're only executed once for every time you tile all
the windows.

Our reality check showed that things seem to work right for four
windows. Let's see what happens if we have three or seven windows. We won't run through the whole mess for each of these; we'll
just see whether things get off to the right start and all the globals
get the correct values.

First, let's check things out for three windows.

```
availHeight := 342 - 8 - 20;   {314 again}
availWidth := 512 - 8; {504 again}
numWindows := 3;
minHeight := 100;
minWidth := 100;
maxWindsCol := 314 div 100; {3, just like last example}
if 100 > (314 div 3)   {¿Que es mas macho?}
     then {100 is less than 104}
     else {we can fit everything in one column};
newWidth := 504;   {big fat windows}
newHeight := (314 div 3) - 16; {but short: 88 pixels}
tiledWindow := FrontWindow;   {first things first}
newPoint.h := 4;{set up for first x-y location}
newPoint.v := 40;
```

If we follow this through, it looks as though we'll get all three windows into one column. Each window will be 504 pixels wide and 88
pixels tall (not including the title bar for each). The first window
will be placed at the same location we always place the first window, at 4,40, which will be tucked up nicely into the upper left corner of the screen. The algorithm still seems all right, so we'll keep
moving along.

Now let's look at what we get if we try for a gaudy seven windows.

```
availHeight := 342 - 8 - 20;   {314 again}
availWidth := 512 - 8; {504 as always}
numWindows := 7;   {a new high}
minHeight := 100;   {we're keeping these the same}
minWidth := 100;
maxWindsCol := 314 div 100; {this stays 3}
if 100 > (314 div 7)   {100 is much more than 44}
      then {figure multi-column info}
         numCols := 7 div 3;   {we'll fill 2 columns...}
         if (7 mod 3) <> 0 {...with two left over...}
            then numCols := numCols + 1; {...so we need 3}
         numWindsCol := 7 div 3; {2 windows per column?}
         if (numWindows mod numCols) <> 0 {no, need more...}
            then numWindsCol := numWindsCol + 1; {3 per column}
newWidth := 504 div 3;   {must squeeze: only 168 wide}
newHeight := (314 div 3) - 16; {just 88 pixels tall, too}
tiledWindow := FrontWindow;   {get the first window}
newPoint.h := 4;     {destination of the first move}
newPoint.v := 40;
```

If we follow the math through this example, we can discover the locations for each of the seven windows. Here's where they'll be:

4,40	172,40	340,40
4,144	172,144	(blank)
4,248	172,248	(blank)

By computing the edge of the windows on the bottom and the right, we can learn how close we're coming to filling the whole screen. The window in the right column starts at 340 and is 168 pixels wide, so it will reach to pixel 508, just in time for our prescribed four-pixel margin at the right edge of the screen. Great! The windows that run across the bottom start at 248 and are 88 pixels high. The bottom ones end at 336, which is very close to 338, the last pixel available before the bottom margin.

After checking out the algorithm a little bit by plugging in some live numbers, we can feel better about how well it will work. If you like you can try working through it with some other sets of numbers. It would be interesting, for example, to see what would happen with a bigger screen, more windows, or a different minimum size. You should also test boundary conditions, such as trying to tile with no windows, one window, or 100 windows (yes, some folks are crazy). If you're interested in trying all these, I guarantee you'll find some bugs in the algorithm you'll get to fix. Have fun looking.

Also, since it was important that this algorithm be easy to explain as we walked through it, you might want to change it around somewhat. In particular, you might want to experiment with when the windows are hidden and shown and when updates are created, to see whether you can speed things up. One idea might be to make all the windows invisible at the same time, then move and resize them, and then make them visible again. You can then see whether this looks faster on the screen than our technique of fixing each window and then showing it. You should spend some time tweaking this technique so that it works exactly as you like.

Following this chapter you'll find Listing 9-1, which includes a window management menu for selecting, zooming, tiling, and stacking windows. It implements the algorithms we've discussed in this section for listing windows in a menu, stacking windows, and flipping through windows. There's even space for you to implement your own version of the tiling algorithm. Joe Bob says check it out.

Stacking and Tiling with Multiple Screens

The Macintosh II and its flexible video impose lots of interesting questions into our programming lives. Usually, Color QuickDraw takes care of much of the worry for you and you don't have to wonder how many monitors you have or what their characteristics are. Sometimes, though, issues come up that do require more information about the expensive collection of monitors plugged into your computer.

One such situation is window stacking and tiling. When you stack or tile your windows, you're spewing them out into all the screen real estate available. The whole idea is to take the maximum advantage of displaying the windows on your screen. How does this relate to the idea of multiple screens? What should happen to your extra screens when you tile or stack windows?

This is really a user interface question. Most users with multiple monitors use one of them most of the time. The others are used to stash whole windows to get them out of the way or to keep tool palettes like the drawing tools in FullPaint, but aren't usually an active part of minute-to-minute usage of the program.

Since most users seem to have created a special use for their secondary (and tertiary, and whatever the fourth, fifth, and so on are called), your tiling and stacking commands should not attempt to use any screens other than the main one for displaying the windows.

Another really good reason to stick by this rule has absolutely nothing to do with the user interface. Using the main screen makes your code much, much simpler, as you'll see shortly. You have to jump through a lot of hoops to find out about additional screens and then you have to make your windows jump through those hoops as you send them all over the place. Of course, if you decide that you absolutely need this kind of feature to make your application a little bit better than the next one, you'll be interested in this section. We'll talk about what kinds of things you have to do in order to make stacking and tiling work with multiple screens.

Using Rectangles

Let's think a bit about how we would tile windows if we had more than one monitor. One possibility is to treat the combined desktop area of all the screens as one big space for tiling. This could turn out to be pretty weird, though, if you think about it. There's no requirement that the desktop be rectangular. What if you have your multiple monitors arranged so that the desktop isn't a rectangle?

If multiple monitors are arranged this way, you can see that figuring out how to spray our tiled windows across the whole desktop is going to be a real challenge. Before we place any window, we have to find out whether we've suddenly moved over to a new screen that may be positioned above or below the one we've been working on. If you try to move directly to the right from one monitor to the other, you'll find yourself drawing windows out into space.

There's another way to place the windows on multiple screens that's a lot easier on your programming time and probably presents a more reasonable user interface than treating all the screens as one desktop. The idea is simply to redo the tiling algorithm for each screen. If you begin by spreading out all the windows to be tiled over all the available screens and then rerun the tiling loop for each screen, things will be much more convenient. The main reason is that each monitor is a rectangle even though the desktop, which is the sum of the screens, may not be a rectangle.

Rounding off.   Strictly speaking, every screen that contains an edge of the desktop is never really a rectangle. Every desktop edge includes a tiny rounded corner. Take a close look at the corners of your Macintosh screen. See the rounded edges? You may have thought these were actual round corners of the video tube and in fact that's exactly how they're supposed to look. But the black corners past the rounded edges are actually capable of being black or white (or color on a color screen). Rounding them off just gives the desktop a more polished appearance. It also means that the desktop is never really a rectangle, nor is any screen that forms a side of the desktop.

If we decide to tile the windows by using each screen separately as a rectangle, we obviously have to know a few things. For one thing we need to know how many screens there are. That's how we'll figure out the way to divide the windows among the screens. We'll need to know the rectangle for each screen as well. To figure out the available space on a screen, we should also find out whether it's the one with the menu bar on it. If it is, we have to subtract some pixels from the top.

How can we find out all this stuff? Color QuickDraw provides some convenient calls to return a lot of the information. For some other things, we'll have to go spelunking directly into the graphics device (gDevice) data structures that tell about the screens.

To find out about the screens' rectangles, we'll have to look at the gDevices that have the information about our monitors. If you're trying something a little unusual or obnoxious when you're programming the Macintosh, you can usually find some convenient trick in the Toolbox or operating system that will help you out.

In this case, our lucky deal is that all the gDevices are kept together in memory in a linked list. One of the fields in a gDevice is called gdNextGD, and it contains a handle to the next gDevice in the list. Just as with window records (and just as you'd expect on the Macintosh), if there are no more gDevices, this field is nil, so we can tell when we're done.

We need to know how big the screen's rectangles are so that we can figure out how many windows we can fit on them. You probably remember that there's a global variable left over from pre–Color QuickDraw days called screenBits that has information about the screen; but what does this mean in the new-wave world of more than one screen?

Almost every application expects screenBits to be the main screen; in fact, most of today's applications were written when every

Macintosh had only one screen. Color QuickDraw keeps it that way. No matter how many screens are being used, screenBits will give you information about the main screen. The main screen is defined as the one with the menu bar on it.

Screening out. How does the Macintosh II figure out which is the main screen, how many screens there are, what their alignment is, and so on? If you were a plain old power user, you'd probably say that the screen configuration is determined by the Monitors setting in the Control Panel. Well, yes, that's how users should configure the screens, but we've got inquiring minds and we want to know how it really works. It's done with resources of course. In this case, there's a resource of type scrn that's kept in the System file. This scrn resource, which has an ID of 0, tells the system about all the attached screens. A lot of the information in the scrn gets put into the gDevices when they're created at system startup time. When you fiddle with the Monitors icon in the Control Panel, you're modifying the scrn 0 resource. The first thing in the scrn is the number of devices; after that, there's a chunk of information for each screen, including the slot, the video mode that the monitor should come up in, and the rectangle that each screen fits into. For more detail about color resources, see Chapter 3.

Since screenBits only gives information about the main screen, we have to find some other way to find out about all the rest of them. For that stuff, we can look at a gDevice field called gdRect, which gives the global rectangle that this screen occupies. This rectangle is given in terms of where it fits into the entire desktop. The main screen will always have its upper left corner at location 0,0.

When we're going through the screens' rectangles trying to figure out how big each one is, we can use the gdRect field in the gDevice records to find out each screen's global rectangle. This really isn't all we want to know, since these rectangles are given as part of the whole giant desktop. What we'd also like to find out is the rectangle in local terms, starting at 0,0. Of course, we can compute that from the global rectangle, but we can save a step if we can find it somewhere already presented the other way.

Well, there is a better way. In the gDevice record, a field called gdPMap holds a handle to the device's pixel map (you may remember that we played around with this field back when we were doing our offscreen drawing business). One of the fields of the pixel map, of course, is the bounds rectangle, which defines the total extent of the pixels. This rectangle will tell us about the size of the screen from a local point of view, beginning with the upper left corner at 0,0.

We also said we needed to know how many screens there were. One way of finding this out would be to look at the beginning of the scrn 0 resource that the system uses to configure the desktop. The first field in the scrn resource is an integer called scrnCount, which contains the number of screen devices. Watch out, though, because this won't always work. In the scrn resource, any device may be marked as inactive, which means that it won't be used. Even if some devices are locked out this way, the scrnCount value includes them in its count. So, looking at this number to find out how many live screens we've got is not a good idea.

What else can we do? We said earlier that each gDevice has a handle called gdNextGD, which we can use to find the next device record. We also said that gdNextGD for the last device in the list was set to nil. With this handy information, we can simply step through the gDevice list and count the number of devices the old-fashioned way, by incrementing a counter. After we reach the gDevice record in which gdNextGD is equal to nil, we'll have the total number of devices, but some of these might still be inactive.

To find out which gDevices are active, we can use another field in the record that gives interesting configuration information about the device. This field, called gdFlags, can tell us whether or not the device is active. If it's not, of course, that means the screen isn't being used and we shouldn't count it in our list of good screens. The gdFlags field is 16 bits long and the flag that tells if a device is active is kept in bit 15, which is called scrnActive.

We're on the air.   The scrn 0 resource also contains the flags word that will tell you whether a device is active or not. It's much easier, though, to step through the gDevice list than to try to decode the scrn resource's data structure. Also, the scrn 0 tells how the screens are to be set up at startup time. If the user changed them with the Control Panel, there's a possibility that the scrn 0 doesn't actually reflect the current state of things. This can happen if the user fools with the Monitor settings in the Control Panel but hasn't yet restarted the Macintosh. So, we should use the information that's actually in the gDevice records since it's more reliable.

One last vital piece of information we need to know is which screen is the main device. There are a couple of ways to figure this out. One idea is to look at the gdRect field (the rectangle in global coordinates) associated with the gDevice and see whether its topLeft value is set to 0,0. If so, this device is guaranteed to be the main screen.

A different way to detect the main screen is to look at another flag in the gdFlags field we discussed. Bit 11 is designated as the flag called mainScrn; if it's set to 1, it means that the device that uses this gDevice record is the main screen. This technique of examining the flags is probably better to use than checking to see whether the global rectangle starts at 0,0. Why? The best reason is that it's more direct. The fact that the main screen starts at 0,0 is very convenient, but the mainScrn bit in gdFlags is expressly made for this purpose, so it's more likely to stay defined that way for the next 50 or 60 years.

The Algorithm

Now that we've figured out how we're going to get all the information we need about every screen in sight, let's see whether we can come up with the algorithm we'll need to tile windows on all our monitors. As we discussed a little bit at the start of this section, the general idea will be to take the windows that need to be tiled and divide them as evenly as possible among all available screens, following the rule that no window can cross screen boundaries. This means, for example, that if we have two screens and four windows to tile, each screen will get two of them, regardless of the size of the screens or the windows.

After we've divided the windows among the screens, we can start chopping up the real estate of each screen to divide it among the windows that are going to get moved there. Once we've gotten to this stage, we're really just going to repeat the single-screen tiling phenomenon we went through earlier, and we already know how to do that.

The rules of this algorithm seem to be pretty simple. First, give each screen the same number of windows. If there are windows left over, spread them around so that every screen's number of windows is within 1 of every other's number. For example, if we have five windows and three screens, we want two of the screens to get two windows each, with the fifth window going on the third monitor. Deciding which monitor gets the extra windows can be interesting. You might want to make it so that the biggest screens get the greater number of windows.

After we've determined how to divide the windows among the screens, we have to perform the tiling on every screen's set of windows. The logic for deciding how big each window should be, how many columns of windows there ought to be, and so on is the same as we figured when we first did the tiling stuff in the previous section.

We have to deal with a couple of new wrinkles when doing the tiling this time. First, we have to know which screen has the menu bar on it, so that we can know not to count the menu bar's pixels when figuring the available space for windows. We can find out which screen has the menu bar by checking the gdFlags field of the gDevice record. As we said earlier, bit 11 is the mainScrn bit; if it's set to 1, the gDevice that you're looking at is the main one and has the menu bar on it.

To place the windows on each screen, we have to know where to MoveWindow them to. MoveWindow takes a point in global coordinates, so we can use the gdRect field of the gDevice record to learn what global rectangle on the desktop is occupied by this screen. When we go through our standard tiling algorithm for each screen, we need to adjust all the MoveWindow destinations by the values in this rectangle.

What about the pixel depth settings and color capabilities for each monitor? We really don't have to worry about them. Color QuickDraw and the Window Manager will ensure that the windows are displayed properly no matter what the pixel depth. If a window with color information is moved to a monochrome screen, the color on the screen will vanish, of course, since not even Color QuickDraw can violate the laws of physics, but the system will make sure that the image stays right. If the window is later put back onto a color monitor, the color information will magically return, since the color information will still be in the pixel map.

The same thing will happen when windows are moved between windows of different pixel depths. The right pixels will automatically be plucked from the pixel maps so that the image is correct on the screen no matter what the pixel depth. If there's multibit gray scale information in the pixel map, and the window's current screen can't handle it, QuickDraw will just map the image into good old black and white.

This discussion of tiling windows on multiple screens is a good example of learning about how something works without having to have a good practical application. You may never really need to worry about tiling windows across multiple screens, but thinking about what you would do to implement it may teach you something or may just be fun and interesting. Either way, these kinds of bizarre exercises can be very useful, if you can find the time to do them after finishing your real work. The best way to find the time is simply to get a job that pays you to write unusual programs for the Macintosh.

Things to Remember

As people get bigger screens and more memory, they start to open lots of windows. You can add some features to your programs that will make life simpler for for users who like to have lots of windows open for convenience. You can construct a menu that lists all the windows, provide automatic tiling and stacking, and make a Command key to flip through the windows.

When you implement these features, be sure to think about such fun problems as multiple screens and desk accessory windows. The best thing to do is just to ignore desk accessory windows in your window-arranging functions and to limit your activity to the main screen.

```
program WindMenu;

{ Listing 9-1  Example of ultra-fancy window management via menus }

  uses
    {$Load Insider:MPW:PInterfaces:Allinterfaces}
    {$U Insider:MPW:PInterfaces:MemTypes.p } MemTypes,
    {$U Insider:MPW:PInterfaces:QuickDraw.p} QuickDraw,
    {$U Insider:MPW:PInterfaces:OSIntf.p   } OSIntf,
    {$U Insider:MPW:PInterfaces:ToolIntf.p } ToolIntf,
    {$U Insider:MPW:PInterfaces:PackIntf.p } PackIntf;

  const
    appleID = 128;      {resource IDs/menu IDs for Apple, File and Edit menus}
    fileID  = 129;
    editID  = 130;
    windowID= 131;

    moveDialog = 1001;  {DLOG ID for move & resize dialog}

    appleM = 1;         {index for each menu in myMenus (array of menu handles)}
    fileM  = 2;
    editM  = 3;
    windowM = 4;

    menuCount = 4;      {total number of menus}

    aboutItem = 1;      {item in Apple menu}

    undoItem  = 1;      {Items in Edit menu}
    cutItem   = 3;
    copyItem  = 4;
    pasteItem = 5;
    clearitem = 6;
```

Listing 9-1 continued

```
      newItem = 1;      {items in File menu}
      closeItem = 3;
      quitItem = 5;

      tileItem = 1;     {items in Window menu}
      stackItem = 2;
      moveItem = 3;

      wName = 'Window ';          {prefix for window names}

      windDX = 25;      {distance to move for new windows}
      windDY = 25;

      leftEdge = 10;    {initial dimensions of window}
      topEdge = 42;
      rightEdge = 210;
      botEdge = 175;

      firstWinItem = 4; {offset from first item in Window menu to first window}

var
      myMenus: array [1..menuCount] OF MenuHandle; {handles to the menus}
      dragRect: Rect;        {rectangle used to mark boundaries for dragging window}
      txRect: Rect;          {rectangle for text in application window}
      textH: TEHandle;       {handle to Textedit record}
      theChar: char;         {typed character}
      extended: boolean;     {true if user is Shift-clicking}
      doneFlag: boolean;     {true if user has chosen Quit Item}
      myEvent: EventRecord;  {information about an event}
      wRecord: WindowRecord; {information about the application window}
      myWindow: WindowPtr;   {pointer to wRecord}
      myWinPeek : WindowPeek;{another pointer to wRecord}
      whichWindow: WindowPtr;{window in which mouse button was pressed}
      nextWRect: Rect;       {portRect for next window to be opended}
      nextWTitle: Str255;    {title of next window to be opened}
      nextWNum: Longint;     {number of next window (for title)}
      savedPort: GrafPtr;    {pointer to preserve GrafPort}
      menusOK: boolean;      {for disabling menu items}
      windowCount: Integer;  {number of open windows}
      itemString: Str255;    {item selected from menu}
      switchWindow: WindowPtr; {new window to select}
      windowName: Str255;    {new window's name}
      curWinName, flipname: Str255;{name of current app. window}
      curWinItem: Integer;   {menu item number of current window}
      flipwin: WindowPtr;
      scrapErr: Longint;
      scrCopyErr: Integer;
```

Listing 9-1 continued

```
procedure SetUpMenus;
{ set up menus and menu bar }

  var
    i: Integer;

  begin
    myMenus[appleM] := GetMenu(appleID);        {read Apple menu}
    AddResMenu(myMenus[appleM],'DRVR');         {add desk accessory names}
    myMenus[fileM] := GetMenu(fileID);          {read file menu }
    myMenus[editM] := GetMenu(editID);          {read Edit menu }
    myMenus[windowM]:=GetMenu(windowID);

    for i:=1 to menuCount do
      InsertMenu(myMenus[i],0);  {install menus in menu bar }
    DrawMenuBar;  { and draw menu bar}
  end;      {SetUpMenus}

function ItemFromName (theName: str255): Integer;

  var
    itemString : str255;
    whichItem : integer;

  begin
    whichItem := firstWinItem; {start at item no. of dashed line}
      repeat
          whichItem := whichItem + 1;
          GetItem (myMenus [windowM], whichItem, itemString);
          until (itemString = theName) or (whichItem > (windowCount+firstWinItem));
    if whichItem > (windowCount+firstWinItem)
      then ItemFromName := 0
      else ItemFromName := whichItem;
  end;



procedure AddWintoMenu (windowName: Str255);

  begin
    InsMenuItem(myMenus[windowM], windowName, firstWinItem);
  end;



procedure RemoveWin (theWindow: WindowPtr);

  var
    winName : Str255;

  begin
    GetWTitle (theWindow, winName);
    DelMenuItem (myMenus [windowM], ItemFromName (winName));
  end;
```

Listing 9-1 continued

```
procedure OpenWindow;
{ Open a new window }

  begin
     NumToString (nextWNum, nextWTitle); {prepare number for title}
     nextWTitle := concat (wName, nextWTitle); {add to prefix}
     myWindow := NewWindow (Nil, nextWRect, nextWTitle, True, noGrowDocProc,
       Pointer (-1), True, 0); {open the window}
     SetPort (myWindow);          {make it the current port}
     txRect := thePort^.portRect;{prepare TERecord for new window}
     InsetRect (txRect, 4, 0);
     textH := TENew (txRect, txRect);
     myWinPeek := WindowPeek (myWindow);
     myWinPeek^.refcon := Longint (textH); {keep TEHandle in refcon}
     OffsetRect (nextWRect, windDX, windDY);{move window down and right}
     if nextWRect.right > dragRect.right {move back if it's too far over}
       then OffsetRect (nextWRect, -nextWRect.left + leftEdge, 0);
     if nextWRect.bottom > dragRect.bottom
     then OffsetRect (nextWRect, 0, -nextWRect.top + topEdge);
     nextWNum := nextWNum + 1; {bump number for next window}
     menusOK := false;
     EnableItem (myMenus [editM],0); {in case this is the only window}
     windowCount := windowCount + 1;
     AddWintoMenu (nextWTitle);

  end; {OpenWindow}


procedure KillWindow (theWindow: WindowPtr);
{Close a window and throw everything away}

  var
     winName : str255;

  begin
     RemoveWin (theWindow);
     TEDispose (TEHandle (WindowPeek (theWindow)^.refcon));
                                {throw away TERecord}
     DisposeWindow (theWindow);  {throw away WindowRecord}
     textH := NIL;               {for TEIdle in main event loop}
     if FrontWindow = NIL        {if no more windows, disable Close}
       then DisableItem (myMenus[fileM], closeItem)
       else
         begin
            theWindow := FrontWindow;
            while (WindowPeek (theWindow)^.windowKind<0)
              do
                theWindow := WindowPtr (WindowPeek (theWindow)^.nextWindow);
            GetWTitle (theWindow, winName);
            curWinItem := ItemFromName (winName);
            curWinName := winName;
         end;
```

Listing 9-1 continued

```
      if WindowPeek (FrontWindow)^.windowKind < 0
                                {if a desk acc is coming up, enable undo}
        then EnableItem (myMenus[editM], undoItem)
        else DisableItem (myMenus[editM], undoItem);
      windowCount := windowCount - 1;

    end; {KillWindow}


  function MyFilter (theDialog: DialogPtr; var theEvent: EventRecord;
      var itemHit: Integer): Boolean;

    var
      theType: Integer;
      theItem: Handle;
      theBox: Rect;
      finalTicks: Longint;

    begin
      if (BitAnd(theEvent.message,charCodeMask) = 13) {carriage return}
        or (BitAnd(theEvent.message,charCodeMask) = 3) {enter}
        then
          begin
            GetDItem (theDialog, 1, theType, theItem, theBox);
            HiliteControl (ControlHandle (theItem), 1);
            Delay (8, finalTicks);
            HiliteControl (ControlHandle (theItem), 0);
            itemHit := 1;
            MyFilter := True;
          end {if BitAnd...then begin}
        else MyFilter := False;
    end; {function MyFilter}


  procedure DoAboutBox;

    var
      itemHit: Integer;

    begin
      myWindow := GetNewDialog (1000, Nil, pointer (-1));
      repeat
        ModalDialog (@MyFilter, itemHit)
      until itemHit = 1;
      DisposDialog (myWindow);
    end; {procedure DoAboutBox}
```

Listing 9-1 continued

```
function NextNoDA (theWindow: windowPeek): windowPeek;

begin
  if theWindow <> Nil
    then
        while (theindow^.windowKind<0) {weed out DAs}
            do theWindow := theWindow^.nextWindow;
NextNoDA := theWindow;
end;

function LastNoDA : windowPeek;
{Finds the rearmost window that's not a DA}
  var
    lastGoodUn : windowPeek;

begin
  if FrontWindow <> Nil
    then begin
        lastGoodUn := NextNoDA (WindowPeek (FrontWindow));
        while NextNoDA (lastGoodUn^.nextWindow) <> Nil
            do lastGoodUn := NextNoDA (lastGoodUn^.nextWindow);
        end;
  LastNoDA := lastGoodUn;
end;

function numFromItem (theDialog: DialogPtr; itemNo: Integer): Integer;
{Given a dialog item number, return its value as an integer}
  var
    itemType: Integer;
    item: Handle;
    box: Rect;
    theText: Str255;
    theNum: Longint;

  begin
    GetDItem (theDialog, itemNo, itemType, item, box); {get item handle}
    GetIText (item, theText);   {get its text}
    StringToNum (theText, theNum);
    numFromItem := theNum;
  end;


procedure DoWinShuffle (theItem: Integer);
      {Handle Stack, Tile, and Move & Resize commands}
      var
        theWindow: WindowPeek;
        mover: WindowPtr;
        nextPos: Point;
        dlogItem: Integer;
        newTop,newLeft,newBot,newRight: Integer;
```

Listing 9-1 continued

```
        theDialog: DialogPtr;

begin
   case theItem of
     tileItem:;
     stackItem:
       begin
         nextPos.h := (((windowCount - 1) * windDX) + leftEdge)
           mod (screenBits.bounds.right - leftEdge);
         nextPos.v := (((windowCount - 1) * windDY) + topEdge)
           mod (screenBits.bounds.bottom - leftEdge);
         theWindow := NextNoDA (WindowPeek (FrontWindow));
         while theWindow <> Nil
           do
             begin
               MoveWindow (windowPtr (theWindow), nextPos.h, nextPos.v, false);
               nextPos.h := nextPos.h - windDX;
               nextPos.v := nextPos.v - windDY;
               if nextPos.h < leftEdge {move back if it's too far over}
                 then nextPos.h := rightEdge;
               if nextPos.v < topEdge
                 then nextPos.v := botEdge;
               theWindow := NextNoDA (theWindow^.nextWindow);
             end;
       end; {case stackItem}
     moveItem:
       begin
         mover := FrontWindow;
         theDialog := GetNewDialog (moveDialog,Nil,pointer (-1));
         repeat
           ModalDialog (@myFilter, dlogItem);
         until (dlogItem = 1) or (dlogItem = 2);
         if dlogItem = 1
           then
             begin
               newTop := numFromItem (theDialog,8);
               newLeft := numFromItem (theDialog,9);
               newBot := numFromItem (theDialog,10);
               newRight := numFromItem (theDialog,11);
               MoveWindow (mover,newLeft,newTop,true);
               SizeWindow (mover,newRight-newLeft,newBot-newTop,true);
             end;
         DisposDialog (theDialog);
       end;

   end {case theItem of}
end; {procedure DoWinShuffle}
```

Listing 9-1 continued

```
procedure DoCommand (mResult: LONGINT);
{Execute Item specified by mResult, the result of MenuSelect}

  var
     theItem: Integer; {menu item number from mResult low-order word}
     theMenu: Integer; {menu number from mResult high-order word}
     name: Str255;      {desk accessory name}
     temp: Integer;


  begin
     theItem := LoWord(mResult); {call Toolbox Utility routines to set }
     theMenu := HiWord(mResult);   { menu item number and menu number}

     case theMenu of              {case on menu ID}

        appleID:
          if theItem = aboutItem
            then DoAboutBox
            else
              begin
                GetItem(myMenus[appleM],theItem,name);
                {GetPort (savedPort);}
                scrapErr := ZeroScrap;
                scrCopyErr := TEToScrap;
                temp := OpenDeskAcc(name);
                EnableItem (myMenus [editM],0);
                {SetPort (savedPort);}
                if FrontWindow <> NIL
                  then
                    begin
                      EnableItem (myMenus [fileM], closeItem);
                      EnableItem (myMenus [editM], undoItem);
                    end; {if FrontWindow then begin}
                  menusOK := false;
                end;       {if theItem...else begin}
        fileID:
          case theItem of

             newItem:
               OpenWindow;

             closeItem:
               if WindowPeek (FrontWindow)^.windowKind < 0
                 then CloseDeskAcc (windowPeek (FrontWindow)^.windowKind)
                 {if desk acc window, close it}
                 else KillWindow (FrontWindow);
                 {if it's one of mine, blow it away}
```

Listing 9-1 continued

```
      quitItem:
        doneFlag := TRUE; {quit}

  end; {case theItem}

editID:
  begin
    if not SystemEdit(theItem-1)
      then
        begin
          case theItem of {case on menu item number}

            cutItem:
              TECut(textH); {call TextEdit to handle Item}

            copyItem:
              TECopy(textH);

            pasteItem:
              TEPaste(textH);

            clearItem:
              TEDelete(textH);
          end;    {case theItem}
          scrapErr := ZeroScrap;
          scrCopyErr := TEToScrap;
        end {if not SystemEdit...begin}
  end;    {editID begin}

windowID:
  begin
    GetItem (myMenus [windowM], theItem, itemString);
    if theItem < firstWinItem
      then DoWinShuffle (theItem)
      else begin
    switchWindow := FrontWindow;
    GetWTitle (switchWindow, windowName);
    while (windowName <> itemString) and (switchWindow <> Nil)
      do
        begin
          switchWindow := WindowPtr (WindowPeek (switchWindow)^.nextWindow);
          GetWTitle (switchWindow, windowName);
        end;
    SelectWindow (switchWindow);
      end; {if theItem < ...else}
      end; {windowID}

  end;    {case theMenu}
  HiliteMenu(0);
end;    {DoCommand}
```

Listing 9-1 continued

```
procedure FixCursor;

   var
      mouseLoc: point;

begin
   GetMouse (mouseLoc);
   if PtInRect (mouseLoc, thePort^.portRect)
      then SetCursor (GetCursor (iBeamCursor)^^)
      else SetCursor (arrow);
end; {procedure FixCursor}


begin         {main program}

   InitGraf(@thePort);
   InitFonts;
   FlushEvents(everyEvent,0);
   InitWindows;
   InitMenus;
   TEInit;
   InitDialogs(NIL);
   InitCursor;

   SetUpMenus;
      with screenBits.bounds do
         SetRect(dragRect,4,24,right-4,bottom-4);
         doneFlag := false;

   menusOK := false;
   windowCount := 0;
   curWinItem := 0;
   nextWNum := 1;    {initialize window number}
   SetRect (nextWRect,leftEdge,topEdge,rightEdge,botEdge);
                     {initialize window rectangle}
   OpenWindow;       {start with one open window}

{ Main event loop }
   repeat
      SystemTask;
      if FrontWindow <> NIL
        then
          if WindowPeek (FrontWindow)^.windowKind >= 0
            then FixCursor;
      if not menusOK and (FrontWindow = NIL)
        then
          begin
            DisableItem (myMenus [fileM], closeItem);
            DisableItem (myMenus [editM], 0);
            menusOK := true;
          end; {if FrontWindow...then begin}
      if textH <> Nil
        then TEIdle(textH);
```

Listing 9-1 continued

```
if GetNextEvent(everyEvent,myEvent)
  then
  case myEvent.what of

    mouseDown:
      case FindWindow(myEvent.where,whichWindow) of

            inSysWindow:
              SystemClick(myEvent,whichWindow);

            inMenuBar:
              DoCommand(MenuSelect(myEvent.where));

            inDrag:
              DragWindow(whichWindow,myEvent.where,dragRect);

            inContent:
              begin
                if whichWindow <> FrontWindow
                  then SelectWindow(whichWindow)
                  else
                    begin
                      GlobalToLocal(myEvent.where);
                      extended := BitAnd(myEvent.modifiers,shiftKey) <> 0;
                      TEClick(myEvent.where,extended,textH);
                    end;    {else}
              end;    {inContent}

            inGoAway:
              if TrackGoAway (whichWindow, myEvent.where)
                then KillWindow (whichWindow);

        end;    {case FindWindow}

    keyDown, autoKey:
      begin
        theChar := CHR(BitAnd(myEvent.message,charCodeMask));
        if BitAnd(myEvent.modifiers,cmdKey) <> 0
          then DoCommand(MenuKey(theChar))
          else if FrontWindow <> Nil
                then TEKey(theChar,textH);
      end; {keyDown, autoKey begin}

    activateEvt:
      begin
      if BitAnd(myEvent.modifiers,activeFlag) <> 0
        then    {application window is becoming active}
          begin
            SetPort (GrafPtr (myEvent.message));
            textH := TEHandle (WindowPeek (myEvent.message)^.refcon);
            TEActivate(textH);
```

Listing 9-1 continued

```
      EnableItem (myMenus[fileM],closeItem);
      DisableItem(myMenus[editM],undoItem);
      scrCopyErr := TEFromScrap;
      if curWinItem <> 0
         then
            begin
               CheckItem (myMenus [windowM],ItemFromName (curWinName), false);
               SetItemCmd (myMenus [windowM], ItemFromName (flipname), chr (0));
            end;
      GetWTitle (WindowPtr (myEvent.message), windowName);
      curWinItem := ItemFromName (windowName);
      curWinName := windowName;
      CheckItem (myMenus [windowM], curWinItem, true);
      if windowCount > 1
      then
         begin
            flipWin := windowPtr (LastNoDA);
            GetWTitle (flipWin, flipname);
            SetItemCmd (myMenus [windowM], ItemFromName (flipname), 'F');
         end;

   end {if BitAnd...then begin}
 else   {application window is becoming inactive}
   begin
   TEDeactivate(TEHandle(WindowPeek(myEvent.message)^.refcon));
   if WindowPeek (FrontWindow)^.windowKind < 0
     then
         EnableItem (myMenus[editM], undoItem)
      else DisableItem (myMenus[editM], undoItem);
   end;   {else begin}
end; {activateEvt begin}

       updateEvt:
         begin
           GetPort (savedPort);
           SetPort (GrafPtr (myEvent.message));
           BeginUpdate(WindowPtr(myEvent.message));
           EraseRect (WindowPtr(myEvent.message)^.portRect);
           TEUpdate(WindowPtr(myEvent.message)^.portRect,
           TEHandle(WindowPeek(myEvent.message)^.refcon));
           EndUpdate(WindowPtr(myEvent.message));
           SetPort (savedPort);
         end;   {updateEvt begin}

     end; {case myEvent.what}

   until doneFlag;
   end.
```

Listing 9-1 continued

```
resource 'MENU' (128) {
    128,
    textMenuProc,
    0x7FFFFFFD,
    enabled,
    apple,
    {   /* array: 2 elements */
        /* [1] */
        "About WindMenu...", noIcon, noKey, noMark, plain;
        /* [2] */
        "-", noIcon, noKey, noMark, plain
    }
};

resource 'MENU' (129) {
    129,
    textMenuProc,
    0x7FFFFFF7,
    enabled,
    "File",
    {   /* array: 5 elements */
        /* [1] */
        "New", noIcon, "N", noMark, plain;
        /* [2] */
        "Open", noIcon, "O", noMark, plain;
        /* [3] */
        "Close", noIcon, "W", noMark, plain;
        /* [4] */
        "-", noIcon, noKey, noMark, plain;
        /* [5] */
        "Quit", noIcon, "Q", noMark, plain
    }
};

resource 'MENU' (130) {
    130,
    textMenuProc,
    0x7FFFFFFC,
    enabled,
    "Edit",
    {   /* array: 6 elements */
        /* [1] */
        "Undo", noIcon, "Z", noMark, plain;
        /* [2] */
        "-", noIcon, noKey, noMark, plain;
        /* [3] */
        "Cut", noIcon, "X", noMark, plain;
        /* [4] */
        "Copy", noIcon, "C", noMark, plain;
        /* [5] */
        "Paste", noIcon, "V", noMark, plain;
        /* [6] */
        "Clear", noIcon, noKey, noMark, plain
    }
};
```

Listing 9-1 continued

```
resource 'MENU' (131) {
    131,
    textMenuProc,
    0x7FFFFFF7,
    enabled,
    "Window",
    {"Tile Windows", noIcon, "T", noMark, plain;
     "Stack Windows", noIcon, "S", noMark, plain;
     "Move and Resize", noIcon, "M", noMark, plain;
     "-", noIcon, noKey, noMark, plain
    }
};

resource 'BNDL' (128) {
    'Scot',
    0,

    {   /* array TypeArray: 2 elements */
        /* [1] */
        'ICN#',
        {   /* array IDArray: 2 elements */
            /* [1] */
            0, 128;
            /* [2] */
            1, 129
        };
        /* [2] */
        'FREF',
        {   /* array IDArray: 2 elements */
            /* [1] */
            0, 128;
            /* [2] */
            1, 129
        }
    }
};

resource 'DLOG' (1000, "About box") {
    {62, 100, 148, 412},
    dBoxProc,
    visible,
    goAway,
    0x0,
    1000,
    "About face"
};
```

Listing 9-1 continued

```
resource 'DLOG' (1001, "Resize") {
    {100, 120, 250, 430},
    dBoxProc,
    visible,
    noGoAway,
    0x0,
    1001,
    "Move me"
};

resource 'DITL' (1001) {
    {   /* array DITLarray: 11 elements */
        /* [1] */
        {110,70,130,125},
        Button {
            enabled,
            "OK"
        };
        /* [2] */
        {110,200,130,255},
        Button {
            enabled,
            "Cancel"
        };
        /* [3] */
        {9, 68, 29, 213},
        StaticText {
            disabled,
            "New size for window"
        },
        /* [4] */
        {44, 19, 64, 50},
        StaticText {
            disabled,
            "top"
        },
        /* [5] */
        {78, 19, 98, 50},
        StaticText {
            disabled,
            "left"
        },
```

Listing 9-1 continued

```
        /* [6] */
        {44, 146, 65, 199},
        StaticText {
            disabled,
            "bottom"
        },
        /* [7] */
        {78, 146, 99, 185},
        StaticText {
            disabled,
            "right"
        },
        /* [8] */
        {44, 59, 64, 119},
        EditText {
            enabled,
            ""
        },
        /* [9] */
        {78, 59, 98, 119},
        EditText {
            enabled,
            ""
        },
        /* [10] */
        {44, 204, 64, 264},
        EditText {
            enabled,
            ""
        },
        /* [11] */
        {80, 204, 100, 264},
        EditText {
            enabled,
            ""
        }
    }
};
```

Listing 9-1 continued

```
resource 'DITL' (1000, "About box") {
    {   /* array DITLarray: 2 elements */
        /* [1] */
        {61, 191, 81, 251},
        Button {
            enabled,
            "OK"
        };
        /* [2] */
        {8, 24, 56, 272},
        StaticText {
            disabled,
            "WindMenu example program\nby Scott Knaster"
            "\nversion 1.0 7/4/87"
        }
    }
};


resource 'FREF' (128) {
    'APPL',
    0,
    ""
};

resource 'FREF' (129) {
    'TEXT',
    1,
    ""
};

resource 'ICN#' (128) {
    {   /* array: 2 elements */
```

Listing 9-1 continued

```
        /* [1] */
        $"FFFF FFFF 8000 0005 FD00 0005 9100 0005"
        $"9100 0005 91EF 0005 9129 0005 912F 0005"
        $"9128 0005 912F 0005 8000 0805 8F00 0805"
        $"8880 0805 8898 C905 8F25 2A05 88A5 2C05"
        $"88A5 2A05 8F18 C905 8000 0005 8000 0005"
        $"9000 0005 9000 E485 9001 0505 9001 0605"
        $"9C90 C405 9290 2605 9290 2505 9CF1 C485"
        $"8010 0005 8010 0005 80F0 0005 FFFF FFFF";
        /* [2] */
        $"FFFF FFFF FFFF FFFF FFFF FFFF FFFF FFFF"
        $"FFFF FFFF FFFF FFFF FFFF FFFF FFFF FFFF"
        $"FFFF FFFF FFFF FFFF FFFF FFFF FFFF FFFF"
        $"FFFF FFFF FFFF FFFF FFFF FFFF FFFF FFFF"
        $"FFFF FFFF FFFF FFFF FFFF FFFF FFFF FFFF"
        $"FFFF FFFF FFFF FFFF FFFF FFFF FFFF FFFF"
        $"FFFF FFFF FFFF FFFF FFFF FFFF FFFF FFFF"
        $"FFFF FFFF FFFF FFFF FFFF FFFF FFFF FFFF"
    }
};

resource 'ICN#' (129) {
    {   /* array: 2 elements */
        /* [1] */
        $"0FFF FE00 0800 0300 09D0 0280 09D0 0240"
        $"09D0 0220 09D0 0210 09D0 03F8 09D0 0008"
        $"09D0 0008 09D0 0008 09D0 0008 09D0 0008"
        $"09F0 0008 0910 0008 0910 0008 0910 0008"
        $"0910 0008 0910 0008 08E0 0008 09F0 0008"
        $"09F0 0008 09F8 0008 09F8 0008 09E8 5FE8"
        $"09F8 0BE8 08D0 3FE8 08F0 FFE8 0870 3FE8"
        $"0819 FFE8 0800 0008 0800 0008 0FFF FFF8";
        /* [2] */
        $"0FFF FE00 0FFF FF00 0FFF FF80 0FFF FFC0"
        $"0FFF FFE0 0FFF FFF0 0FFF FFF8 0FFF FFF8"
        $"0FFF FFF8 0FFF FFF8 0FFF FFF8 0FFF FFF8"
        $"0FFF FFF8 0FFF FFF8 0FFF FFF8 0FFF FFF8"
        $"0FFF FFF8 0FFF FFF8 0FFF FFF8 0FFF FFF8"
        $"0FFF FFF8 0FFF FFF8 0FFF FFF8 0FFF FFF8"
        $"0FFF FFF8 0FFF FFF8 0FFF FFF8 0FFF FFF8"
        $"0FFF FFF8 0FFF FFF8 0FFF FFF8 0FFF FFF8"
    }
};
```

Listing 9-1 continued

```
data 'Scot' (0) {
    $"1853 686F 776F 6666 2063 7265 6174 6564"    /* .WindMenu created */
    $"2031 322F 3235 2F38 35"                      /*  7/4/87 */
};
```

APPENDICES

New machines and system software. 68020 microprocessor overview. Macintosh Technical Note #110.

APPENDIX A

New Machines and System
Software

This appendix discusses new Macintosh develop-
ments that Apple released in 1987. Specifically, we'll
talk about the Macintosh SE and Macintosh II comput-
ers, which completely redefined the product line, and
System files version 4.1 and later, which added a lot of
features to the Macintosh Plus as well as the new com-
puters.

Macintosh SE

In March 1987, Apple began shipping the Macintosh SE, which immediately became the best-selling member of the Macintosh product line. When the SE was conceived at Apple, it was called the "Plus Plus," which is exactly what it was intended to be—an evolution of the successful Macintosh Plus.

The Macintosh SE has the following features and characteristics.

1. Two basic models are available from Apple. One comes with two internal floppy disk drives, the other with one floppy drive and one 20-megabyte hard disk drive. Both systems come with one megabyte of RAM. In the summer of 1987, Apple was reportedly selling 85 percent of Macintosh SEs in the hard disk configuration, and you can bet that a good percentage of the folks who weren't buying hard disks from Apple were getting hard disks from third-party developers rather than sticking with floppy-based systems. For those who want more than 20 megabytes or a faster drive, several manufacturers offer internal hard disks for the Macintosh SE. Since Apple doesn't ship the SE with fewer than two drives, those who want a different internal hard disk have to buy the two-floppy version and figure out how to convert the internal floppy to an external one; alternatively, they can use it as a hood ornament.

2. There is a choice of keyboards. The Macintosh SE doesn't come with a keyboard, as the box proudly tells you: "Keyboard not included. Mouse included." You can use the Apple Keyboard, which has virtually the same layout as the Macintosh Plus, or the Apple Extended Keyboard, which is modeled after the IBM PC RT keyboard and includes lots of function keys and obscure things like Scroll Lock and Alt. These are Apple's first Macintosh keyboards to include Control and Escape keys. You can also choose from several alternatives offered by third-party developers.

3. Both keyboards, as well as the mouse, connect to the computer through a scheme called Apple Desktop Bus (ADB), which allows the Apple II and Macintosh product lines to share input devices and also makes it somewhat easier for third parties to develop alternate keyboards, mice, tablets, and other electronic thingies to get data into the computer. This has the unfortunate side effect of preventing owners of Macintosh Plus and earlier machines from using the new keyboards. On the back of the Macintosh SE, there are two connectors for Apple Desktop Bus, one

for the mouse and one for the keyboard. Interestingly enough, both of Apple's keyboards pass the ADB signals through and have a connector on each side, which means you can also plug the mouse directly into the keyboard. Both ways of plugging in the mouse work equally well; you can use whichever way you like.

4. The Macintosh SE has an expansion slot inside, making it the first truly hardware-expandable Macintosh. The reason it has only one slot is that it's real crowded in there. "Only" one slot, though, has provided lots of expansion opportunities for Macintosh SE owners: large screens, accelerator cards with 68020 microprocessors and 68881 coprocessors, debugging boards, and specialized hardware. Of course, most of these things are also available for previous Macintoshes, but they're a lot easier to design and install for the SE.

5. The Macintosh SE has ROM version $76. This ROM implements the changes necessary to support the new hardware in the Macintosh SE, such as the second built-in disk drive and the slot; in addition, it has some user interface toolbox changes, such as support for the new version of TextEdit. The ROM contains about 192K of code in a 256K-byte pair of chips. The rest of the ROM is either empty or filled up with grainy, digitized pictures; the pictures are of people who worked on the Macintosh SE, people who helped the people who worked on the Macintosh SE, and other people who were around when the pictures were made. It seems that Apple could have filled the remaining ROM space with commonly used resources, but this isn't what happened. See the section on Toolbox and operating system changes in this appendix for more information on the new toolbox routines.

6. The Macintosh SE can be upgraded to several levels of RAM just by plugging in special modules called SIMMs (single inline memory modules) and clipping a resistor. SIMMs are available in two varieties: 256K and 1M. The SE (like the Macintosh Plus) has four SIMM sockets and you have to install them in pairs—that is, you can't have three of one size and one of another. Given these rules, you can have the following RAM totals:

- Four 256K, for one megabyte.
- Two 256K, two 1M, for 2.5 megabytes.
- Four 1M, for four megabytes.

7. The Macintosh SE isn't beige. Hey, don't laugh. Not only has case color been elevated to the esteemed postion of Religious Issue inside Apple, it really raised a stir in the Macintosh world when all the computers and peripherals were switched to a light gray color called platinum in early 1987. This was done as

part of the effort to give a more uniform look to Apple's entire product line, which previously had consisted of some beige (Macintosh, Apple IIe, ImageWriter) and some refrigerator white (Apple IIc, LaserWriter, ImageWriter II) cases. Since the Apple IIgs and for the foreseeable future, everything is platinum. Of course, if you don't like it, several companies will give your Macintosh a custom paint job, carefully disassembling it, painting, and putting it back together, for the techie who has everything.

Little-known feature.   The Macintosh SE differs radically from earlier models in another important way: it has a high-capacity power supply and a cooling fan. The Macintosh community (which is located near Santa Cruz, California) has had lots of reports of power supply failures over the past couple of years. The Macintosh SE power supply and fan are designed to make sure the system won't overheat or run out of oomph. Since there's a fan the old venting slots across the top of the other Macintoshes aren't needed any more, so they've been filled in. This adds a very handy feature to the Macintosh SE: you can pile papers, compact discs, and small toys on the top without fear of making the computer overheat.

That's it. Those are the most significant differences in the Macintosh SE.

Apple has a pretty good history of providing upgrades to allow its customers to add the features of new machines to their existing ones. For example, anyone with one of the original Macintosh 128K models could move all the way up to a Macintosh Plus with the appropriate upgrade hardware from Apple. To give an example from another product line, an Apple IIe owner can get to the next generation, the Apple IIgs, with an upgrade kit. This helps customers stay loyal, and it's good business for Apple, since upgrade kits make money, too.

When the Macintosh SE came out, Apple didn't provide a way to upgrade existing products. The reason for this is the total redesign of the Macintosh that made the SE possible. If you're comfortable slicing open your Macintosh, you might want to compare the guts of the Plus with the SE. You'll see how different they really are, as the SE uses a custom VLSI chip to perform most of the logic functions and uses the extra room for the slot.

One reason the lack of an upgrade path for the SE isn't such a bad thing is that except for the slot, most of the SE's capabilities can be had with a Macintosh Plus. The new user interface features in the SE's ROM are available in System 4.1 for the Macintosh Plus, so there's virtually no software that works on an SE and not a Plus.

In fact, from a programmer's point of view, the most interesting thing about the Macintosh SE is that you should rarely have to think about the fact that it's a different model of Macintosh. For an application programmer, the real interesting differences are those contained in System file versions 4.1 and later, which provide new features to the entire Macintosh line of computers and which we'll talk about later in this appendix.

Macintosh II

The Macintosh II, which Apple announced in March 1987 and shipped in May of that year, made several radical changes in the Macintosh product line. One of the toughest things about making the Macintosh II was that it could not be a completely new computer; it had to be an extension of the Macintosh product line.

To the credit of its designers and engineers, it has many of the features that have become famous on the earlier models. The Macintosh II still runs almost all the software that works on earlier machines and Apple has kept the same operating system working across the entire current line while still taking advantage of many of the Macintosh II's advanced features, a feat that seems to have eluded other computer manufacturers.

Here are the features and characteristics of the Macintosh II.

1. Two configurations are available from Apple. One model includes one megabyte of RAM and one floppy disk drive; the high-end unit comes with a megabyte of RAM, a floppy drive, and a 40-megabyte internal hard disk.

    Although these are the only ways it ships from Apple, you can get lots of options. An additional internal floppy drive is available. You can choose an internal hard disk of 20, 40, or 80 megabytes. Memory upgrade options are also available. The Macintosh II has eight SIMM slots and it requires that you install memory in groups of four SIMMs. These are the possible memory configurations for the Macintosh II, using 256K and 1M SIMMs:

    *   Four 256K, four empty slots, for one megabyte.
    *   Eight 256K, for two megabytes.
    *   Four 1M, four empty slots, for four megabytes.

- Four 1M, four 256K, for five megabytes.
- Eight 1M, for eight megabytes.

2. The Macintosh II, like the SE, comes with a mouse but no key-board and uses Apple Desktop Bus. You can choose from either of Apple's keyboards or you can use a third-party ADB model.

3. Probably the most significant thing that makes the Macintosh II different from its other family members is that it has six expan-sion slots inside. These slots, which support the standard NuBus connection scheme, allow you to add things to your Macintosh II that aren't built into the machine. You do this by plugging in NuBus expansion cards, which are available from Apple and lots of third-party developers.

    One thing that's not built into the Macintosh II that you'll probably want to add right away if you want to get much work done is video output. For maximum flexibility, the II doesn't gen-erate video output all by itself. Instead, you plug in a NuBus card that connects to a monitor; the card and the monitor get to-gether with QuickDraw and the Slot Manager to show you what's happening.

    Apple sells two monitors, a video card, and an upgrade kit for the video card. The monitors are a 12-inch black and white and a 13-inch color, both of which display 640 pixels across and 480 down. The video card will support up to 16 colors on the color monitor, or 16 gray shades on the monochrome. With the video card upgrade kit, you can have 256 colors or shades of gray on the screen at the same time.

    A monitor is controlled by a video card in a slot and the Mac-intosh II has six slots, so someone working on the Macintosh II thought it would be clever to work out a way to let you use more than one monitor at a time. This idea became reality in Color QuickDraw, in which the desktop can consist of as many moni-tors as you've got plugged in.

    A Macintosh II user can put windows anywhere on any screen or even have them straddle two or more screens, and the magic is handled by Color QuickDraw. Using the Control Panel, the user can choose a monitor's display settings, such as whether a color monitor should be displaying color or not, and how many colors or shades of gray should be used.

4. The Macintosh II has a 68020 microprocessor and a 68881 floating point coprocessor as standard equipment. The 68020 is an im-proved version of the good old 68000 that's used in the other Ma-cintoshes. It can push around twice as much information at a time as the 68000, and in the Macintosh II it's run at twice the speed of the earlier machines. With these numbers, we can crudely es-

timate that programs run about four times as fast on a II as they do on a 68000-based Macintosh. Although that's too simple a method to be real, it provides a reasonable approximation.

The 68881 floating-point coprocessor is a special chip that speeds up real arithmetic (that's math with numbers that aren't integers) by a huge factor. Most microprocessors, including the 68000 and even the mighty 68020, can perform arithmetic only on integers; real number math has to be done in software, which is much slower than encoding it right in the microprocessor.

On the Macintoshes before the II, floating-point math is done in the Standard Apple Numerics Environment package (SANE). On the Macintosh II, most applications still go through SANE, which knows how to take advantage of a 68881 if one is present. The 68881 is a slick invention from Motorola, makers of the whole 68000 family, which can do a wide range of real number math. We're not just talking addition and subtraction here, either: the set of functions is very complete, including trigonometric functions, logarithms, square root, exponentiation, and other big math-type words.

The main advantage to using the 68881 instead of SANE is a remarkable speed improvement. By using the 68881 directly, calculations can be several hundred times faster than when using SANE. This shows the power of having features built into a microprocessor or coprocessor. It's interesting to note that in some cases, SANE provides better accuracy than the 68881. This happens with some transcendental and trigonometric functions.

5. The Macintosh II has 256K bytes of ROM. This ROM starts with the Macintosh SE version and adds code to take care of the slots, the color video capabilities, and various new user interface features. The Macintosh II ROM is filled to its 256K limit with code and some often-used resources; there's no room for anybody's picture.

Even though the Macintosh II has lots of features that aren't in any other Macintosh, it's still quite easy to write software that's compatible with the whole product line. Of course, to do that you have to use the lowest common denominator, but that really isn't very low. About the only general features you have to sacrifice for easy compatibility are 256-color mode (also called eight-bit color) and direct access to the 68881. The Macintosh operating system lets you take full advantage of big screens, multiple screens, larger memory, and multitasking, without having to write special-case code.

Toolbox and Operating System Changes

When the Macintosh II shipped, Apple also started shipping System version 4.1 with all Macintosh computers. This new version was cooked up especially to support the II and the SE, but it also contains enhancements for the Macintosh Plus. In this section, we'll talk about the new system software features that are provided by System 4.1 and the ROMs in the SE and the II.

In some cases, a new feature is implemented partially in ROM and partially by patches in the system file; an example of this is the new version of TextEdit. For features like this, it's not really significant to a programmer whether the routine is defined in ROM or in the system file. It works the same way in either case.

For each new feature discussed, you can assume that all three of the current Macintoshes (Plus, SE, II) support that feature, unless otherwise noted. Although System 4.1 works with the Macintosh 512K Enhanced, it requires a larger system heap, cutting down on the amount of RAM available to applications. If an application can still fit in a 512K Enhanced with System 4.1, it can take advantage of the new features provided by the new system file.

We'll go over the new Toolbox features thoroughly, but most of the other new stuff (Script Manager, Sound Manager, and so on) is just given a quick overview. To go into depth on everything would require a great deal of space, enough to fill an entire book— a book called *Inside Macintosh, Volume V*, in fact, which is the place to turn if you're hungry for more information on these features.

Menu Manager

The new version of the Menu Manager has added a bunch of features that extend the user interface. Menu items can now contain menus themselves, through a scheme called hierarchical menus. This is useful for lists of similar things, like fonts or font sizes. Instead of having to clutter up a whole menu with a list of fonts, you can place this list in a submenu and it will be seen only when the user is holding down the mouse button on the associated menu item.

The Menu Manager now supports popup menus, which are menus that can appear anywhere on the screen at the click of a mouse. This is really just a generalization of what happens when a hierarchical menu appears, so it was added to the Menu Manager at the same time.

User interface corner.   Usually, popup menus are used to select from a list within a dialog. This is pretty much the same thing you do with a list of radio buttons or with a scrolling list: you can use all three of these in very similar situations. Which one should you use? One criterion is the amount of screen space you have. Popup menus are handy when you're pressed for space, since the lists of items are hidden until they pop out in front of the other stuff on the screen. Scrolling lists can be as big as you want, allowing the user to see at least a few choices. A group of radio buttons lets you show all the available choices.

The menu bar used to be drawn by hard code in the ROM. Now, there's a new definition procedure called the menu bar defproc that lets you fool around with the appearance of the menu bar. Like with other defprocs, this one gives you the ability to do lots of bizarre custom things with the menu bar. Your menu bar defproc lets you define exactly what your menu bar looks like, where it will appear, how menus are drawn, and almost everything else about a menu bar's behavior.

There are several cosmetic changes and additions to the Menu Manager, too. When a menu has enough items to scroll, it now displays a nice black triangle at the bottom of the menu indicating there's more than meets the eye. As you scroll down, a triangle will appear at the top of the menu to remind you there are more items in that direction.

The Macintosh system software has been greatly enhanced to support languages and writing systems that are very different from English; in particular, we're talking about writing from right to left, as in Arabic and Hebrew, and languages with thousands of different characters, such as Chinese and Japanese. To support this, the Menu Manager does its part by displaying font names for international writing systems (called **scripts** by Apple) in the appropriate script, rather than in the usual Chicago (which is in the United States) font; for example, fonts associated with the Chinese script system will be shown in Chinese.

When the user lets the mouse up on a disabled menu item, the Menu Manager used to just return a 0 in the MenuSelect routine and you had no way of knowing what had happened, only that no valid menu choice was made. Now, a routine called MenuChoice will tell you the menu and disabled item that the user chose. This can be useful for implementing a neat help feature where you can nicely explain to the user just why the menu item is disabled.

The Menu Manager also supplies support for lots of color in your menus if you're using a Macintosh II. It's very non-obtrusive about it, though. The only color you get automatically, without asking, is the six-color Apple logo as the title of the Apple menu. Everything else is drawn in black and white by default, but you can really go wild by adding various resources that tell the Menu Manager to draw in color.

The Menu Manager lets you specify separate colors for lots of different parts of your menus. You can choose different colors for all these things:

- The menu bar's background.
- Each pulled-down menu's background.
- Each menu's title.
- Each item's name.
- Each item's Command key.
- Each item's mark character (usually a check mark).

Color blind. As you can see, you can really go wild with color in your menus, but you should control your urges in the interests of preserving your users' sanity and their eyesight. Even though you can do all this fancy stuff with colors in menus, most users will probably prefer to stick with legible, boring black and white in their menus. In general, you should leave it up to them to color their menus if they want to.

The new version of the Menu Manager fixes an interesting limitation of preceding versions. In the original Menu Manager, each menu contained a long integer that was used as a set of flags to enable each item and the menu itself. One bit was used to decide if the menu was enabled and the remaining 31 bits in the long word determined whether items were enabled. This meant that if you had more than 31 items in a menu, disabling an item would also disable the item that came 32 positions later in the menu, since they would share the same flag.

For compatibility reasons, the size of the flag's long word couldn't be changed in the new Menu Manager. Instead, new code was added that makes sure you can only disable the first 31 items in a menu. Items past number 31 are always enabled. Since most menus that have that many items are lists of fonts and since there's rarely a reason to disable a menu item in a font menu, this little trick works out pretty well.

New Menu Manager routines.

```
Procedure InitProcMenu (resID: Integer; aVariant: Integer);
```

If you've defined your own custom menu bar defproc, you should call this routine instead of InitMenus. This will initialize the menu bar properly with the resource ID and variant you specify. Since InitWindows calls InitMenu to draw the menu bar, be sure you call InitProcMenu before calling InitWindows.

```
Procedure GetItemCmd (menu: Menuhandle; item: Integer;
VAR cmdChar: Char);
```

```
Procedure SetItemCmd (menu: Menuhandle; item: Integer;
cmdChar: Char);
```

These two procedures give you an easy way to look at and change the Command-key equivalent associated with a menu item. When a menu item has a submenu, it will have a "Command key" of $1B, so these routines can also be used to monkey around with hierarchical menus.

```
Function PopUpMenuSelect (menu: MenuHandle; top, left,
popUpItem: Integer): Longint;
```

This call makes a popup menu appear anywhere on the screen and lets the user start tracking through it. The menu parameter is a handle to a standard menu, which you can create with Rez or ResEdit. The top and left parameters give the point where you want the selected item in the menu to appear. The popUpItem gives the number of the item that was selected the last time this menu was used. This should be set up so that if the user just clicks the mouse button and doesn't track through the menu, the choice remains the PopUpItem. For a good example of how the user interface for popup menus should work, check out how Commando works in the Macintosh Programmer's Workshop.

```
Function MenuChoice: Longint;
```

As we said earlier, you can call this routine after getting back a 0 from MenuSelect. If the user had the mouse button on a disabled menu item when the button went up, MenuChoice will give you the menu ID and item number of the item that the mouse pointer was touching.

Macintosh II only:

```
     Procedure SetMCEntries (numEntries: Integer; menuCEntries:
MCTablePtr);
     Function GetMCEntry (menuID, menuItem: Integer): MCEntryPtr;
     Procedure DelMCEntries (menuID, menuItem: Integer);
```

These three calls are used to fool around with the menu color information table, which is the data structure that tells what colors to use when drawing a menu bar and its menus. The SetMCEntries call lets you set up color information from an array of color entries. Each entry in the array can have information for the menu bar, a menu, or an item. Here's the format of each element in the array.

```
type mcEntry = Record
                 mctID, mctItem: Integer; {menu and item ID}
                 mctRGB1: RGBColor; {title or mark color}
                 mctRGB2: RGBColor; {background or item color}
                 mctRGB3:RGBColor; {item or Command color}
                 mctRGB4: RGBColor; {menu bar or background color}
                 mctReserved: Integer; {used by Mr. Menu}
               end;
```

The mctID and mctItem are used to tell what you're interested in coloring. If both values are 0, the entry is used for the menu bar. For this kind of entry, the first RGB color is the default color for menu titles; the second is the default for the background of pulled-down menus; the third is the default for menu items, Command keys, and marks; and the last RGB is used to draw the menu bar itself.

If mctItem is 0 and mctID isn't, then the table entry is for the menu that has an ID of mctID. The first RGB is the color of the menu's title; RGB2 is used internally; RGB3 is the default color for items in that menu; and RGB4 is the background color for the pulled-down menu.

If both mctItem and mctID are non-0, the table entry has information for a single menu item, specified by using mctID as the menu ID and mctItem as the item number. For this kind of entry, the first RGB color is used for the item's mark (usually a check mark); the second RGB is the color for the item's name; the item's Command-key equivalent is drawn with RGB3; and the fourth color is used internally.

The menuCEntries parameter in the SetMCEntries call is a pointer to an array of these color entries. You should construct a dummy entry with an mctID of –99 to indicate the end of the table. You can use DelMCEntries to remove the color information for any menu bar, menu, or item. GetMCEntry will return the color stuff for any colored menu structure.

Macintosh II only:

```
Procedure SetMCInfo (menuCTbl: MCTableHandle);

Function GetMCInfo: MCTableHandle;

Procedure DispMCInfo (menuCTbl: MCTableHandle);
```

These three calls let you change, examine, and throw away the color information for an entire menu bar all in one shot. The data structure that you're dealing with in each case is an entire MCTable (even though you know that stands for menu color table, aren't you tempted to call it a McTable?).

TextEdit

One of the original ideas behind the design of the Macintosh Toolbox was to provide consistency across different applications. The idea was to give programmers a standard way of displaying windows, a standard way of implementing pull-down menus, and so on. This way, the theory went, users would have an easier time figuring out how to move from one application to another—a theory that proved to be absolutely right.

One of the central elements of that consistency is text-editing ability. In the Macintosh ROM, TextEdit is used for virtually all simple text entry and editing. Users quickly learn the rules about cut, copy, and paste, clicking to select, backspacing, double-clicking to select a word, and so on. These rules work in almost every application.

TextEdit provides all the basic editing most applications need, but the wonderful Macintosh capabilities of multiple fonts, sizes, and faces (like bold, outline, and italic) really make you want more. TextEdit, however, is very limited in that area: each TextEdit record must display all its text the same way.

In the early days of the Macintosh, the solution for those who wanted more advanced text editing was a package called CoreEdit. This package did a lot of fancy things TextEdit couldn't do, such as mixing different fonts, sizes, and faces in a single record and implementing a smarter cut and paste. Apple's intention originally was to include CoreEdit as a package in the system file, but as it evolved it became less and less general-purpose and grew larger and larger. Eventually, Apple decided that it was too big, too specific, and possibly too fragile to be distributed and so it was removed from the system file.

The lack of an editing package that could deal with anything more than one font was a common complaint from Macintosh developers. So, in both of the 256K ROM versions and in System 4.1, Apple revised TextEdit to include support for multple fonts, sizes, and faces in a single text record. Since TextEdit was being remodeled at the same time that color was being added to the Macintosh, the new TextEdit also lets you set a color for each character in the text.

Of course, the most important goal in retrofitting TextEdit with these new features was to make sure that old applications worked just as before, but the really exciting parts of the new TextEdit are the fancy style capabilities. TextEdit now allows you to apply different font information to runs of text within a single record.

> **Terminology corner.** Most Macintosh programmers refer to possible variations in text (bold, italic, outline, underline, shadow, condense, and extend) as styles. However, the new TextEdit uses the term *style* to mean the entire set of variations on text, including the things just listed and font, size, and color tweaks. To avoid confusion, this section uses *style* to mean what the new TextEdit means; another term, *face*, is used for bold and friends.

To use these new tricks with TextEdit, you have to start with a new-version text record. Once you've got the text record, you can dress it up with style information in various ways. TextEdit uses a clever trick to indicate that a new-version record is being used. The old txSize field, which used to give the font size for the entire record, is now used simply as a flag; it's set to –1 to show that this is a new-version record. This works fine, since the size will never be negative on an old-version record; on a new-version record the text size can vary throughout the record and is kept somewhere else.

TextEdit uses a similar trick to deal with the multiple fonts, faces, and sizes the record can hold. In old-version TextEdit records, there are two fields, txFont and txFace, which hold the font ID and the text face for the entire record. In new-version text records (which can easily be spotted because they have –1 in the txSize field, remember), these fields are glued together and used as a handle to a **style record,** a thing that keeps track of the different styles used in the text.

The new TextEdit reads and writes a new type of scrap information, called styl, which includes the style characteristics of a chunk of text. If your application supports the new TextEdit, you'll be able to exchange formatted text with other programs that are as smart as yours. TextEdit writes the styl type whenever you call TECut or TE-Copy with a new-version record. It also writes type TEXT to be compatible with the masses.

New TextEdit calls.

```
Function TEStylNew (destRect, viewRect: Rect): TEHandle;
```

This is the call to use instead of TENew. It creates a text record in the new format. Like TENew, the destRect and viewRect are used to tell TextEdit how to draw and how to display the text.

```
        Procedure TESetStyle (mode: Integer; newStyle:
TextStyle; redraw: Boolean; hTE: TEHandle);

        Procedure TEGetStyle (offset: Integer; VAR theStyle:
TextStyle; VAR lineHeight, fontAscent: Integer; hTE: TEHandle);
```

These procedures are used to change and look at the style settings for a selection. You can use TESetStyle when you want to set the current selection to a new style. The mode parameter tells what characteristics you want to change. You can change a selection's font, face (bold, italic, and so on), size, or color. There's also a mode that changes all of these at once and a mode that increases or decreases the font size by a given number of points.

Here are the constants for the modes.

```
const    doFont = 1;      {set a new font ID}
         doFace = 2;      {change to bold, italic, or whatever}
         doSize = 4;      {set a new point size}
         doColor = 8;     {set the color}
         doAll = 15;      {change everything, one swell foop}
         addSize=16;      {change the point size}
```

The textStyle parameter holds style information in the following format.

```
type TextStyle = Record
                    tsFont : Integer;    {font ID}
                    tsFace: Style;       {style set}
                    tsSize: Integer;     {point size}
                    tsColor: RGBColor;   {color record}
                  End;
```

The redraw parameter to TESetStyle tells whether you want TextEdit to redraw the text in the new style; usually you'll want to do this. When you call TEGetStyle, you pass an offset parameter that gives the character position to look at in the text and the standard TEHandle to the record. You'll get back a style record like the one we just talked about plus, as a free added bonus, you'll get the line-height and font ascent for that character.

```
Procedure SetStylHandle (theHandle:TEStyleHandle; hTE: TEHandle);

Function GetStylHandle (hTE: TEHandle): TEStyleHandle;
```

These two calls are used when you want to deal with the style information for an entire new-version text record. They're mainly used when you want to save a new-version text record to disk and then bring it back later. A style record (the thing at the end of the TEStyleHandle) is really only usable on the text record it was created with, since it ties style information to specific runs of text in the record.

```
Procedure TEReplaceStyle (mode: Integer; oldStyle,
newStyle: TextStyle; redraw: Boolean; hTE: TEHandle);
```

You can use this procedure to selectively change all the text that's in one style into a different style. For example, you could use TEReplaceStyle to change all the text in Helvetica bold 9-point in red into Courier 12-point outline in mauve, assuming you know the RGB values for mauve. The mode parameters are the same as for TESetStyle. Only text that matches all the attributes you specify in the mode parameter is matched.

```
    Procedure TEStylInsert (text: Ptr; length: Longint; hST:
StScrpHandle; hTE: TEHandle);

    Procedure TEStylPaste (hTE: TEHandle);
```

These procedures let you grab and use formatted text information that's on the clipboard in a styl scrap type. Instead of calling TEInsert, use TEStylInsert to keep the formatting in the text. You can get the hST parameter by using the GetScrap function to read the styl information from the scrap. If you're inserting into an old-style record, don't worry; it will work just like TEInsert.

When the user wants to paste into a text record, you should call TEStylPaste. This will stick the style information into the record if it's a new-version record and there's styl information on the scrap. Otherwise, it'll work just like TEPaste, so you have nothing to lose.

```
Function GetStylScrap (hTE: TEHandle) : StScrpHandle;
```

This function is used to copy the selection's style information into the data at the end of the StScrpHandle. You can then write it to the scrap if you want by calling PutScrap. When you call TECopy or TECut and the text record you're working on is a new-version one, the style information will be written automatically along with the text, so you may not need to use this call. You could use it if you wanted to implement a feature that allowed style information only to be copied and pasted.

```
Function TEGetOffset (pt: Point; hTE: TEHandle) : Integer;

Function TEGetPoint (offset: Integer; hTE: TEHandle) : Point;
```

These two handy functions really have nothing to do with the fancy style functionality that has been added to TextEdit. They just provide a couple of convenient utilities for helping to figure out what's going on in your text record. They work with both old and new-version records. If you know a point in your text and you want to find out what character lies at that point, you can call TEGetOffset and it will tell you what character you're in. This is useful for finding out what the user has clicked on in a text record.

The TEGetPoint function does the inverse: if you know a character offset into your text record and you want to find out where that character is drawn on the screen, it will tell you. The point returned is the bottom left of the character, the position where QuickDraw normally starts drawing text.

```
Function TEGetHeight (endLine, startLine: Longint; hTE:
TEHandle) : Longint;
```

This function is useful for figuring out how much vertical space any chunk of text takes up in your record. Given two lines in the text record, it totals up the space from the top of startLine to the bottom of endLine and returns the answer as the function result. You can use this call on old-version records, even though you can also calculate it just by multiplying the line height by the number of lines, since all lines are the same height in old records.

Window Manager

The new version of the Window Manager has been changed mainly by the addition of support for color and multiple screens, and both of these things are only available in the Macintosh II ROM. There are only a couple of new general-purpose calls in the Window Manager, and even these don't really add any new functionality.

A few existing routines work a little differently now so that they do the right thing in a world that might contain multiple screens and a color desktop pattern. The original Window Manager drew non-window things, like the menu bar and window titles and frames, in a special grafport called the Window Manager port or WMgrPort. For the Macintosh II, grafports that support the new color model have to be a new kind, called color grafports. So, the Window Manager also makes a new structure called the WMgrCPort when it starts up and it draws any new-version windows in this port.

When you use MoveWindow to slide a window (or part of a window) from one screen to another, it doesn't automatically redraw the window's structure, as it used to do back in the primitive days of one screen per computer. Now, it will only redraw the part of the window structure that stays on the same screen. Any part that gets moved to a new screen is drawn when the next update event happens.

The routines that drag windows and regions around (DragWindow, DragTheRgn, DragGrayRgn) work a little differently on the Macintosh II. Instead of limiting the dragging to the rectangle that you pass, these routines will now examine your rectangle. If it looks like your limiting rectangle came from screenBits.bounds (strictly speaking, the left, right, and bottom coordinates have to be within six pixels of screenBits, and the top coordinate must be within 36 pixels of screenBits), the dragging calls will let the user drag around all the screens. A region that comprises all the screens put together is stored in the global variable called GrayRgn.

GrowWindow still limits the user to the rectangle you specify when resizing a new window. There's a power-user trick that can override your limits and let the adventurous user make a window that touches more than one screen: holding down the Command key while resizing the window removes the limits on the window's size. Of course, depending on the application, this may cause big problems, but most programs seem to handle it OK. When you're writing your application, be sure to anticipate that your windows might get very stretched. As long as you're ready for big windows, you shouldn't have to do anything special for multiple screens.

The Window Manager has invented some new things to support the new color model. There's a new data structure called a color window record. It's identical to the original window record, except that the old grafport field is now a color grafport. A new structure, called an **auxiliary window record,** holds the colors that are used to draw the window's structure.

Every color window record can have an auxiliary window record that tells about its colors. Unfortunately, no field is available in the window record to point to the auxiliary window record. Every auxiliary record contains a field that points to its owner.

Any color window record that doesn't have a corresponding auxiliary record is colored according to a resource of type wctb and ID 0. If there's no wctb 0 in any open resource file, you'll get the one in ROM, which simply sets the window up in beautiful black and white. The format of a wctb is the same as a window color table, which we'll talk about very soon.

When you call InitWindows, the Window Manager uses the first wctb 0 resource it finds to set up an auxiliary record. Since each auxiliary record points to its owner, every window that uses colors other than the default has to have its own auxiliary record, even if it uses the same colors as another window.

All the auxiliary records are connected together in a linked list. There's a field in each one that contains a handle to the next one in the list. The last auxiliary record is the one that was created from the first wctb found in the resource chain. You can tell it's the default record because its link to the next record (the awNext field) is nil.

Here's a look at all the fields in the auxiliary window record:

```
type AuxWinRec = record
                awNext: AuxWinHndl;
                awOwner: WindowPtr;
                awCTable: CTabHandle;
                dialogCTable: Handle;
                awFlags: Longint;
                awResrv: Longint;
                awRefCon: Longint;
            end;
```

We've already said that the awNext field contains a handle to the next auxiliary window record in the chain or nil if this is the default record (which, conveniently enough, is also the last record in the list). The awOwner field contains a pointer to the window that uses this record. The awCTable field has a handle to the color table for this window. The color table tells which parts of the window get which colors. We'll explore it in just a moment.

If this auxiliary record is used by a dialog, the Dialog Manager will put some of its stuff at the end of the dialogCTable handle. The next two fields, awFlags and asResrv, aren't used in this version of the ROM and are saved for future fun, so you shouldn't mess around with them. The last field, awRefCon, is reserved for your application's use, just like the other refcon fields throughout the Toolbox.

Now, as promised, here's the window color table the auxiliary record points to.

```
type WinCTab = Record
                wCSeed: Longint;
                wCReserved: Integer;
                ctSize: Integer;
                ctTable: Array [0..4] of ColorSpec;
            end;
```

This table holds the information that tells how to color the structure parts of the window. The first two fields aren't used for windows (technically, they're reserved by Apple, so you shouldn't use them either). The ctSize field gives the array index of the last entry in the table. For windows, there are five things that you can color, so there are usually five entries in the table; since the first entry has index 0, ctSize is usually 4. If you write your own custom window definition function, you may have a different number of parts to be colored.

The last field matches RGB values to parts of the window's structure. Each ColorSpec record contains an integer and an RGB value. The integer in every ColorSpec has a value that tells what part of the window should get the RGB from that record. These are the values for the window's parts:

```
cons   twContentColor = 0;    {content region's background}
       wFrameColor = 1;       {the window frame}
       wTextColor = 2;        {the window's title}
       wHiliteColor = 3;      {hilit close and zoom boxes}
       wTitleBarColor = 4;    {title bar background}
```

Let's say you wanted to set up a window to have a white content, a black frame, red text, blue highlighting for the close and zoom boxes, and a green title bar (sounds lovely). Here's how you would set up the window color table:

```
{VAR aTableHdl : WCTabHandle}
aTableHdl := WCTabHandle (NewHandle (sizeOf (WinCTab)));
with aTableHdl^^ do
   begin
      ctSize := 4;   {five elements in color table}
      with ctTable [0] do
         begin
            value := wContentColor; {we want this part white}
            rgb.red := 65535;   rgb.green := 65535;
            rgb.blue := 65535; {Pump it Up to white}
         end;

      with ctTable [1] do
         begin
            value :=  wFrameColor; {set this to black}
            rgb.red := 0;  rgb.green := 0;  rgb.blue := 0;
            {Can't get Less than Zero}
         end;

      with ctTable [2] do
         begin
            value :=  wTextColor;  {this should be red}
            rgb.red := 65535;  rgb.green := 0;  rgb.blue := 0;
            {The Angels Wanna Wear my Red Shoes}
         end;
```

```
with ctTable [3] do
   begin
      value :=  wHiliteColor;  {Set this one blue}
      rgb.red := 0;  rgb.green := 0;  rgb.blue := 65535;
      {Almost Blue?  No, completely blue!}
   end;

with ctTable [4] do
   begin
      value :=  wTitleBarColor; {Green it}
      rgb.red := 0;  rgb.green := 65535;  rgb.blue := 0;
      {Green Shirt}
   end;

end; {with aTableHdl^^ do}
```

This code will construct the color table we want for the window. We could call AddResource to put the table into a wctb resource and then use it with GetNewCWindow. We could also assign it directly to a window that's already around using the SetWinColor routine discussed below.

Look up.   Remember that the actual color you'll see on the screen depends on the monitor and settings that the user has chosen. If the user has a device that uses a lookup table, like the Apple Color Monitor, several levels of filtering will occur. To pick your ideal color, you specify an RGB value. The one displayed on the screen may be slightly different, depending on how many bits per pixel the monitor is set up for and whether any entries are available in the color table. The Color Manager will try hard to make the color very close to the one you want.

New Window Manager routines.
Macintosh II only:

```
Function NewCWindow (wStorage: Ptr; boundsRect: Rect;
title: Str255; visible: Boolean; procID: Integer;
behind: WindowPtr; goAwayFlag: Boolean; refCon: Longint) :
WindowPtr;

Function GetNewCWindow (windowID: Integer; wStorage:
behind: WindowPtr) : WindowPtr;
```

These calls are like their non-colored counterparts, except that they set up new-version window records. When you call GetNewC-Window, the Window Manager will look for a wctb resource with the same ID as the the WIND resource you're getting. If it finds one, it will create an auxiliary record and make it point to this window. If there's no corresponding resource, this window will get the default colors (the ones that live in wctb 0).

If you use NewCWindow, the Window Manager won't make an auxiliary record for the window, and it'll just use the default colors. You can assign an auxiliary record to this window with another call, though, which we'll discuss next.

Macintosh II only:

```
    Procedure SetWinColor (theWindow: WindowPtr;
newColorTable: WCTabHandle);
```

You can use this procedure to change the color table for a color window. This is especially useful after you call NewCWindow, where you can't just specify a wctb resource with the color information. You can just set up the color table and then use SetWinColor to make a new auxiliary record and tie it to the window.

If you create a colorless window with NewCWindow and immediately add color to it by calling SetWinColor, the window will first be drawn in black and white and then again in color, which is not a particularly classy way to do it. Instead, you can specify that the window be invisible when you create it, give it an auxiliary record, then make it visible.

Macintosh II only:

```
    Function GetAuxWin (theWindow:WindowPtr;awHndl:
AuxWinHndl): Boolean;
```

This routine will look through the auxiliary window records and find the one that's used for the window given in the theWindow parameter. If the window you pass only gets to use the default colors (that is, it has no auxiliary record), awHndl will have a handle to the default record, and the function result will be false.

Macintosh II only:

```
Procedure CGetWMgrPort (VAR wMgrCPort: CGrafPtr);
```

As we said earlier, the Window Manager now makes a new-version grafport (a color grafport) for drawing all the window's structures. This procedure will give you a pointer to that grafport.

> Although this procedure provides a clean, compatible way to get a pointer to the color Window Manager port, you should avoid drawing into it, since Apple's multitasking operating system means that you don't own the whole screen if other applications are running. Of course, the thing that makes the Window Manager port so attractive (the ability to draw anywhere on the screen) is exactly what makes it dangerous. If you decide to draw into it to add a neat trick to your application, you may mess up another application that's around.

```
Function GetGrayRgn: RgnHandle;
```

This new function is part of Apple's overall cleanup effort to convince you to stay away from low-memory globals. Using this call, you can get a handle to the gray region, the area making up the desktop, which may have more than one screen on the Macintosh II. This means you shouldn't have to look directly at the GrayRgn global.

```
Function GetWVariant (theWindow: WindowPtr): Integer;
```

This is an interesting little function: it returns the variant code for a window. In case you've forgotten, a window's variant code is the value that tells the window definition just how the window should look. For example, the standard window definition function has five variants including a standard document window, called documentProc; a standard alert box, called dBoxProc; and a window without a size box, named noGrowDocProc.

Usually, the window definition functions put the variant code into the high byte of the windowDefProc field of the window record. The low three bytes of this field contain a handle to the definition function itself. At first glance, this function seems pretty innocuous and fairly obscure. Why does there have to be a function to return this variant, when you can simply look in the windowDefProc field to find it?

The answer is that Apple wants to move the Macintosh operating system toward full 32-bit operation. Currently, several parts of the system use the high byte of pointers and handles to stash important stuff, like the variant code, for example. To use all 32 bits of the pointers and handles for addresses, the other stuff that's crammed in will have to be moved elsewhere.

To prepare for the great day when the Macintosh operating system uses 32-bit addresses, Apple is beginning to put in calls that will let them move the values that are presently stashed in high-order bytes of pointers and handles, limiting them to 24 bits. By using the GetWVariant call to find a window's variant code, Apple can move the variant information somewhere else and you'll still be assured of getting the right information.

Control Manager

The Control Manager now has the ability to draw controls in lots of different colors. Other than that, it's pretty much unchanged. Like the Window Manager, there's a new data structure called the **auxiliary control record,** which is used for color information about controls.

Auxiliary control records work very much like their window counterparts. When you call InitWindows, the Control Manager looks for a resource of type cctb and ID 0 to build a default auxiliary control record. If there isn't one, it will find the one in ROM that sets up controls for black and white. A cctb resource looks just like a control color table record: a long integer and an integer, which aren't used; an integer telling the number of entries in the table minus one; then, the table entries, each one consisting of an integer giving the part code for the control (the constants are listed below), then one integer each for the red, green, and blue magnitude.

This is the structure of an auxiliary control record.

```
type AuxCtlRec = Record
                acNext:  AuxCtlHndl;
                acOwner:  ControlHandle;
                acCTable:  CCTabHandle;
                acFlags:  Integer;
                acReserved:  Longint;
                acRefCon:  Longint;
              end;
```

The fields in an auxiliary control record have just the same meanings as in an auxiliary window record. The control color table (type CtlCTab) is just like a window color table, too, except that there are only four different parts of a control that can be colored, so there are four ColorSpec records instead of five.

Here are the constants you can use to color the four parts of a control.

```
const    cFrameColor = 0;         {frame, arrows, scroll shaft}
         cBodyColor = 1;          {buttons background, arrow &
                                    shaft foreground}
         cTextColor = 2;          {button title}
         cThumbColor = 3;         {interior of scroll box}
```

To get access to all the new model colors, you have to draw your controls in a window that was created with NewCWindow or Get-NewCWindow. Otherwise, the controls will be drawn in an old-version grafport and only the eight original QuickDraw colors can be used.

New Control Manager routines.

```
Function GetCVariant (theControl: ControlHandle): Integer;
```

This call is the Control Manager's new way to find out the variant code for a control without looking directly in the contrlDefProc field of the control record. You should use it so that your application will work right when a 32-bit version of the Macintosh operating system becomes available.

Macintosh II only:

```
Procedure SetCtlColor (thecontrol: Controlhandle;
newColorTable: CCTabHandle);
```

```
Function GetAuxCtl (theControl: ControlHandle acHndl:
AuxCtlHndl): Boolean;
```

When you create a new control by calling GetNewControl, the Control Manager will search for a cctb resource that has the same ID as the CNTL resource you're using. If it finds one, it will use it to create an auxiliary control record with color information. Otherwise, the new control will have the default colors.

When you call NewControl, you have no way to instantly attach an auxiliary record to the control. Instead, you have to use the SetCtlColor call to add the color information and an auxiliary record will be constructed to your exact specifications. To make your life easier, these things work just like their counterparts in the Window Manager.

When you create a new control that doesn't have a cctb resource, it'll be drawn in the default colors, usually black and white. If you then add color with SetCtlColor, it will be erased and drawn again with the new color information. You can avoid this by making the control invisible when it's created and calling ShowControl after you've added the color.

With GetAuxCtl, you can get a handle to the auxiliary record for any control. You can use this handle to find out what colors are being used to draw the control, or you can change the record. If the control uses the default colors, the function will return false and the value of acHndl will be nil.

Dialog Manager

The Dialog Manager has remained unchanged from the outside, except for the addition of color support on the Macintosh II. Programs running on classic black and white Macintoshes shouldn't notice any difference in the way the Dialog Manager behaves. New programs for the Macintosh II that want to take advantage of color in dialogs really get a lot of flexibility in coloring things.

On the Macintosh II, all the elements of your dialogs or alerts can be colored. When you call GetNewDialog, the Dialog Manager tries to find a resource of type dctb with the same ID as the DLOG resource; if it does, it calls NewCWindow for the dialog and uses the dctb for color information. The format of the color information in a dctb is the same as in a wctb resource, which we've already talked about, and you've certainly memorized by now. If there's no dctb, the dialog gets the default colors.

When you make any of the Dialog Manager calls that create new alerts (Alert, CautionAlert, StopAlert, and NoteAlert), the Dialog Manager will look for an actb resource, which works just like the dctb we just went over. If you call CouldDialog or CouldAlert, the associated dctb or actb resource will be loaded along with all the others.

As you may remember from your basic studies of *Inside Macintosh*, five fundamental kinds of items can appear in dialogs and alerts: controls, text (static and editable), icons, pictures, and user items. When you're using a color dialog or alert, each of these items can carry color information. The format of the color information differs for each kind of item. We'll talk about how to color each one.

The color information you provide for a control is simply the control color table, in the same format you would use for a cctb resource or a call to SetCtlColor. You can get a little fancier with text items: not only can they be colored, but because the Dialog Manager uses TextEdit to display text, you can now take advantage of fancy style variations for your text. In addition to the TextEdit options for font, face, size, and color, you can also set the background color behind the text. To make sure your text is drawn in the right font, you can even include the font's name, just in case the fonts are renumbered by Font/DA Mover.

To use color in an icon item, you should create a cicn resource, then put its resource ID into the dialog item list (usually a DITL resource). When you create the dialog box, the Dialog Manager will grab the cicn resource to use as the icon. Displaying color pictures is even easier, since pictures can have color information recorded in them, of course. The Dialog Manager simply draws the picture with the approprate resource ID, so if there's color information, you get color.

The fifth kind of thing you might want to color in a dialog is a user item. Getting color in a user item is entirely up to you, since you get to install a procedure to draw the user item. If you want color in your user item, just draw in color in your procedure. That's all there is to it.

We've just discovered that icons, pictures, and user items can have color goodies associated directly with them, so there's no need to add color information to the dialog record. Controls and text items have extra stuff, though, like a color table or font information. Where do we put this extra stuff?

The answer, as you probably guessed, is a new data structure, called a **dialog item color table.** This thing contains all the special color information for text and control items in the dialog. The dialog item color table is a pretty complicated structure. It's usually set up with an ictb resource that has the same ID as the DITL for a dialog. In fact, the item color table's structure is so wacky that, like some other Toolbox structures, it can't be declared with legitimate Pascal syntax (although Rez has no problem with it).

Don't let me be misunderstood.   Note that the ictb is a unique data structure; it doesn't look like anything else used in the Toolbox. All the other color table resources that work with the color Toolbox (wctb, dctb, cctb, and so on) are real color tables as defined by Color QuickDraw. That is, they have the following Pascal declaration.

```
ColorTable = Record
          ctSeed:  Longint;
          transIndex:  Integer;
          ctSize:  Integer;
          ctTable:  Array [0..0] of ColorSpec;
       end;
```

For color Toolbox resources, the first two fields are usually not used. The third field tells how many color entries there are in the table (less one, since the count is zero-based). Each entry in the ctTable array has an integer value, which is used to match a part code or bit value, and an RGB value that tells which color goes with the integer value.

Here's a description of the item color table, in classic *Inside Macintosh* style.

Number of bytes	Contents	
	For each item:	
2 bytes	if item type is:	content is:
	ctrlItem	length in bytes of color info
	statText, editText	flags for TextEdit (see below)
	other types	0
2 bytes	ctrlItem, statText, editText	offset to this item's color info (from start of item color table)
	other types	0
	For each item:	
	if item type is:	content is:
(for ctrlItems, number of bytes is shown in length field above)	ctrlItem	color control table
2 bytes	statText, editText:	font ID or offset to font name
2 bytes		text face
2 bytes		text size
6 bytes		RGB for text
6 bytes		RGB for background
2 bytes		text mode (usually srcOr)
Optional:		
n bytes		list of font names

TextEdit flags.   For text items, the first field contains flags that determine the item's style. If a flag bit is set, then the color entry contains information for that attribute. The flags integer is composed of the following bits.

Number of bits	Contents
1 bit	font ID field contains an offset to a font name instead
1 bit	set text mode
1 bit	set background color
9 bits	unused (reserved)
1 bit	set text color
1 bit	set text size
1 bit	set text face
1 bit	set font

There are constants defined for each of these bits to make it easy to set them. Since the item control table structure is so difficult to play with, you probably won't be using the constants in your programs, but for your information, here they are.

doFontName = 32768	doMode = 16384
doBackColor = 8192	doTextColor = 8
doSize = 4	doFace = 2
doFont = 1	

When you construct an ictb, you have to include an entry for every item in the dialog, whether it's getting colored or not, even if it carries its own color information (like icons and pictures). For items that don't have a color entry, use 0 for the length and offset values in the item color table. Note that you can use an item color table just to set style information for your text items, even if you don't color them. If you do this, you still have to have a complete ictb, with entries for every item in the dialog. Any text or control item that doesn't have its own color entry will be drawn in default colors.

If you call GetNewDialog, the Dialog Manager will try to find a dctb with the same ID as the DLOG and an ictb with the same ID as the DITL. If it finds the dctb, it creates a color window, and if the ictb is there too, you're in business with color items. You can also use a new routine to build a color dialog from scratch, just as with New-Dialog.

New Dialog Manager routine.
Macintosh II only:

```
    Function NewCDialog (dStorage: Ptr; boundsRect: Rect;
title: Str255; visible: Boolean; procID: Integer; behind:
WindowPtr; goAwayFlag: Boolean; refCon: Longint; items:
Handle): CDialogPtr;
```

This routine lets you create a color dialog without specifying a DLOG resource, just like the original NewDialog call. When you use this call, you'll get a new color dialog, but there won't be any color window or color item information, so it'll just be drawn in the default colors (usually black and white). To colorize the dialog, you have to create an auxiliary window record for it. The easiest way to do this is to build a window color table and then call SetWinColor to set up the auxiliary window record. Note that this colorizes the dialog window's structure, not the items themselves.

If you want to attach an item color table structure to the dialog, you have to first get it into memory, usually by calling GetResource to load it from an ictb resource or by building it up from scratch (not for the faint of heart). Then, you have to plug the item color information into the auxiliary record. There's a field in the auxiliary record just for this purpose called dialogCTable. Just put the handle to the item color table into the dialogCTable field of the auxiliary record. The code would look something like this.

```
    theDialog := NewCDialog (dStorage, boundsRect, title, false,
procID, behind, goAwayFlag, refCon, items);
    {create dialog, make it invisible}
    {assumes we've set up a window color table}
    SetWinColor (WindowPtr (theDialog), newColorTable);
    itemCTblHdl := GetResource ('ictb', ID); {load an 'ictb' resource}
    temp := GetAuxWin (WindowPtr (theDialog), awHndl);{get aux handle}
    awHndl^^.dialogCTable := itemCTblHdl;  {attach item color table}
    ShowWindow (WindowPtr (theDialog));
```

This makes the new color dialog (initially invisible), gives it an auxiliary window record so that the structure will be colored, loads in an item color table from a resource, puts a handle to it in the auxiliary record, and then displays the whole mess. For an example of how to build a window's color table, see the Window Manager section earlier in this appendix. As we said, you can also construct the item color table programmatically right in memory, but you have to be really fond of munging around in memory to do it.

Font Manager

Just like the rest of the user interface toolbox, the Font Manager now has the ability to support color. In addition, the Font Manager has gotten smarter about which font it gives you if the one you ask for isn't available. As with other parts of the system, your existing programs should work the same with the new Font Manager, except for the new font search technique and some bugs that have been fixed.

When you ask for a font that the Font Manager can't find, it now tries very hard to give you a font as close as possible to the requested one. First, it looks for a FOND resource, and if there aren't any, it tries for a FONT resource that matches the request. If the font can't be found hiding anywhere in any open resource files, the Font Manager will try to give you the application font. Sometimes even that font isn't around, in which case you'll get the system font. Since some applications use a different system font and load it into RAM, there's even a chance it may not be available. If that happens, the Font Manager just pulls the Chicago 12 font out of ROM.

The Font Manager now provides support for fonts that appear in color or gray scale. When you define a font, you can now use multiple bits to describe each pixel, just like when you're defining a pixel map. The Font Manager's flexibility actually allows you to define a different color for every pixel in a character. Using resource type NFNT, you can define fonts in all the depths currently supported by Color QuickDraw: one, two, four, or eight bits per pixel.

The Font Manager uses a scheme that's a lot like the one the rest of the Toolbox uses to define fonts with mutiple bits per pixel. Each different color or gray scale value is specified with a different bit pattern; two-bit fonts (what a derogatory-sounding term) can have four different colors, while eight-bit fonts can contain 256 different colors.

In the font definition, each pixel is specified with a bit pattern representing the color you want. This bit pattern is called the index. You can supply an additional resource that's yet another kind of color table, a **font color table** or fctb resource, naturally. This color table is in the standard format, as defined by Color QuickDraw.

The color for each pixel in the font is determined by finding the value field in a ColorSpec record that matches the index for that pixel. For example, in a four-bit font, all the pixels that have an index of 0110 (six decimal) will be drawn in the color that has 6 as the index value in its ColorSpec record.

The Font Manager does some smart things when your fctb doesn't define all the index values used in the font. For index values that aren't in the table, it will average the unknown colors between the grafport's foreground and background colors. This can be especially interesting if the user is set up for gray scales instead of color. If there's no fctb at all, the Font Manager will still assign different colors or grays to each index, ranging from the foreground color to the background color.

To keep things moving along swiftly, the Font Manager tries to find an NFNT resource that matches the current screen depth. If it can't find one, though, it will take what it has and crunch it up to fit the current screen. If the screen depth and the font depth don't match, the Font Manager constructs a new image of the font at the proper depth. This new life form is called a **synthetic font.**

The Font Manager has to keep track of each font's depth and color information so that it can know what to do when it's time to draw with that font. The Font Manager puts several bits of the font record to work that were previously unused. Bits 2 and 3 are used to hold the depth of the font: 0 is one-bit, 1 is two-bit, 2 is four-bit, and 3 is eight-bit depth. Bit 7 is set if the font has an fctb resource that provides color information. Bit 8 is set by the Font Manager if this font is a synthetic one that had to be created especially for this screen depth. Bit 9 is set as a reminder to the Font Manager for a font that has colors (other than black).

New Font Manager routine.

```
Procedure SetFractEnable (fractEnable: Boolean);
```

When the Macintosh Plus and ROM version $75 were introduced, the Font Manager included a new feature that allowed the use of fractional character spacing. This idea allowed character positions to be recorded in fractions of a pixel. Although you couldn't actually draw characters at fractional pixel positions on the screen, a printer like the LaserWriter, with four times the screen's resolution in each direction, could make use of this information.

Apple originally tried to make the fractional character spacing happen automagically, but it caused too many applications to fail. So, the feature was turned off and a global called FractEnable was required to turn it back on. To make it easier for high-level language programmers to enable this feature, a call named SetFractEnable was implemented in the MPW Pascal and C interfaces. The new version of SetFractEnable simply implements this call as a trap in ROM, so that all developers, including folks working in assembly language, can take advantage of it. This is also another example of Apple providing a higher-level interface to a global, which means that the global might change its meaning in the future. So be sure to use SetFractEnable to turn fractional character spacing off and on.

Resource Manager

From the outside, the Resource Manager in the Macintosh SE and Macintosh II is virtually the same one found in the Macintosh Plus. There are some additional resources that have been added to the ROM, and there's one new routine that makes it easier to get resources from the ROM.

If you were the Resource Manager, here's a list of the resources that you'd find in the Macintosh SE ROM.

Resource type	ID	Contents
CDEF	0	Button/check box definition procedure
CDEF	1	Scroll bar definition procedure
CURS	1	Text cursor ("I-beam")
CURS	2	Cross cursor
CURS	3	Plus cursor
CURS	4	Watch cursor
LISA	0	Precursor
DRVR	3	Sound driver (.Sound)
DRVR	4	Disk driver (.Sony)
DRVR	9	low-level AppleTalk driver (.MPP)
DRVR	10	AppleTalk transaction protocol driver (.ATP)
DRVR	40	AppleTalk file server support (.XPP)
FONT	0	System font name (Chicago)
FONT	12	System font, 12-point (Chicago)
FONT	384	Geneva font name
FONT	393	Geneva font, 9-point
FONT	396	Geneva font, 12-point
FONT	512	Monaco font name
FONT	521	Monaco font, 9-point
MBDF	0	Menu bar definition procedure
PACK	4	Floating-point math (SANE)
PACK	5	Transcendental functions
PACK	7	Binary-decimal conversions
SERD	0	Serial drivers
WDEF	0	Standard window definition function
WDEF	1	Round-cornered window definition

The Macintosh II ROM has all these resources plus a few more, mostly to support color. Here are the additional resources in the Macintosh II.

Resource type	ID	Contents
NFNT	2	Chicago font, 12-point, 4-bit depth
NFNT	3	Chicago font, 12-point, 8-bit depth
NFNT	33	Geneva font, 9-point, 4-bit depth
cctb	0	Control color table for black and white
clut	127	Color lookup table for old 8 colors
gama	0	Color correction table for monitor
mitq	0	Used by MakeITable call
wctb	0	Window color table for black and white

New Resource Manager routine.

```
Function RGetResource (theType: ResType; theID: Integer) : Handle
```

The Macintosh Plus ROM introduced the concept of ROM-based resources, but the technique for getting at them was a little weird. In order to retain compatibility with existing applications that didn't expect any resources to be ROM-based, the Resource Manager only searched the ROM resource file if it was explicitly inserted at the front of the chain of open resource files by setting a low-memory global.

The new routine RGetResource provides a different kind of functionality in a much simpler way. This routine will search through the chain of open resource files for a resource; if it can't find the one you want, it will look in the ROM as a last resort. If you want to grab the ROM-based resource first, you still have to mess around with globals, but if you just want to be sure you've tried the ROM as well, you can use this new routine.

Script Manager

The Script Manager is a whole new chunk of code Apple supplies with System 4.1. It's a clever combination of callable routines and lots of system patches, a real guerrilla piece of software that could only be implemented on a Macintosh.

Most programmers who've heard of the Script Manager think of it as having something to do with localizing applications for use with non-Roman writing systems, like Chinese, Japanese, Arabic, Hebrew, Korean, Laotian, Maldivian, and Telugu (the first person who writes me a letter in Telugu, with an English translation, will get a special mention in the next printing of this book).

It's true that the heart of the Script Manager is designed for this, but a lot of Script Manager routines are reasonably general-purpose utilities for dealing with text. You can use these utilities for any text manipulation needs you have and get the added bonus that these calls will work with different script systems.

Good old all-American ASCII has room for 256 different characters, since a character has to fit into a single byte. Although that's plenty for English and other Latin-based languages like French, Spanish, and Italian, it's not even close for something like Kanji (written Japanese), which has more than 40,000 characters.

So, one basic change that the Script Manager implements is that characters can take up two bytes instead of just one. Obviously, this could cause great confusion if your application assumes that all characters are one byte long. The Script Manager provides calls to help you figure out what's going on in your text in a way that works with both one-byte and two-byte characters.

One of the most interesting things that changes for some writing systems is the direction of writing. In Hebrew and Arabic, for example, characters are written from right to left. Of course, your basic Toolbox routines just aren't set up to deal with this, so the Script Manager applies some of its patching magic. The Script Manager maintains a low-memory global called TESysJust that tells whether the direction of text should be left to right or right to left .

Lots of decisions are made based on the value of this global. If TESysJust is set for right to left, it will affect text drawn with TextEdit, text in menus, and labels on radio buttons and check boxes. If you're just drawing text, as with DrawChar or DrawText, the Script Manager convinces QuickDraw to draw the characters in the opposite direction from the usual.

In addition to the all-new Script Manager, the International Utilities Package has been overhauled to be more flexible and to work properly with the Script Manager. Instead of using the old INTL resources with IDs 0 and 1, there are some new resources that allow you to switch between multiple scripts installed in the same system.

The new resources are types itl0, itl1, and itl2. The first two contain pretty much the same information that was in the old INTL 0 and 1. Since there can be many resources of type itl0 in the system, you can have lots of scripts to switch between. The new itl2 resource allows you to customize character comparisons to a very high degree.

The International Utilities provide a few new ways to format the existing day and time information. For the time format, you can now specify a value of 1 that will cause midnight and noon to be represented as 0:00. There are three new formats for short dates: month-year-day, day-year-month, and year-day-month.

There are new ways to format the long date, too. The old values of 0 and 255 are still respected; if the value is anything else, the format byte is used to determine the order of the elements in a long date. Each two-bit field in the byte corresponds to a field in the long date. Bits 0 and 1 specify the first thing in the date, 2 and 3 the second, 4 and 5 the third, and 6 and 7 the last. A value of 0 indicates where the day of the month will appear; 1 is for the day of the week; 2 indicates the month; 3 is for the year.

The new International Utilities also allow you to suppress any parts of the long date. There's a bit that corresponds to each of the four parts of a long date, and setting that bit causes the associated part of the date to be suppressed from the long date. Bit 0 is for the day of the month; bit 1 is used for the day of the week; bit 2 is used to suppress the month; bit 3 keeps the year away.

Script Manager routines.   Only a few routines are listed.

```
Function FontScript : Integer;
Function IntlScript : Integer;
Procedure KeyScript (code: Integer);
```

These routines let you find out and set various information about the current state of the system from the Script Manager's point of view. FontScript tells you the font number of the font that's currently being used. IntlScript tells which script system is in use from an Apple-assigned list of more than 30 writing systems.

The KeyScript routine lets you set the keyboard to work in one of the script systems installed on the startup disk. When you do this, the Script Manager will draw the icon for the script system you've chosen on the far right edge of the menu bar, just to remind you and alleviate any surprise that might result from seeing Mongolian characters suddenly appear in the middle of your new novel.

```
Function CharByte (textBuf: Ptr; textOffset: Integer): Integer;
Function CharType (textBut: Ptr; textOffset: Integer): Integer;
```

These two functions can help you figure out whether a particular byte in a chunk of text is part of a two-byte character. To use them, set textBuf to the address of the first character in your text and set textOffset to the byte position in the text that you want to examine. By calling CharByte, you can find out whether the byte is a one-byte character (the function returns 0) or the first byte (–1) or second byte (1) of a two-byte character.

The CharType function gives you a way to find out more about a byte in a run of text. The function result from CharType is composed of five fields, all crammed into that one integer value. Bits 0 through 3 contain the character type, which can be a standard AS-CII text or number character (1), a punctuation character (0), or a "European" non-standard ASCII character (7). Bits 8 through 11 tell whether the character is a number (1), a text character (0), or a symbol (2). Bit 13 tells whether the character is part of left to right (0) or right to left (1) text. Bit 14 says whether the character is upper (1) or lower (0) case. Bit 15 indicates whether the byte is part of a one-byte (0) or two-byte (1) character.

Printing Manager

The Printing Manager has added a couple of interesting new features, one of them hidden and one functional. The new hidden feature is that most of the Printing Manger's routines, which have always been added through a linked file, are now in ROM. They're accessed through a single trap called _PrGlue, and the interfaces for MPW have been changed appropriately. The new functional feature of the Printing Manager is a procedure that allows printer drivers to communicate with the application. This new call is listed next, so read on for details.

New Printing Manager routine.

```
Procedure PrGeneral (pData: Ptr);
```

This call provides a generic, printer-independent way to find out some things about the printer you're using without having to look directly into the print record. Finding out secret things about the printer by looking into the print record is a time-honored tradition among Macintosh software developers, but it's not one that's likely to be well-respected by Apple as the printing code's architecture changes in the future.

Although the fields of the print record were fully documented in the early days of the Macintosh, when the original ImageWriter was the only available printer, Apple soon realized that lots of things would have to change to support vastly different devices like the LaserWriter. So, the Printing Manager chapter of *Inside Macin-*

tosh was changed to specify a bunch of fields "used internally," where more detail was once available.

Of course, the horse was already out of the barn, as they say, and closing the door didn't really stop it. Once the information was out in the world, it got used, reused, and passed on like a chain letter. Now, as Apple works on improving future printing software, it's very likely these fields will change again. Those who depend on them will probably fail with the new software, just as many applications failed to work with the LaserWriter at first—something to look forward to. To avoid having this tragedy befall your application, you should try to steer clear of peeking into the print record. To help your self-control in this area, PrGeneral was invented as a clean way of finding out some facts about the current printer.

The structure of PrGeneral is very, uh, general in that it allows lots of different kinds of operations to be specified. The pData parameter points to a block of things that tell exactly what information you're looking for. Here's the Pascal declaration for the parameter block.

```
type TGnlData = Record
                iOpCode: Integer;  {call number}
                iError: Integer; {error code returned here}
                lReserved: Longint; {reserved by Apple}
            {additional data, different for each call}
                End;
```

The first part of the record is the call number. This determines which of PrGeneral's functions you're asking for. Currently, there are five PrGeneral calls, and we'll talk about each of them in a minute. The next field contains the error code returned by the PrGeneral call. The reserved field is just that. Each PrGeneral call also defines some additional call-specific fields we'll talk about soon.

The following are the five calls supported by PrGeneral.

* GetRslDataOp (call number 4) returns data about the printer's resolution capabilities.
* SetRslOp (call number 5) sets the current printer's resolution.
* DraftBitsOp (call number 6) allows you to print bitmaps with draft printing.
* NoDraftBitsOp (call number 7) turns off bitmaps during draft printing.
* GetRotnOp (call number 8) lets you find out if the user has chosen vertical (portrait) or horizontal (landscape) paper orientation.

The getRslDataOp call lets you find out about the resolutions supported by the current printer, usually specified by the user in the page setup dialog. For example, the LaserWriter can print as small as 25 percent of actual size, as large as 400 percent, or anything in between; the ImageWriter can print in 72 by 72, 144 by 144, 80 by 72, or 160 by 144 resolution, and only those values. The getRslDataOp call will tell you if the printer supports discrete resolution only, and which values if so; for variable resolution, it will give you the range.

The setRslOp call can be used to set the printer's resolution directly, without having to rely on the user to do it right with the print dialogs. The idea here is to obtain a resolution that's supported by using the getRslDataOp call and then use setRslOp to plug in the new value. If you use values that aren't right, the Printing Manager will set the resolution to the printer's default.

The draftBitsOp routine lets you pull off a neat trick: prining bitmaps in draft mode on the ImageWriter. Normally, draft mode disables all bitmaps, as well as fonts and font styles. By calling PrGeneral with the draftBitsOp constant, bitmaps will be printed when the user has selected draft mode. If you're going to use this call, you should do it before calling PrJobDialog or PrStlDialog, because it locks the user out of certain choices. Specifically, it forces the printing choices to be draft mode and portrait orientation if the user is going to print to an ImageWriter. On a LaserWriter, this call doesn't do anything, since the LaserWriter's draft mode is its only method of printing.

When you use this call, each bitmap will be printed in turn, from top to bottom, and paper motion is always forward. If you have two bitmaps side by side, you'll have a problem, because the Image-Writer will finish drawing the first bitmap and then will not be able to print the second one, since the print head will be too far down on the page and the ImageWriter driver won't move it back up for this kind of printing.

To avoid this problem, you have to make sure you print your bitmaps from the top of the page to the bottom. If the top of any of them overlaps the bottom of another, you'll have to combine them by CopyBitsing them into the same image and then printing the combined image. Oh well.

When you're all done printing bitmaps in draft mode, you should call PrGeneral with the noDraftBitsOp constant. This will turn off bitmap printing in draft mode and will return draft mode printing to its usual text-only, single-font, boring self.

Terminology corner. When the Macintosh and its printing software first appeared, the ImageWriter was the only printer supported. There were two printing methods: draft and spool printing. In draft printing, the printing happened immediately, without writing an intermediate file to disk, and only text was printed, using only the printer's built-in standard font. In spool printing, a file containing a QuickDraw picture was created on disk and then sent to the printer, and this picture could contain any graphics or font changes you wanted. The reason for the creation of spool printing was that printing pictures directly required too much memory for the old 128K Macintosh: the picture, the code to draw it, and the code to print it all had to be loaded at the same time. By creating an intermediate file, the application's imaging code could be placed in a segment and then unloaded when it was time to print. When Apple introduced the LaserWriter, which only worked with Macintoshes containing 512K of RAM or greater anyway and which only knew one way to print—beautifully—the words *draft* and *spool* didn't really work right anymore. Now, *draft* meant "printed with no intermediate file," and *spool* meant "printed with an intermediate file," which never happened on a LaserWriter. This is why we now have such interesting variations as a LaserWriter that always prints in draft mode (which just means no intermediate disk file is created) and an ImageWriter that can print bitmaps in draft mode (again, meaning no disk file is created).

The last of the PrGeneral calls is getRotnOp, which tells you if the user has selected portrait or landscape orientation. It simply returns a boolean value. If it's true, the document is set up for landscape; otherwise, it's portrait.

These are the only PrGeneral calls supported now, but there will probably be more in the future. As Apple adds more functionality to the Printing Manager and implements new high-level ways to deal with it you should probably pay close attention, since the high-level interface will probably be the only one that continues to work the same way over the next couple of years.

Operating System Utilities

As the Macintosh product line has grown and diverged over the last few years, it's gotten harder and harder to figure out what features are available in the machine your application is running on. System 4.1 includes a new call that can help you figure out some things about the environment your application is living in.

New Operating System Utilities routine.

```
Function SysEnvirons (versionRequested: Integer; VAR
theWorld: SysEnvRec): OSErr;
```

There are all sorts of globals, tricks and techniques inside your Macintosh that you can use to find out about what kind of Macintosh you've got, what's plugged into it, what ROM version it has, and so on. Now, for the first time, all of your favorite configuration stuff has been gathered together for convenient one-stop shopping in the SysEnvirons call.

In one shot, this call will tell you all the following information:

- What kind of Macintosh you've got (128K/512K, XL, 512Ke, Plus, SE, II, or something from beyond).
- The version of the System file that's open (4.1 or later only).
- Which microprocessor is running the computer (68000, 68010, 68020, or science fiction).
- Whether the computer has an Apple-installed 68881 floating-point coprocessor.
- Whether Color QuickDraw is in the ROM.
- What keyboard is attached (original, original numeric pad, Macintosh Plus, Apple Keyboard [ADB-based], Apple Extended Keyboard [ADB-based], or something unrecognizable).
- The version of the AppleTalk drivers.
- The reference number of the current System file's folder (a WDRefNum) or volume (a VRefNum).

What a bargain! All that stuff for just one call. In addition, this call is designed to be extended when necessary. When you call it, you pass along a version number. SysEnvirons responds with that version number if it can and the nearest one otherwise. This will allow Apple to add new fields of information to this call in the future, making it an even bigger deal for finding out what you've got in your Macintosh.

Sound Manager

In versions $69 and $75 of the Macintosh ROM (the 64K and 128K ROMs), the Sound Driver allowed you to carry a tune on your Macintosh. On the Macintosh II, the sound capabilities have been enhanced so much that the Sound Driver has been promoted to management—it's now the Sound Manager.

The biggest news about the Sound Manager for non-musical types is the invention of a resource type that holds sound information (which can be music, speech, a message to your dog, or the theme from "Pee-Wee's Playhouse"). While you have to know what you're doing to create these resources, which are type 'snd,' it's easy to write code to copy, paste, and play them in your programs.

Sound Manager routine. Not all routines are listed.
Macintosh II only:

```
    Function SndPlay (chan: SndChannelPtr; sndHdl: Handle;
async: Boolean): OSErr;
```

This is the magic call that lets even us total music zeroes play music in our programs. The easy way to use this routine is to pass nil for the chan parameter, which will create a new channel or queue to pass the music commands to. The sndHdl parameter should be a handle to an 'snd ' resource that you got from a friend who knows how to play piano or that you digitized, and you should pass false for the async parameter.

If you learn a little more about how the Sound Manager works, you can create your own sound channels and use them for fancier effects like stereo. You can use some of the other Sound Manager commands to control exactly what you want to do. The Sound Manager lets you have various synthesizers, or drivers, that can process special formats like plain notes, wave tables, or MIDI data. For a great demo of the Macintosh II's sound capabilities, check out the alert sound that's a stereo recording of an elephant trumpeting. It'll make your eyes water.

Shutdown Manager

The Shutdown Manager is a little collection of code that makes sure your Macintosh is all ready to be turned off when you're done working. Most users see it when they choose Shut Down from the Finder's Special menu. For those lucky enough to have a Macintosh

II, this turns the computer's power off; otherwise, it puts up the alert that tells you it's OK to turn the computer off yourself.

The Restart command in the Finder is also performed with the help of the Shutdown Manager. When you do a restart, all the housekeeping things that take place on a Shut Down command are handled; instead of killing the power or putting up the alert, though, the computer is restarted.

If you want something in particular to happen when the Shutdown Manager is called, you can install a procedure that will be called when the user shuts down or restarts, or at both times. This is handy for such things as signing off a mail server on AppleTalk, parking the heads on a hard disk, or playing the chorus from "Shut Down" by the Beach Boys ("Tach it up, tach it up . . . ").

Shutdown Manager routines.   Not all routines are listed.

```
      Procedure ShutDwnInstall (shutDwnProc: ProcPtr; flags:
Integer);

      Procedure ShutDwnRemove (shutDwnProc: ProcPtr);
```

The ShutDwnInstall procedure is used to stick a procedure into the queue to be executed when the Shutdown Manager is called on to turn off or restart the machine. You can specify just when in the shutdown process you want your routine to be called: before unmounting volumes, before closing drivers, or just before restarting or shutting down. The second routine is used to take something out of the queue.

That's it. As long as we're talking about shutting down, we might as well end our discussion of the new stuff here. Following this, you'll find Listing A-1, which uses the new versions of TextEdit and the Menu Manager to do some tricks.

```
program NewHiyer;

{Listing A-1   Example of hierarchical menus and stylish TextEdit}

   uses
      {$LOAD Insider:MPW:PInterfaces:AllInterfaces}
      {$U Insider:MPW:PInterfaces:MemTypes.p } MemTypes,
      {$U Insider:MPW:PInterfaces:QuickDraw.p} QuickDraw,
      {$U Insider:MPW:PInterfaces:OSIntf.p  } OSIntf,
      {$U Insider:MPW:PInterfaces:ToolIntf.p } ToolIntf,
      {$U Insider:MPW:PInterfaces:PackIntf.p } PackIntf;
```

Listing A-1 continued

```
const
   appleID = 128;      {resource IDs/menu IDs for menus}
   fileID  = 129;
   editID  = 130;
   textID              = 131;
   fontID  = 132;
   sizeID  = 133;
   styleID = 134;

   appleM = 1;         {index for each menu in myMenus (array of menu handles)}
   fileM  = 2;
   editM  = 3;
   textM  = 4;
   fontM  = 5;
   sizeM  = 6;
   styleM = 7;

   menuCount = 7;      {total number of menus (incl. hierarchical)}

   aboutItem = 1;      {item in Apple menu}

   undoItem  = 1;      {Items in Edit menu}
   cutItem   = 3;
   copyItem  = 4;
   pasteItem = 5;
   clearitem = 6;

   newItem = 1;        {items in File menu}
   closeItem = 3;
   quitItem = 5;

   fontItem = 1;       {items in Text menu}
   sizeItem = 2;
   styleItm= 3;

   wName = 'Window ';  {prefix for window names}

   windDX = 25;        {distance to move for new windows}
   windDY = 25;

   leftEdge = 10;      {initial dimensions of window}
   topEdge = 42;
   rightEdge = 210;
   botEdge = 175;

var
   myMenus: array [1..menuCount] OF MenuHandle; {handles to the menus}
   dragRect: Rect;          {rectangle used to mark boundaries for dragging window}
   txRect: Rect;            {rectangle for text in application window}
   textH: TEHandle;         {handle to Textedit record}
   theChar: char;           {typed character}
   extended: boolean;       {true if user is Shift-clicking}
   doneFlag: boolean;       {true if user has chosen Quit Item}
   myEvent: EventRecord;    {information about an event}
   wRecord: WindowRecord;   {information about the application window}
```

Listing A-1 continued

```
      myWindow: WindowPtr;    {pointer to wRecord}
      myWinPeek : WindowPeek;{another pointer to wRecord}
      whichWindow: WindowPtr;{window in which mouse button was pressed}
      nextWRect: Rect;        {portRect for next window to be opended}
      nextWTitle: Str255;     {title of next window to be opened}
      nextWNum: Longint;      {number of next window (for title)}
      savedPort: GrafPtr;     {pointer to preserve GrafPort}
      menusOK: boolean;       {for disabling menu items}
      scrapErr: Longint;
      scrCopyErr: Integer;
      theStyle: TextStyle;    {for setting TE style}
      itemString: Str255;     {font name selected}
      familyID: Integer;      {for setting font ID}
      fontSize: Longint;      {for setting font size}

procedure SetUpMenus;
{ set up menus and menu bar }

   var
     i: Integer;

   begin
      myMenus[appleM] := GetMenu(appleID);        {read Apple menu}
      AddResMenu(myMenus[appleM],'DRVR');         {add desk accessory names}
      myMenus[fileM] := GetMenu(fileID); {read file menu }
      myMenus[editM] := GetMenu(editID);          {read Edit menu }
      myMenus[textM] := GetMenu(textID);

      myMenus[fontM] := NewMenu(fontID,'Font');
      AddResMenu(myMenus[5],'FONT');
      myMenus[sizeM] := GetMenu(sizeID);
      myMenus[styleM]:= GetMenu(styleID);

      for i:=1 to 4 do
        InsertMenu(myMenus[i],0);   {install menus in menu bar }

      InsertMenu (myMenus[fontM],-1);  {install hierarchical menus}
      InsertMenu (myMenus[sizeM],-1);
      InsertMenu (myMenus[styleM],-1);

      DrawMenuBar;        { and draw menu bar}
   end; {SetUpMenus}


procedure OpenWindow;
{ Open a new window }

   begin
      NumToString (nextWNum, nextWTitle); {prepare number for title}
      nextWTitle := concat (wName, nextWTitle); {add to prefix}
      myWindow := NewWindow (Nil, nextWRect, nextWTitle, True, noGrowDocProc,
        Pointer (-1), True, 0); {open the window}
      SetPort (myWindow);       {make it the current port}
      txRect := thePort^.portRect;{prepare TERecord for new window}
```

```
      InsetRect (txRect, 4, 0);
      textH := TEStylNew (txRect, txRect);
      theStyle.tsSize := 12;
      TESetSelect (0, 32767, textH);
      TESetStyle (doSize, theStyle, true, textH);
      myWinPeek := WindowPeek (myWindow);
      myWinPeek^.refcon := Longint (textH); {keep TEHandle in refcon!}
      OffsetRect (nextWRect, windDX, windDY);{move window down and right}
      if nextWRect.right > dragRect.right {move back if it's too far over}
        then OffsetRect (nextWRect, -nextWRect.left + leftEdge, 0);
      if nextWRect.bottom > dragRect.bottom
        then OffsetRect (nextWRect, 0, -nextWRect.top + topEdge);
      nextWNum := nextWNum + 1; {bump number for next window}
      menusOK := false;
      EnableItem (myMenus [editM],0); {in case this is the only window}
   end; {OpenWindow}


procedure KillWindow (theWindow: WindowPtr);
{Close a window and throw everything away}

  begin
     TEDispose (TEHandle (WindowPeek (theWindow)^.refcon));

                            {throw away TERecord}
     DisposeWindow (theWindow);        {throw away WindowRecord}
     textH := NIL;          {for TEIdle in main event loop}
     if FrontWindow = NIL     {if no more windows, disable Close}
       then DisableItem (myMenus[fileM], closeItem);
     if WindowPeek (FrontWindow)^.windowKind < 0
                            {if a desk acc is coming up, enable undo}
       then EnableItem (myMenus[editM], undoItem)
       else DisableItem (myMenus[editM], undoItem);

  end; {KillWindow}


function MyFilter (theDialog: DialogPtr; var theEvent: EventRecord;
    var itemHit: Integer): Boolean;

  var
     theType: Integer;
     theItem: Handle;
     theBox: Rect;
     finalTicks: Longint;

  begin
     if (BitAnd(theEvent.message,charCodeMask) = 13) {carriage return}
       or (BitAnd(theEvent.message,charCodeMask) = 3) {enter}
       then
```

Listing A-1 continued

```
        begin
          GetDItem (theDialog, 1, theType, theItem, theBox);
          HiliteControl (ControlHandle (theItem), 1);
          Delay (8, finalTicks);
          HiliteControl (ControlHandle (theItem), 0);
          itemHit := 1;
          MyFilter := True;
        end {if BitAnd...then begin}
      else MyFilter := False;
  end; {function MyFilter}


procedure DoAboutBox;

  var
    itemHit: Integer;

  begin
    myWindow := GetNewDialog (1000, Nil, pointer (-1));
    repeat
      ModalDialog (@MyFilter, itemHit)
    until itemHit = 1;
    DisposDialog (myWindow);
  end; {procedure DoAboutBox}

procedure MakeStyle (theItem: integer; VAR theStyle: TextStyle);

begin
  with theStyle do
    case theItem of
      1 : tsFace := [];
      2 : tsFace := [bold];
      3 : tsFace := [italic];
      4 : tsFace := [underline];
      5 : tsFace := [outline];
      6 : tsFace := [shadow];
      7 : tsFace := [condense];
      8 : tsFace := [extend];
    end; {case theItem}
end; {procedure MakeStyle}


procedure DoCommand (mResult: LONGINT);
{Execute Item specified by mResult, the result of MenuSelect}

    var

    theItem: Integer; {menu item number from mResult low-order word}
    theMenu: Integer; {menu number from mResult high-order word}
    name: Str255; {desk accessory name}
    temp: Integer;
```

Listing A-1 continued

```
begin
    theItem := LoWord(mResult); {call Toolbox Utility routines to set }
    theMenu := HiWord(mResult); { menu item number and menu number}

    case theMenu of              {case on menu ID}

      appleID:
       if theItem = aboutItem
         then DoAboutBox
         else
           begin
             GetItem(myMenus[appleM],theItem,name);
             {GetPort (savedPort);}
             scrapErr := ZeroScrap;
             scrCopyErr := TEToScrap;
             temp := OpenDeskAcc(name);
             EnableItem (myMenus [editM],0);
             {SetPort (savedPort);}
             if FrontWindow <> NIL
               then
                 begin
                   EnableItem (myMenus [fileM], closeItem);
                   EnableItem (myMenus [editM], undoItem);
                 end; {if FrontWindow then begin}
             menusOK := false;
           end;  {if theItem...else begin}
      fileID:
        case theItem of

          newItem:
            OpenWindow;

          closeItem:
            if WindowPeek (FrontWindow)^.windowKind < 0
              then CloseDeskAcc (windowPeek (FrontWindow)^.windowKind)
              {if desk acc window, close it}
              else KillWindow (FrontWindow);
              {if it's one of mine, blow it away}

          quitItem:
            doneFlag := TRUE; {quit}

        end; {case theItem}

      editID:
        begin
          if not SystemEdit(theItem-1)
            then
              case theItem of {case on menu item number}

                cutItem:
                  TECut(textH); {call TextEdit to handle Item}
```

Listing A-1 continued

```
                copyItem:
                  TECopy (textH);

                pasteItem:
                  TEStylPaste (textH);

                clearItem:
                  TEDelete (textH);

              end;     {case theItem}
          end;     {editID begin}

        fontID:
              begin
                GetItem(myMenus [fontM], theitem, itemString);
                GetFNum(itemString, familyID);
                theStyle.tsFont := familyID;
                {theStyle.tsSize := 12;   {fix to set right size}
                TESetStyle (doFont+doSize, theStyle, true, textH);
              end; {fontID: begin}

        sizeID:
              begin
                GetItem(myMenus [sizeM], theitem, itemString);
                StringToNum (itemString, fontSize);
                theStyle.tsSize := fontSize;
                TESetStyle (doSize, theStyle, true, textH);
              end; {sizeID: begin}

        styleID:
              begin
                MakeStyle (theItem, theStyle);
                TESetStyle (doFace+doSize, theStyle, true, textH);
            end; {sizeID: begin}


      end;     {case theMenu}
    HiliteMenu(0);
  end;   {DoCommand}


procedure FixCursor;

      var
        mouseLoc: point;

    begin
      GetMouse (mouseLoc);
      if PtInRect (mouseLoc, thePort^.portRect)
        then SetCursor (GetCursor (iBeamCursor)^^)
        else SetCursor (arrow);
    end; {procedure FixCursor}
```

Listing A-1 continued

```
begin          {main program}

  InitGraf(@thePort);
  InitFonts;
  FlushEvents(everyEvent,0);
  InitWindows;
  InitMenus;
  TEInit;
  InitDialogs(NIL);
  InitCursor;

  SetUpMenus;
     with screenBits.bounds do
       SetRect(dragRect,4,24,right-4,bottom-4);
       doneFlag := false;

  menusOK := false;
  nextWNum := 1;       {initialize window number}
  SetRect (nextWRect,leftEdge,topEdge,rightEdge,botEdge);
                       {initialize window rectangle}
  OpenWindow;          {start with one open window}

{ Main event loop }
  repeat
     SystemTask;
     if FrontWindow <> NIL
       then
          if WindowPeek (FrontWindow)^.windowKind >= 0
             then FixCursor;
     if not menusOK and (FrontWindow = NIL)
       then

          begin
             DisableItem (myMenus [fileM], closeItem);
             DisableItem (myMenus [editM], 0);
             menusOK := true;
          end; {if FrontWindow...then begin}
     if textH <> Nil
       then TEIdle(textH);

     if GetNextEvent(everyEvent,myEvent)
       then
       case myEvent.what of

          mouseDown:
             case FindWindow(myEvent.where,whichWindow) of

                   inSysWindow:
                     SystemClick(myEvent,whichWindow);

                   inMenuBar:
                     DoCommand(MenuSelect(myEvent.where));

                   inDrag:
                     DragWindow(whichWindow,myEvent.where,dragRect);
```

Listing A-1 continued

```
      inContent:
        begin
          if whichWindow <> FrontWindow
            then SelectWindow(whichWindow)
            else
              begin
                GlobalToLocal(myEvent.where);
                extended := BitAnd(myEvent.modifiers,shiftKey) <> 0;
                TEClick(myEvent.where,extended,textH);
              end;   {else}
        end;   {inContent}

      inGoAway:
        if TrackGoAway (whichWindow, myEvent.where)
          then KillWindow (whichWindow);

    end;     {case FindWindow}

keyDown, autoKey:
  begin
    theChar := CHR(BitAnd(myEvent.message,charCodeMask));
    if BitAnd(myEvent.modifiers,cmdKey) <> 0
      then DoCommand(MenuKey(theChar))
      else TEKey(theChar,textH);
  end; {keyDown, autoKey begin}

activateEvt:
  begin
  if BitAnd(myEvent.modifiers,activeFlag) <> 0
    then   {application window is becoming active}
      begin
        SetPort (GrafPtr (myEvent.message));
        textH := TEHandle (WindowPeek (myEvent.message)^.refcon);
        TEActivate(textH);
        EnableItem (myMenus[fileM],closeItem);
        DisableItem(myMenus[editM],undoItem);
        if WindowPeek (FrontWindow)^.nextWindow^.windowKind < 0
          then scrCopyErr := TEFromScrap;
      end {if BitAnd...then begin}
    else   {application window is becoming inactive}
      begin
        TEDeactivate(TEHandle(WindowPeek(myEvent.message)^.refcon));
        if WindowPeek (FrontWindow)^.windowKind < 0
          then
            begin
              EnableItem (myMenus[editM], undoItem);
              scrapErr := ZeroScrap;
              scrCopyErr := TEToScrap;
                    end {if WindowPeek...then begin}
                  else DisableItem (myMenus[editM], undoItem);
                end; {else begin}
              end; {activateEvt begin}
```

```
        updateEvt:
          begin
            GetPort (savedPort);
            SetPort (GrafPtr (myEvent.message));
            BeginUpdate(WindowPtr(myEvent.message));
            EraseRect(WindowPtr(myEvent.message)^.portRect);
            TEUpdate(WindowPtr(myEvent.message)^.portRect,
            TEHandle(WindowPeek(myEvent.message)^.refcon));
            EndUpdate(WindowPtr(myEvent.message));
            SetPort (savedPort);
          end; {updateEvt begin}

      end;  {case myEvent.what}

   until doneFlag;
end.
```

Listing A-1 continued

```
resource 'MENU' (128) {
    128,
    textMenuProc,
    0x7FFFFFFD,
    enabled,
    apple,
    {   /* array: 2 elements */
        /* [1] */
        "About Showoff...", noIcon, "", "", plain,
        /* [2] */
        "-", noIcon, "", "", plain
    }
};

resource 'MENU' (129) {
    129,
    textMenuProc,
    0x7FFFFFF7,
    enabled,
    "File",
    {   /* array: 5 elements */
        /* [1] */
        "New", noIcon, "N", noMark, plain;
        /* [2] */
        "Open", noIcon, "O", noMark, plain;
        /* [3] */
        "Close", noIcon, "W", noMark, plain;
        /* [4] */
        "-", noIcon, noKey, noMark, plain;
        /* [5] */
        "Quit", noIcon, "Q", noMark, plain
    }
};

resource 'MENU' (130) {
    130,
    textMenuProc,
    0x7FFFFFFC,
    enabled,
    "Edit",
    {   /* array: 6 elements */
        /* [1] */
        "Undo", noIcon, "Z", "", plain,
        /* [2] */
        "-", noIcon, "", "", plain,
        /* [3] */
        "Cut", noIcon, "X", "", plain,
        /* [4] */
        "Copy", noIcon, "C", "", plain,
        /* [5] */
        "Paste", noIcon, "V", "", plain,
        /* [6] */
        "Clear", noIcon, "", "", plain
    }
};
```

Listing A-1 continued

```
resource 'MENU' (131) {
    131,
    textMenuProc,
    0x7FFFFFFF,
    enabled,
    "Text",
    {   /* array: 3 elements */
        /* [1] */
        "Font", noIcon, "\0x1B", "\0x84", plain,
        /* [2] */
        "Size", noIcon, "\0x1B", "\0x85", plain,
        /* [3] */
        "Style", noIcon, "\0x1B", "\0x86", plain
    }
};

resource 'MENU' (133) {
    133,
    textMenuProc,
    0x7FFFFFFF,
    enabled,
    "Size",
    {   /* array: 9 elements */
        /* [1] */
        "9", noIcon, noKey, noMark, plain;
        /* [2] */
        "10", noIcon, noKey, noMark, plain;
        /* [3] */
        "12", noIcon, noKey, noMark, plain;
        /* [4] */
        "14", noIcon, noKey, noMark, plain;
        /* [5] */
        "18", noIcon, noKey, noMark, plain;
        /* [6] */
        "24", noIcon, noKey, noMark, plain;
        /* [7] */
        "36", noIcon, noKey, noMark, plain;
        /* [8] */
        "48", noIcon, noKey, noMark, plain;
        /* [9] */
        "Other...", noIcon, noKey, noMark, plain
    }
};
```

Listing A-1 continued

```
resource 'MENU' (134) {
    134,
    textMenuProc,
    0x7FFFFFFF,
    enabled,
    "Style",
    {   /* array: 8 elements */
        /* [1] */
        "Plain", noIcon, noKey, noMark, plain;
        /* [2] */
        "Bold", noIcon, noKey, noMark, bold;
        /* [3] */
        "Italic", noIcon, noKey, noMark, italic;
        /* [4] */
        "Underline", noIcon, noKey, noMark, underline;
        /* [5] */
        "Outline", noIcon, noKey, noMark, outline;
        /* [6] */
        "Shadow", noIcon, noKey, noMark, shadow;
        /* [7] */
        "Condense", noIcon, noKey, noMark, condense;
        /* [8] */
        "Extend", noIcon, noKey, noMark, extend
    }
};


resource 'BNDL' (128) {
    'Scot',
    0,
    {   /* array TypeArray: 2 elements */
        /* [1] */
        'ICN#',
        {   /* array IDArray: 2 elements */
            /* [1] */
            0, 128,
            /* [2] */
            1, 129
        },
        /* [2] */
        'FREF',
        {   /* array IDArray: 2 elements */
            /* [1] */
            0, 128,
            /* [2] */
            1, 129
        }
    }
};
```

Listing A-1 continued

```
resource 'DITL' (1000, "About box") {
    {   /* array DITLarray: 2 elements */
        /* [1] */
        {61, 191, 81, 251},
        Button {
            enabled,
            "OK"
        },
        /* [2] */
        {8, 24, 56, 272},
        StaticText {
            disabled,
            "NewHiyer example program\nby Scott Knaster"
            "\nversion 1.0  10:55:43 PM  6/23/87"
        }
    }
};

resource 'DLOG' (1000, "About box") {
    {62, 100, 148, 412},
    dBoxProc,
    visible,
    goAway,
    0x0,
    1000,
    "New Dialog"
};

resource 'FREF' (128) {
    'APPL',
    0,
    ""
};

resource 'FREF' (129) {
    'TEXT',
    1,
    ""
};

resource 'ICN#' (128) {
    {   /* array: 2 elements */
        /* [1] */
        $"FFFF FFFF 8000 0005 FD00 0005 9100 0005"
        $"9100 0005 91EF 0005 9129 0005 912F 0005"
        $"9128 0005 912F 0005 8000 0805 8F00 0805"
        $"8880 0805 8898 C905 8F25 2A05 88A5 2C05"
        $"88A5 2A05 8F18 C905 8000 0005 8000 0005"
        $"9000 0005 9000 E485 9001 0505 9001 0605"
        $"9C90 C405 9290 2605 9290 2505 9CF1 C485"
        $"8010 0005 8010 0005 80F0 0005 FFFF FFFF",
        /* [2] */
```

```
            $"FFFF FFFF FFFF FFFF FFFF FFFF FFFF FFFF"
            $"FFFF FFFF FFFF FFFF FFFF FFFF FFFF FFFF"
            $"FFFF FFFF FFFF FFFF FFFF FFFF FFFF FFFF"
            $"FFFF FFFF FFFF FFFF FFFF FFFF FFFF FFFF"
            $"FFFF FFFF FFFF FFFF FFFF FFFF FFFF FFFF"
            $"FFFF FFFF FFFF FFFF FFFF FFFF FFFF FFFF"
            $"FFFF FFFF FFFF FFFF FFFF FFFF FFFF FFFF"
            $"FFFF FFFF FFFF FFFF FFFF FFFF FFFF FFFF"
        }
    };

    resource 'ICN#' (129) {
        {   /* array: 2 elements */
            /* [1] */
            $"0FFF FE00 0800 0300 09D0 0280 09D0 0240"
            $"09D0 0220 09D0 0210 09D0 03F8 09D0 0008"
            $"09D0 0008 09D0 0008 09D0 0008 09D0 0008"
            $"09F0 0008 0910 0008 0910 0008 0910 0008"
            $"0910 0008 0910 0008 08E0 0008 09F0 0008"
            $"09F0 0008 09F8 0008 09F8 0008 09E8 5FE8"
            $"09F8 0BE8 08D0 3FE8 08F0 FFE8 0870 3FE8"
            $"0819 FFE8 0800 0008 0800 0008 0FFF FFF8",
            /* [2] */
            $"0FFF FE00 0FFF FF00 0FFF FF80 0FFF FFC0"
            $"0FFF FFE0 0FFF FFF0 0FFF FFF8 0FFF FFF8"
            $"0FFF FFF8 0FFF FFF8 0FFF FFF8 0FFF FFF8"
            $"0FFF FFF8 0FFF FFF8 0FFF FFF8 0FFF FFF8"
            $"0FFF FFF8 0FFF FFF8 0FFF FFF8 0FFF FFF8"
            $"0FFF FFF8 0FFF FFF8 0FFF FFF8 0FFF FFF8"
            $"0FFF FFF8 0FFF FFF8 0FFF FFF8 0FFF FFF8"
            $"0FFF FFF8 0FFF FFF8 0FFF FFF8 0FFF FFF8"
        }
    };

    data 'Scot' (0) {
        $"1853 686F 776F 6666 2063 7265 6174 6564"          /* .NewHiyer created */
        $"2031 322F 3235 2F38 35"                           /*  6/23/87 */
    };
```

A P P E N D I X B

68020 Microprocessor Overview

The Macintosh II is run by a Motorola 68020 microprocessor, the latest evolution in the 68000 family (although the 68030 is close behind). This is the first Macintosh that Apple has produced with something other than the 68000 as the standard microprocessor. There are several third-party products that will add a 68020 to your Macintosh, if you want one.

In this short appendix, we'll talk about what it means to have a 68020 under the hood, how it affects software, and some of its features. For this appendix, and especially for the last part, it would help if you have an understanding of assembly language and the 68000, but even if you don't, you can still take a look at it—after all, you paid for the whole book.

Clock Speed and Data Bus

There's a common misconception that the Macintosh II and the third-party 68020 upgrades are fast just because they have a 68020. That's just not true. If you designed a Macintosh Plus that was exactly the same as the existing one except that the microprocessor was a 68020 instead of a 68000, it would be barely faster.

There are two big reasons why the Macintosh II is so fast: **clock speed** and **bus size.** Clock speed is the rate at which the microprocessor performs its tasks. Every microprocessor instruction requires a precise amount of time defined in **cycles.** A cycle is the time required to perform one step of an instruction, such as storing data or adding numbers.

The 68000 in the Macintoshes before the II had a clock speed of approximately eight megahertz or eight million cycles per second. You can also run a 68020 at this speed and you'd get a system that performs a lot like it did with a 68000. The Macintosh II runs its 68020 at about 16 megahertz or twice the speed of a Macintosh Plus. It's an oversimplification to say that this doubles the machine's raw speed, although it actually does do just about about that.

The other factor in the speed of the Macintosh II is the amount of data that's pushed around at once, called the data bus size. With a 68000, 16 bits of information can be sent at one time between the internal parts of the system, such as from the microprocessor to RAM. The 68020 doubles that, letting you slam 32 bits around the system at once. Again, we can't strictly say that doubling this number doubles the speed of the system, but it's a reasonable estimate.

You can't add a 32-bit data bus to a system just by dropping in a 68020 microprocessor. The size of the data bus affects a large part of the design of the system, and the Macintosh II was built to accommodate the 32-bit bus right from the start. The wider data bus and the faster clock speed combine to give the Macintosh II much of its speed improvement over the models that came before.

Instruction Cache

You're probably familiar with the concept of a cache. All the recent Macintosh models have included the ability to use a portion of RAM as a cache for stuff that's usually on the disk. You can control the size of this cache by using the Control Panel.

The 68020 has its own version of caching. Built right into the microprocessor is a cache for machine language instructions. As the microprocessor executes instructions, it keeps them in this cache, which can hold up to 256 bytes. Before fetching the next instruction, it checks to see whether it already has it in the cache. If so, it doesn't have to bother getting it from memory, and it can execute the instruction much faster from the cache than from memory. This technique is especially useful when running through small loops, in which the same few instructions are executed again and again.

> The 68020's instruction cache works by keeping track of the addresses that it has grabbed instructions from and then comparing them to the addresses of instructions that it's about to execute. If your code modifies itself, you could be in trouble, because the 68020 may have cached the old version of your code, and then try to execute it. The best way to avoid this is to avoid self-modifying code, a good idea in the Macintosh world anyway. The Macintosh Operating System, which has to move code segments around all day, gets around this problem by invalidating the cache whenever it needs to with a 68020 instruction.

Coprocessor Interface

The 68020, like most microprocessors, doesn't do floating-point arithmetic. It has a close cousin, though, called the 68881, which does do floating-point arithmetic and does it very fast. The 68881 is called a floating-point coprocessor, since it works in close alliance with the microprocessor. Real number calculations with the 68881 are up to 200 times faster than without it. We're not talking about 200 percent faster, which would mean twice as fast, but 200 times faster.

You can use a 68881 with a 68000, but it's really designed to work best with a 68020. The coprocessor interface with the 68020 is very clean. Instructions that drive the 68881 look like 68020 instructions and they can be written directly in your code. The Macintosh II includes a 68881 as standard equipment in every unit.

Addressing Modes

The 68000 defines a pretty rich set of addressing modes for programmers. In fact, most programmers never get to use all of them. The

68020 adds a few more you'll want to try and a few others you'll never get to, either.

The most interesting new mode for Macintosh programmers is known technically as **memory indirect** addressing. In the 68000, you can only use a register as an indirect address—never memory itself. The 68020 adds the ability to use a memory location as a base for the effective address. Since you also get to specify the memory address itself indirectly, usually through an address register, this amounts to double-indirection, which matches very nicely with the way handles work in the Macintosh.

You can combine memory indirect addressing with another new feature, called **scaled index.** By using scaled index mode, you can have an index into an array of bytes, words, long words, or double-long words, and the instruction will automatically multiply the index by one, two, four, or eight, depending on the size of the elements in your array.

By combining memory indirect addressing with scaled index, you can have amazing flexibility in specifying the effective address. For example, in the memory indirect post-indexed mode, you can write an instruction like this:

```
MOVE.L ([8,A1],D1*4,36), D2
```

This instruction starts by getting the value in register A1 and then adding eight to it (called the base displacement). The number that results is called the indirect memory address, and in this case it would probably be the start of an array or table of values. The 68020 then gets the value in *that* address and adds the value from register D1 multiplied by four; since we're multiplying by four, this would suggest that the values in the array are four bytes each. Finally, 36 is added to this value, giving the effective address at last. The 36 is called the **outer displacement,** and it gives us one last shot at indexing into an array. In an anticlimax, the value in this location would then be moved into register D2.

Don't worry about all this. Any of the values in this addressing mode can be 0, so you'll usually write something much simpler, like this:

```
MOVE ([A1],48), 252(A5)
```

If you have a handle to an object stored in a register (A1 in this example), you can use a single instruction to move the word that's 48 bytes into the relocatable object to the location at 252 off A5. Obviously, this can really help when you're writing Macintosh code.

Instructions

The 68020 defines a few new instructions that you can use to enhance your programs. A bunch of instructions have been enhanced to support 32-bit displacements, where only 16-bit dispacements are allowed on the 68000. These include the branch instructions (BEQ, BCC, and so on), and the LINK instruction that's used to build stack frames. Several instructions now work with larger values. The multiply instructions (MULS and MULU) now allow 32-bit operands; the divide instructions (DIVS and DIVU) work with 32-bit and 64-bit operands; and the CHK instruction can have 32-bit operands.

There are also a lot of brand new instructions. The biggest collection of them are the bit field instructions, which allow you to directly examine and manipulate individual bits or groups of bits within bytes. For example, you can use the BFINS (bit field insert) instruction to move a group of bits directly into the middle of a byte. There's also a BFTST (bit field test) instruction which you can use to see if a bit field is zero or not. Probably the best name for a 68020 instruction is BFFFO (bit field find first one), which will find the first bit that's a one in a bit field, but more importantly, you can pronounce this instruction either "biffo" or "boffo." Both are acceptable.

Things to Remember

The 68020 makes a computer fast because it's usually clocked at a fast speed and because it can support a 32-bit data bus. The 68020's instruction cache also helps speed up your programs, but you have to watch out for self-modifying code, or your programs may get a not so nice surprise.

The 68020 has a very tight coprocessor interface, which works very well with the 68881 floating-point coprocessor. The 68020 also has new addressing modes, including one in which you can place a handle in an address register and pull in bytes directly from the relocatable object. There are also a lot of new instructions for working with bit fields and enhancements to existing instructions that let you work with larger values.

A P P E N D I X C

Macintosh
Technical Note #110

Late in 1986, a very unusual and mysterious technical note appeared
on various Macintosh bulletin board systems. It looked like an official Macintosh Technical Note from Apple. Although the note
listed me as the author, I didn't have anything to do with writing it
and I was pretty surprised to see my name on it, especially since it
contained a pretty bizarre parody of technical notes in general.

This technical note, which was listed as number 110, was filled
with satirical comments and puns, but it was done with subtlety. Although it was obvious to most people familiar with the Macintosh
world that the note was a parody, a few folks inside Apple didn't
see it that way and decided that it was a really bad idea to have
this thing be an official-looking document from Apple. While various factions recommended everything ranging from a public dis-
claimer to litigation to tactical nuclear weapons, Jean-Louis Gassée
had the best idea, as he often does. "Write one of your own," he said,
"that's so bizarre that it will obviously be a joke."

So I did, and subtlety was not, as they say in product development, part of the design center. Here are the original note, whose au-
thorship is now suspected but still unclaimed, and the "corrected"
version.

Macintosh Technical Notes

#110: Processor Compatibility

See also: Technical Note #2—Macintosh Compatibility Guidelines

Written by: Scott Knaster   December 2, 1986

This document is a brief look at compatibility problems in applications whose code assumes they're running on a 68000 processor.

Many applications which work on existing Macintosh architectures have encountered problems when running on processors other than the 68000, such as third-party processor boards and prototype machines at Apple. To be fully compatible with these CPUs, your application will have to observe the rules discussed here.

Caching Considerations

The 68020 has a 256-byte, on-chip "instruction cache." This automatically caches only those memory locations fetched as instructions, and thus is read-only. Operations which alter code (such as impure tables in code) or move code segments (as naturally occurs in Macintosh memory management) *must invalidate the cache's contents*. This invalidation should not be done frivolously, as it's important to maintain cache flow.

The CCR—Condition Code Register—on the 68000 is the Cache Control Register on the 68020, or Cache Register for short. Motorola has redefined the "C" flag (the "Carry" condition code) to serve a dual purpose, keeping backwards compatibility but also using the flag to signal whether the cache is valid. This double-duty bit is now called the Cache/Carry flag.

Memory Alignment

Word- and long-sized memory operands must be even-aligned in the 68000. The 68020 has no such restrictions, but you should continue to observe them so your application will work with older architectures.

Apple is considering low-end architectures, including a home version of the Macintosh (the "Mac Jr.") using the 68008, which is essentially a 68000 with an eight-bit internal architecture. Unfortunately, VLSI design constraints forced Motorola to swap the numbering of bytes within a word, so the memory organization closely resembles the Intel processor family. The processor will automatically compensate for this when fetching instruction operands, and RAM-based patches to the Resource Manager will be available. However, all other in-memory data structures will require byte-swapping before using them.

On-Site Hardware Upgrades

In my recent book *How to Write Macintosh Software,* I discussed the need to prevent applications from depending on the location of subroutines in ROM. The Toolbox interface is intended to maintain this independence. As pointed out on page 368, "Apple guarantees that the ROM will not change while your application is running." While this will probably be true in future architectures, Apple is considering applications which will need hardware upgrades *during the time an application is running.* Systems such as file servers, life-support monitors, and MazeWars servers can't interrupt operation just for an upgrade.

It is possible to suspend the processor by driving the HALT signal (pin #54) high. At this point, future architectures may provide hardware facilities for swapping processors, or adding peripheral chips such as MMUs or FPUs. Applications need to know that this has occurred, especially when the transition is from a 68020 to a less powerful chip (as might happen when a failing 68020 processor's only available replacement is a 68000).

To handle this, new ROMs will detect when the HALT signal has been used for any reason and give the application the option of receiving notification by storing the address in a hook for this purpose.

```
JcpuHALT.EQU $81B      ; cpu-HALTed hook [pointer]
```

Note that this hook is valid only in ROMs where ROM85 is $3FFF or less. Other ROMs cannot guarantee to detect and notify the condition.

Actually, Apple is considering provisions for dynamically updating ROMs in a similar manner. Since this would invalidate all addresses obtained through GetTrapAddress, it may cause problems for existing applications. You may want to keep ROM addresses in handles, since the ROM will be able to easily find and correctly update all master pointers which point into ROM.

Macintosh Technical Notes

#110: Processor Compatibility

See also: Technical Note #2:   Macintosh Compatibility Guidelines
                                       Motorola MC68020 Reference Manual
                                       Random House Almanac, 1957 Edition
                                       The Baseball Encyclopedia
                                       Star Trek Concordance

Not written by:	Scott Knaster	ever
Written by:	Mike Morton	December 2, 1986
Modified by:	Scott Knaster	January 7, 1987
	John Smallberries	November 1, 1938

This document is a brief look at compatibility problems in applications whose code assumes they're running on a 68000 processor. It includes recent modifications intended to make the intent and meaning of this note clear to even the casual reader.

Many applications which work on existing Macintosh architectures have encountered problems when running on processors other than the 68000, such as third-party boards containing a 68010, a 68020, a 68008, a Z-80, or an Intel 8080. To be fully compatible with these CPUs, your application will have to observe the rules discussed here. Failure to do so would be bad.

Caching in the Chips

The 68020 utilizes VLSI technology to support many advanced features directly on the chip, and implements these features in its **dual-inline package** (DIP). This "chip in a DIP" technique, as real engineers call it, is used to implement a 256-byte, on-chip instruction cache. This instruction cache can be used to speed up processing, or for other special applications, such as fault-tolerant operation, in which computers are kept running even when they're about to fail. In well-documented experiments at Xerox PARC in 1981, for example, a technique was perfected to reliably cache a failing Star, but the costs of the associated hardware continued to telescope until they became astronomical.

In normal operation, the cache fills with instructions as they are fetched. The cache makes no provisions for code which modifies itself (known as "self-abusive code"). Any code which modifies itself can cause problems with cache flow if the code may be executed repeatedly. To help with this problem, some versions of the 68020 contain a special instruction which automaticaly disables the cache "conditionally on warning"; that is, if the code has been modified. Assembler information for this Cache Conditionally on Warning instruction (which was inexplicably left out of the official Motorola documentation) is provided here:

CACHE COW   Cache Conditionally on Warning

Instruction format:

bit	#15	14	13	12	11	10	9	8	7	6	5	4	3	2	1	0
value	1	1	1	1	1	1	1	0	1	1	0	0	1	1	1	0

To accommodate new features, the condition codes register (CCR) has been broken up. The main part of CCR, known as the JF (John Fogarty), has become a solo register, and has issued two implementations thus far. The reassignment of the other former members of CCR has not yet been determined, except that the carry bit of the CCR is now also a valid indicator of the cache status, so this bit has been renamed the cache and carry flag.

Memory Alignment

In the 68000, word- and longword-sized operands must begin at an even address, or an address error will occur. The 68020 has no such restriction; however, a new Toolbox Manager, called The Masochist, implements a technique known as "front-end alignment" which will force an address error under the following circumstances:

1. An odd memory reference was made for a word- or longword-sized operand.
2. A rather odd chunk of code was executed.
3. A pretty odd programmer tried to execute some code.
4. Every now and then, at random intervals, depending upon the Venusian calendar.

As a possible future enhancement, Apple is considering a new microprocessor, the V-8, which almost perfectly emulates the 68000, but with much higher performance. The most significant difference in programming the V-8 is that it utilizes the AOK (approximations are OK) protocol, which means that all values include a possible error of 3,448,332,884 plus or minus. Your code should include error-checking techniques to verify that you have the right values.

Algorithm and Blues

The latest system release, version 4.0, includes a new, powerful version of the PackBits utility which compresses data. This call is named PackMan and its parameters are the same as PackBits. The packing algorithm used for this new call is efficient enough to guarantee that the packed data will be no longer than one byte, regardless of the length of the unpacked data. Here is the calling format:

```
PROCEDURE PackMan (VAR srcPtr,dstPtr: Ptr; srcBytes: INTEGER);
```

A corresponding call to unpack the data is forthcoming.

G L O S S A R Y

A-trap A 68000 instruction that begins with $A; on the Macintosh, it calls the system software.

allocation block The smallest unit of space that can be allocated to a disk file.

analog Continuously variable over a range, like a standard clock or gas gauge.

auxiliary control record A data structure that correlates each part of a color control to an RGB value.

auxiliary window record A data structure that correlates each part of a color window to an RGB value.

b-tree A technique used for creating an index into a large collection of data.

bit image A group of bits in memory that represent a graphical image enclosed by a rectangle.

bitmapped Represented by bits, as the Macintosh display.

blessed folder The directory that contains the copy of System and Finder that are used to start up a disk.

blitting   Moving bit images from one place to another.

boot blocks   System startup information located in the first two blocks of a volume.

bottleneck   A QuickDraw low-level processing routine.

bus size   The number of bits that can be transferred at one time between memory and the microprocessor.

chunky   A model of color representation that uses adjacent bits in RAM to form each pixel in an image.

clock speed   The rate at which a microprocessor executes instructions.

closed architecture   A computer design technique that prevents expansion.

color lookup device   A device, usually a chip on a video card, that relates index values to colors.

color specification   A Color QuickDraw data structure that contains a value and an RGB record.

color table   A Color QuickDraw data structure that contains a unique identifier called a seed, a transparent pixel index, and an array of color specifications.

comment kind   The value that defines a QuickDraw comment.

definition function   A routine that determines the precise appearance and behavior of a Toolbox element, such as a menu or window.

depth   The number of bits per pixel.

design center   The set of goals and definitions that specify a product.

dialog item color table   A data structure that determines the colors for items in a dialog.

digital   Represented by discrete values only, like a digital clock or a TV channel indicator.

directory   A part of a volume that can contain files; also called a folder.

directory ID   A number, unique on a volume, that indicates a directory.

dirID   Shortcut for directory ID.

dithering   A technique that combines two or more colors in adjacent pixels to produce the effect of a new color.

drive queue   A data structure that contains an entry for each drive attached to a Macintosh.

easy to learn   Characterized by simple, straightforward operation, with all basic functions easily understood and accessible.

easy to use   Characterized by shortcuts, features, and techniques for users to become more productive as they learn a program.

file control block   A data structure that contains information about each open file.

file control buffer   A block in the system heap that contains the file control blocks.

font color table   A data structure that contains the color specifications for a font.

forgiveness   The user interface principle that permits users to undo or correct operations.

full pathname   A form of file specification that specifies a volume name, all appropriate directory names, and a file name.

gDevice   A Color Manager device, also called a graphics device.

general   A description of software that incorporates flexibility and can be modified for future enhancements.

global consistency   Similar behavior among different applications.

GrowZone function   A function implemented by an application program that provides a technique for freeing up memory when there are no bytes free.

hook A pointer to a routine that can modify the behavior of a system routine.

job dialog The dialog that asks for information about a printing job.

local consistency Logical, consistent behavior in all parts of an application.

local ID A local identifying number attached to a resource in a BNDL, such as an icon list.

low-memory global A Macintosh system variable that's stored in the first few thousand bytes of RAM.

macro A series of commands that can be recorded and replayed.

mask A bit image that is used to modify a cursor or icon when it's drawn.

memory indirect A 68020 addressing mode that allows a memory location to be used as a base for an indirect address.

memory-mapped video A design technique that represents the video screen with some part of RAM.

message A call made to a definition function that causes it to perform some action.

multi-launch For an application, the ability to be run from a shared volume by several users at the same time.

noun-verb The user interface technique in which the user selects an object, then an action.

outer displacement In the memory indirect addressing mode, the final displacement value.

paradigm A user interface technique or concept.

partial pathname A file specification that does not contain a volume name.

patch A modification to a Macintosh system routine.

picture comment Data that's recorded with a picture and usually ignored by QuickDraw, but which can be used by other software, such as the LaserWriter driver.

pixel A single dot on the screen (from "picture element").

pixel image A group of bits, which represent a graphic image that may contain more than one bit per pixel.

pixel map A Color QuickDraw data structure that defines a pixel image and its characteristics.

pixel patterns A variable-sized pixel image, used to define a repeating color or design.

planar A model of color representation that separates each pixel into separate planes, with one bit per pixel of information in each plane.

pointer arithmetic A programming technique that involves moving a pointer through a data structure by directly modifying the pointer.

PostScript escape font A font in which all text is treated as PostScript commands when printed to a LaserWriter.

print dialog Either of the two Printing Manager dialogs, the job dialog or the style dialog.

reality check A debugging technique in which the programmer manually verifies that information is sensible.

recursion See *recursion*.

RGB value A specification for a color, which consists of magnitude values for its red, green, and blue components.

root directory The directory that corresponds to a volume on a disk. All files that are not in a folder are in the root.

script A system for writing and typing in a particular language and set of characters.

seeded Given pre-release, prototype equipment under special agreement.

sexy A modern marketing term that indicates an allegedly clever or interesting concept.

shell A program that controls the launching of other programs.

signature resource A resource whose type is the same as the owner's signature.

special case A programming situation that is handled by code that's specifically written for that purpose.

stack A window management technique that makes a portion of each window's title bar visible.

style dialog The dialog that sets the page information for printing.

style record A TextEdit data structure that contains information about text's font, face, size, and color.

synthetic font A font that was specially constructed for the current screen's depth.

system startup information Configurable information that's stored in the first two blocks (the boot blocks) of a volume.

tiling A window management technique that divides the screen space among all open windows.

transfer mode One of a set of logical functions that are performed when QuickDraw combines two bit images.

trap A call to the Macintosh system software, also called an A-trap.

trap dispatcher The part of the Macintosh system software that converts trap numbers to memory addresses and calls the routines.

unimplemented instruction trap The 68000 feature that's used to capture instructions that start with $A (see A-trap) and send them to the trap dispatcher.

User Interface Toolbox The part of the Macintosh system software that implements the user interface features.

venerable Commanding reverence by virtue of position or age.

verb-noun   The user interface technique in which the user selects an operation first, such as insertion or deletion, then the object.

vertex   A corner of a polygon.

volume control block   A data structure in memory that contains information about a volume.

volume information block   Information about a volume stored on the volume itself.

volume reference number   A unique number that's assigned to a volume when it's mounted.

vRefNum   See *volume reference number*.

working directory   A technique in the Hierarchical File System for referring to a volume and a disk directory with a single integer.

working directory control block   A data structure maintained by the Hierarchical File System, which keeps track of a working directory.

working directory reference number   A number that's assigned to a working directory, which can be used in file system calls.

Index